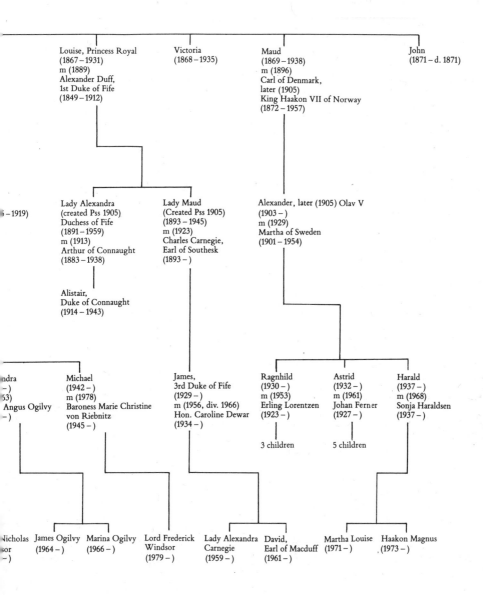

Louise, Princess Royal
(1867 – 1931)
m (1889)
Alexander Duff,
1st Duke of Fife
(1849 – 1912)

Victoria
(1868 – 1935)

Maud
(1869 – 1938)
m (1896)
Carl of Denmark,
later (1905)
King Haakon VII of Norway
(1872 – 1957)

John
(1871 – d. 1871)

i – 1919)

Lady Alexandra
(created Pss 1905)
Duchess of Fife
(1891 – 1959)
m (1913)
Arthur of Connaught
(1883 – 1938)

Lady Maud
(Created Pss 1905)
(1893 – 1945)
m (1923)
Charles Carnegie,
Earl of Southesk
(1893 –)

Alexander, later (1905) Olav V
(1903 –)
m (1929)
Martha of Sweden
(1901 – 1954)

Alistair,
Duke of Connaught
(1914 – 1943)

ndra
–)
53)
Angus Ogilvy
–)

Michael
(1942 –)
m (1978)
Baroness Marie Christine
von Riebnitz
(1945 –)

James,
3rd Duke of Fife
(1929 –)
m (1956, div. 1966)
Hon. Caroline Dewar
(1934 –)

Ragnhild
(1930 –)
m (1953)
Erling Lorentzen
(1923 –)

3 children

Astrid
(1932 –)
m (1961)
Johan Ferner
(1927 –)

5 children

Harald
(1937 –)
m (1968)
Sonja Haraldsen
(1937 –)

Nicholas
sor
–)

James Ogilvy
(1964 –)

Marina Ogilvy
(1966 –)

Lord Frederick
Windsor
(1979 –)

Lady Alexandra
Carnegie
(1959 –)

David,
Earl of Macduff
(1961 –)

Martha Louise
(1971 –)

Haakon Magnus
(1973 –)

piled by Marlene Eilers

ALEXANDRA

ALEXANDRA
PRINCESS AND QUEEN

David Duff

COLLINS
St James's Place, London
1980

William Collins Sons and Co Ltd
London · Glasgow · Sydney · Auckland
Toronto · Johannesburg

First published 1980
ISBN 0 00 216667 4
Set in VIP Bembo

Printed by W. & G. Baird Ltd at Greystone Press, Antrim
Bound by Robert Hartnoll Ltd, Bodmin

CONTENTS

LIST OF
ILLUSTRATIONS

7

ACKNOWLEDGMENTS

I am indebted to Her Majesty the Queen for permission to reproduce certain photographs and pictures from the Royal Collection.

I was encouraged to write this book by the late Earl Mountbatten of Burma, who gave me permission to reproduce an extract from his father's unpublished reminiscences. Arrangements were in hand for the completed manuscript to be sent to him for approval after his summer holiday in Ireland of 1979, a holiday which ended in such tragic circumstances.

My thanks are due to many who have helped me in my researches, and in particular to Her Royal Highness Princess Margrethe de Bourbon, Queen Alexandra's niece, for looking through the manuscript. The Duke of Beaufort, whose wedding Queen Alexandra attended, recalled her ever present charm. Miss Penelope Boscawen and Mrs Alison Ingwersen helped me with information concerning Danish matters and read the relevant chapters. Mrs Alexandra Loch, granddaughter of King Edward's agent, Captain Frank Beck, assisted me with information regarding Sandringham. For historical research my thanks are due to Miss Barbara Duff and to Mr Cecil Barclay who helped me with research on the life of Prince Albert Victor, Duke of Clarence. For expert advice, always willingly given, my thanks are due once again to Miss Jennifer Hassell.

I am deeply grateful to Miss Marlene Eilers for compiling the genealogical tables, to Miss Sarah Clay for typing a difficult manuscript faultlessly and with patience and Miss Christine Bernard for editorial help.

Lastly, my deep thanks are due to Mr Robin Baird-Smith, of Collins, who edited with infinite care, was always ready with advice and who assisted with the choice of illustrations.

David Duff

PREFACE

The part played by Alexandra, consort of Edward VII, as an influence on the Royal Family and on the British people, deserves far more emphasis than it has ever received. This portrait is an attempt to give the beautiful Danish princess who came to us the recognition that is her due both as a woman and as Queen.

Young, poor and foreign, she arrived in Britain with a daunting future ahead, as wife to the heir to a long-postponed throne and as daughter-in-law to Queen Victoria. To her initial handicaps was soon added the burden of ill-health; a serious illness in 1867 left her both slightly lame, and deaf. Yet she overcame all her difficulties – the frequent criticisms from the different factions at court and in society, the problems within her marriage, the death of two of her sons – to earn the respect of all who knew her.

Within the Royal Family it was she who helped to turn back the British tide of affection to Queen Victoria. For many years following the death of Prince Albert, Victoria was not a popular Queen, being seen as an embittered recluse. During the early years of Alexandra's marriage there was continual friction between herself and her mother-in-law, mainly because the Princess of Wales deplored all things German; but in the 1880s the relationship changed. The Queen herself has recorded how Alexandra's example softened her responses; and through her last years Victoria gained a renewed hold on the hearts and affection of the British people. On the Diamond Jubilee drive to St Paul's, as she sat in a carriage with her daughter-in-law and the deafening cheering brought tears to the old lady's eyes, Alexandra wiped them away. Victoria owed a great deal to Alexandra.

As a wife her conduct was exemplary within an incompatible marriage. She endured her husband's aberrations with dignity, compassion and courage, she put the family first, she showed the true meaning of loyalty and, in the words of that brilliant Liberal, Bernal Osborne, kept the throne safe for Queen Victoria's heir.

11

Preface

Alexandra was in many ways a modern thinker; many of her humane views were criticized by conventional members of society. She did not relish mass slaughter of game; out hunting, she openly expressed the hope that 'the poor fox would escape'. She was opposed to corporal punishment, then considered an essential part of the school curriculum. She believed in widening the field of learning for the young to include subjects such as music, metal work and embroidery, at a time when many favoured the instillation of only the minimum of knowledge, a broader education, it was felt, leading to unwanted and advanced ideas. Alexandra fought the use of children as chimney sweeps. In the spheres of welfare, nursing, education and politics, she was a century ahead of her time.

Alexandra played a significant part in the First World War – the war she had foreseen so clearly. She was no tired old lady, no shadowy mother of the king. She worked tirelessly for the war effort, especially in the care and entertainment of the ordinary serviceman, pressing for better conditions for the blinded and the shell-shocked.

The British monarchy has to a large extent survived because of the love and respect which Britain has held for its Queens – Victoria, 'the great-I-am'; Alexandra herself; Mary; Elizabeth, who rose from the smoke and the fire of the Abdication; and our present Queen. But we owe a special tribute to the understanding and the humanity stemming from the lovely princess who came from Denmark with only a few pounds to her name, in 1863.

Her presence can still be felt at Sandringham, where she was always happiest, and where now crowds in their thousands walk in her gardens, browse in her rooms, pray in her church. When asked, as a child, what her ambition was, she answered: 'To be loved.' Her dream came true and by the turn of the century she had earned a special place in the hearts of the British people. Her own love extended far beyond her family, to disabled children, and the ill, the wrongdoer and the poor, indeed to all living creatures.

To this woman, who combined so many rare qualities – among them steadfastness, courage and dignity – we owe much, as did her family and contemporaries.

ONE

Poverty in a Palace

Prince and Princess Christian of Schleswig-Holstein-Sonderburg-Glücksburg had six children. Frederick, the eldest, arrived in 1843. On 1 December 1844 a daughter was born in the Gûle (yellow) Palace in Copenhagen and was christened Alexandra Caroline Maria Charlotte Louisa Julia. There followed William George, Dagmar, Thyra, and Waldemar who made a belated appearance in 1858. They matured into an 'international brigade', having loyalties to Denmark, Great Britain, Russia, Greece, Germany, Sweden, Norway and France.*

Alexandra was an ugly baby. When the nurse showed the infant to her father, he winced and said, 'Take the thing away'. She grew into a very plump child – 'great puppy cheeks and fat arms', as she later described herself.[1] And she was violent.[2] But at the age of fourteen there came a complete change: she blossomed into loveliness, dazzlingly fair, with eyes of that deep shade of blue which in some lights looks violet, and grew tall and slim (in contrast with the daughters of Queen Victoria, who were pert and pretty until they reached puberty, when they became fat and podgy and inclined to spots).

Prince Christian, Alexandra's father, was an army officer. Although he was a lineal descendant of George II of England, he was not in direct line to the Danish throne. In fact, he was a poor

---

* Frederick: Frederick VIII of Denmark, married Louise, Princess of Sweden and Norway. Alexandra: Married Albert Edward, Prince of Wales. William: George I of the Hellenes, married Grand Duchess Olga of Russia. Dagmar: Married Alexander III of Russia, and became Empress Marie Feodorovna. Thyra: Married Ernest Augustus, Duke of Cumberland, Crown Prince of Hanover. Waldemar: Married Princess of Bourbon-Orleans.

relation, not having a penny of his own. Born in 1818 and orphaned when he was thirteen, he was cared for by his uncle, Frederick VI of Denmark. At eighteen he was appointed Captain of the Horse Guards. Tall and well built, he danced well, was a superb horseman, and was bent on having a good time; his one drawback being that he was not very intelligent. But here was an obvious attraction to any young lady not worried about his lack of money and brains.

In 1837 William IV of England died and was succeeded by his niece, Victoria. The Danish King decided to send an Ambassador Extraordinary to London to congratulate her, and picked upon Christian for the job. There was then born in the high places of Copenhagen a scheme to bring about a marriage between Victoria and Christian. He was a year older, of royal birth, personable – why not? The advantages were obvious, both financially and politically. Prussia had her eyes on the Duchies in the south of Denmark and a union with England would prove both a safeguard and a deterrent. The English minister in Copenhagen was brought in and plans were hatched.

But the idea of converting Queen Victoria into an in-law had not escaped the attention of other families with growing sons, lured not only by the power and the glory thus to be obtained, but also by the thought of the £50,000 a year which it was expected that the Queen's consort would receive from the long suffering British public.

The Tories wanted her to marry her cousin, Prince George of Cambridge, an army officer and of the same age. But George was a ladies' man and a flirt; he was not attracted by the dumpy Queen, with her poor complexion, protruding eyes and authoritarian outlook. Yet at present he was considered to be a 'runner', though in the event he took the first opportunity to withdraw, bolting to the Mediterranean shores until the matter was settled. The other main contender was a student Prince from Coburg, highly intelligent, ambitious, though physically of poor stock; but he was a nephew of both the Queen's mother and the wily King Leopold of the Belgians. Leopold was already in receipt of £50,000 a year as a result of marrying Princess Charlotte, only daughter of the Prince Regent and losing her soon after in child-birth. He had every intention of increasing the

Coburg family funds by installing young Albert at Windsor, and there was a no more cunning schemer than Uncle Leopold.

Christian arrived in London early in the morning and woke the Danish ambassador from his slumbers. Not being able to speak a word of English, he was lost. The ambassador took one look at his clothes, shuddered, and after breakfast took him to the tailor. The tailor also shuddered. Christian's outfit, and in particular his awful high hat, was hidden well out of sight and he was re-kitted. The result was highly satisfactory.

Christian was a social success in London. He had lunch with the Queen and the two chatted away animatedly until late in the afternoon. She seldom met young men of royal rank who were both good looking and fun. Those about the court who were anti-Coburg – and there were plenty – beamed with delight. He was asked to the best houses, saw the sights and each night danced through to the dawn. This was very tiring for the ambassador who accompanied him, but who often retired in the early hours, leaving the young man to his own devices. He reported:

> The Prince seems to please everyone mightily. And it is not at all certain that he has not made some impression on the Queen. He is invited out to every meal, and dances almost every evening till far into the night. One of his Court invitations prevented his attending a show where a man was to give a parachute demonstration and lost his life in the process.[3]

He met with only one hostile reception. That was when he visited the Duchess of Kent, the Queen's mother, at Kensington Palace. And Christian made one silly mistake – he confided in the Duchess of Cambridge, to whom he was related, that he was much attracted by Queen Victoria. Back in Copenhagen, his thoughts centred upon his next visit to London. The chance came with the coronation the following year, the Danish King choosing Christian as his representative. His backers had urged upon him the importance of learning English before his return visit, but this he neglected to do.

Victoria was delighted to see him again. 'To the great annoyance of the various Ambassadors, at the Court concert the Queen sent the Lord High Chamberlain to summon the Prince

15

and motioned him to a seat by her side.'[4] It seemed now as if Christian was all set to win and the royal relations treated him with great respect and swamped him with invitations. But he paid too much attention to the balls and the parties and not enough to the rehearsal of his duties. On the occasion when the representatives of the various courts introduced themselves to the Queen, and had done their piece, they were instructed to bow deeply to her, take two steps backwards and bow again, and so a third time, all the while keeping their eyes on Her Majesty. Christian managed the first bow all right and stepped back. But he had not noticed that a sofa was standing on his line of retreat. He ended, arms waving, deep in the folds of that sofa. The Queen roared with laughter, but court officials were not amused.

The Coburgs, now deeply alarmed, made the most of Christian's boobs and deficiencies. They despatched Albert on a tour of Italy, to sharpen him up and increase his manly image, urging him to learn the ways of women, while King Leopold himself visited Britain to further Albert's cause. The Danish ambassador in London, watching events closely, informed Copenhagen he feared that Prince Christian's chances were fading away. He was correct in his fears, for in 1840 Queen Victoria married Prince Albert.

In 1839 Frederick of Denmark died. He was succeeded by Christian VIII, bringing Prince Christian one step nearer to the throne. In 1841 Prince Christian fell in love with Princess Louise of Hesse-Cassel and the following year married her. They were cousins, Christian's grandfather having been Landgrave of Hesse. They met at her family home, the beautiful castle of Rumpenheim on the River Main. They were ideally suited, she being dainty, intelligent and musical and fully able to manage her husband and to hold his affections. They set up home in the Yellow Palace.

Officially No. 18, Amaliegade was more a large town house than a palace, a grace and favour property for which the Christians paid no rent. The front door opened directly on to the street. A hundred yards to the right stood the royal Palace of the Amalienborg, and it was only a short walk to the Langelinie, Copenhagen's fashionable waterfront promenade. Prince Chris-

Poverty in a Palace

tian's income was around £800 a year, little enough on which to raise a family, and he relied largely on the bounty of the King and his in-laws. As his children came of educational age, he instructed them in drawing, gymnastics and riding, while his wife cared for languages, music and the domestic arts. With the responsibilities of fatherhood Christian became a stern disciplinarian. He insisted on the importance of learning, but his eldest daughter found the absorption of knowledge difficult. She excelled at riding and turning cartwheels, and inherited from her mother a love of music. Fortunately for her, she liked sewing and was soon making her own day dresses and bonnets. In later life she attributed the ease with which she could retain an upright sitting position at long public ceremonies to having been trained as a child not to lean back in her chair, for fear of creasing her frock.[5]

Punctuality was insisted upon at the Yellow Palace, but Alexandra could not master time, and never learned to. When the bell rang for dinner she was never ready and raced along the corridor. If she missed the reading of the blessing by her father she had to stand behind his chair during the first course. It was not going without the food which upset her but the ragging which she had later to endure from the servants. It was a very democratic household, with none of the sharp line of demarcation between Upstairs and Downstairs that existed at courts such as Windsor. On the servants' days off Alexandra and her sister. undertook their duties, and they also learned the ways of the kitchen.

Food was good but plain, the mid-day meal being on a 'help yourself' basis. Breakfast was substantial, the chief attraction being the beer-broth called ølebröd. It was made of black bread boiled in black beer – a kind of porter – and served steaming hot from a soup tureen. A layer of brown sugar was spread over the plates and the broth poured over it, and stirred until the sugar was melted. Then thick cream was added. In summer there was Rødgrød,* raspberry jelly swamped with sugar and cream.[6]

Life was spartan, however, and there was no money for decorating the Yellow Palace, no baths, partial submersion in a

* Any red fruit, cooked with potato flour, to make a jelly-like gruel.

17

tub once a week being the only assistance to personal cleanliness. In the summer the situation was improved by carriage drives to Klampenborg to bathe in the sea. In an uneventful childhood, Alexandra's outstanding memories were of the occasions when Hans Christian Andersen called and told her fairy stories before she went to bed.[7]

One of the subjects that dominated conversation at the Yellow Palace concerned the future of the Duchies of Schleswig and Holstein. They lay in the narrow tongue of land to the south which separated Denmark from Germany; their North Sea and Baltic shores were of great economic and strategic importance, and were administered by the King of Denmark, who held the title of Duke of Schleswig-Holstein. The majority of the Schleswig population was Danish, those in Holstein being German. Arguments had been going on for centuries: some of the inhabitants wished to remain under Danish rule, some preferred German; some wished for the return of the hereditary leading families, others wanted independence on a democratic basis. As always happens when there are divided loyalties, the Duchies were a seedbed of intrigues, hopes and schemes. The rest of Europe did not understand either the labyrinthine dynastic claims or the ethnic differences. But the point remained that Denmark without the Duchies would be reduced to an area somewhat small for an independent kingdom. This was the problem for Prince Christian, doubly involved through family ties.

Another source of endless discussion at the palace was Crown Prince Frederick, heir to the throne. Born in 1808, he turned out to be a problem prince: he was licentious, had a lamentable taste in companions and had been in endless trouble. His diet consisted of vast quantities of pea soup and bacon, washed down with equally vast quantities of beer and *akavit*.[8] Not surprisingly, he was grossly fat. He had been married twice, each time disastrously. His ex-wives must have talked, for it was common knowledge that he was infertile. When King Louis Philippe of the French was informed that Frederick's wife was expecting a child, he remarked, 'Well, God bless the father, whoever he may be!'[9] But the ordinary people had a liking for him, since his views were democratic, in contrast to his father, a die-hard and a

18

martinet. A patriot and a dreamer, Frederick had somehow convinced himself that he had taken part in the great battles of the Napoleonic wars; when it was pointed out to him that he was then only a small boy, he replied that he had trotted along beside the soldiers – he remembered well! When Frederick met Louise Rasmussen, a dancer at the Royal Opera House, she immediately cast a spell over him. Enchanted by her, he soon took her to live with him at his fine country home, Jaeger Priso.

Louise was a well-educated girl who had had a varied career. After a post as governess in Norway, she entered the fashion business in Paris. This apparently did not satisfy her, for she took up dancing. It was this career which had brought her to Copenhagen. Becoming the mistress of Berling, a printer and newspaper publisher,[10] she had a son by him. (The boy was given the surname of Jacobsen. He was sent in secret to England for an agricultural training and later farmed at Weybread, Suffolk. He was killed in a motor accident in 1908.) Berling introduced her to the Prince. In time she proved to be a restraining influence and was the only person who could prevent him from wild bouts of excessive drinking, but combating his diet proved too much for her and she soon became as fat as he was.

In 1848, a time when revolutionary waves swept across Europe, Christian VIII died. The demands for more democratic rule were loud in Denmark. After a public procession of protest on 21 March, Frederick, now king, replied that he intended to renounce the absolute rule and that he had already taken steps towards forming a Government responsible to the representatives of the people. He then married Louise Rasmussen (and gave her the title Countess Danner) and retired to his country home.

Although Frederick's reforms were popular in Copenhagen they met with resistance in the Duchies of Schleswig and Holstein; it was not long before war was declared. Frederick, forbidden to approach the fighting line, nevertheless strutted around with his arm in a sling, pretending he had been wounded in the heat of battle. Two years later the Danes gained the ascendency and an uneasy peace lay over the Duchies. The great powers, worried about the succession in Denmark, called a conference in London. It was there decided that Prince Christian should be the King's heir. Both his mother-in-law and his wife, who had prior

19

claim, surrendered their right to him. Thus he now became known as Prince of Denmark, and Bernstorff Palace, a few miles from the centre of the capital, was allotted to him as a residence.

These events affected young Alexandra in three ways: she rose in status, now being the eldest daughter of the heir; she moved to the country; and, most important to a child, she was affected by the social vendetta applied to the King's morganatic wife. The leading ladies of Denmark, and in particular Princess Christian, refused to recognise or meet Countess Danner. She was ostracised, with the result that the Copenhagen court was exclusively male. This meant that Alexandra was robbed of the very necessary training in court procedure, attending no ceremonies or festivities. Across her family life lay the dark shadow of 'the Danner woman'.

Meanwhile Louise Danner was hard at work consolidating her position as the king's wife, but was meeting with little success. She demanded the rank of Duchess, but the Government refused. She insisted that the Prince and Princess be ordered to receive her, but Princess Christian refused. But the ministers tolerated Louise for she had an astute political mind and was the only person who could control the King. When, after quarrelling with Frederick because her demands had not been met and storming out of the palace (briefly) he immediately started to drink heavily again – until her return. But Louise was also a clever business woman and accumulated considerable riches, while the Christians remained poor and proud. Thus did Alexandra learn early of the bitterness of Palace intrigue.

But she also gained something of great value: this new stage of her life was set in the tranquil countryside in and around Bernstorff. From its windows could be seen the spires of Copenhagen to the south, the Sound to the east, the forest of Fortunen to the north and the village of Gentofte to the west. Avenues of lime trees crossed the park[11] and led to the yellow-washed house, its steeply pitched roof embellished with dark blue tiles and dormer windows. It had been built in the eighteenth century for the Bernstorff family by a French architect, and was a charming reminder of the great châteaux outside Paris. The Bernstorffs had been keen horticulturists and the gardens were sheer delight. Here Alexandra grew up, giving her love to the house, a love she later transferred to Sandringham.

She was passionately fond of riding. An Englishman who saw her when she was fourteen, galloping along the avenues, laughing with delight, her hair flying in the wind, reported home that he had never seen anything so lovely in his life. Her attractions proved too much for a young officer of the guard and he was posted away. Her mother told her she would have her face smacked if she became a coquette like her cousin, Mary of Cambridge (the Duchess of Teck).[12]

A mile away from Bernstorff lay the village of Gentofte, with rows of thatched cottages and trim, white villas. Each Sunday the family walked across the park to the red brick church there, just as generations of the British Royal Family have followed the path through the grounds of Sandringham to the church of St Mary Magdalene. In fact Alexandra's role at Sandringham was but a continuation of her experiences in Bernstorff. She was soon adopted by the village women, picturesque in large bonnets, striped petticoats and aprons. She ran in and out of the cottages, played with the children, read to the old and cared for the sick. It was this deep and democratic humanity that she carried with her to Norfolk arousing a love which lasts until today.

She learned English from the English chaplain at Copenhagen, the Revd Mr Ellis,[13] and was confirmed in the Palace of the Christianborg. At sixteen she was given a room of her own and a dress allowance of £20 a year.[14] At about this time she was photographed, posed before a sylvan back-drop. Her mother sent copies to her relations, one going to the Duchess of Cambridge at Kew. One day Albert Edward, Prince of Wales, called upon the Duchess. Seeing the photograph on the chimney piece,[15] the nineteen-year-old asked, in the semi-sophisticated tone of voice which his parents so deplored, 'Who is the rustic beauty?'[16]

TWO

❧❧

Seven Brides

Prince Albert Edward, known in the family as 'Bertie' and referred to by his mother, when displeased, as 'You-know-who', posed many problems. He was starved of love, understanding, sympathy and encouragement, all of which he greatly needed. The result was that he became a poseur, a dilettante, and was often very unpleasant. It was to compensate for his deficiencies that his parents, Queen Victoria and Prince Albert, sought the perfect wife, with all the plus values.

Bertie was unfortunate in that he was born to a role that early demanded endless study and concentration, a reasoning mind and a strong constitution. A sense of discipline and the gift for thinking of others was essential. He had none of these things. Work held no attraction for him. He was interested in fancy waistcoats and the cheap novelettes to be bought at railway stations. His leaning towards the pleasures of drinking, smoking and associating with women was soon revealed.

Both Victoria and Albert came to the conclusion that the trouble with Bertie lay 'in the head'. They engaged a phrenologist to examine his bumps, but remained none the wiser. The Queen then decided that the reason for the mental weakness was that she had had Bertie too soon after the birth of her eldest child, Victoria, known as 'Vicky'. But the real causes were genetic. The line was suspect on both sides. Queen Victoria's grandfather, George III, had porphyria which finally overwhelmed him. Of her uncles, George IV was a physical wreck for the greater part of his reign and many people had expected William IV to end in a strait-jacket. On the paternal side, there was haemophilia, tuberculosis and syphilis. As a child, Prince Albert

had been a weakling, suffering from nightmares, croop and fever-
ish colds: he was prematurely aged by the time he was twenty-
five, plagued by rheumatism and constipation; by forty he was an
old man, a victim of periodic depression, the nerves twitching
in his face. The inherited defects showed most clearly in the elder
children of Victoria and Albert, the failing not being apparent
in the younger ones of the brood, two of whom reached ninety.

Bertie's inability to concentrate and study did not appear in
either of his parents. Albert was a glutton for work, could master
any subject and greatly enjoyed a reasoned argument. Bertie
simply could not stand up to the Germanic pressure applied by
Prince Albert and his tutors. Portents of the coming storm were
recognizable – the downcast eyes, the feet shuffling on the floor:
then suddenly all control went. Screams rent the lesson hour,
china and clocks flew through the window, books and papers
filled the air and anyone within range became a target for kicks
and punches.

Bertie was a quiet and a loving child until submerged in the
stern educational programme laid down. Then he took indis-
criminate revenge for the strain imposed upon him. He poured a
jug of water over his valet. Seeing a housemaid's wedding dress
laid out on her bed, he smeared it with red ink. On a walking tour
in the West Country, he went completely berserk among a flock
of sheep, scattering them far and wide. The answer was clear to
many people, but not to his parents. So he opted out. For him,
life was the present, an ever-changing kaleidoscope of pleasures
and interests, amusements and sport, designed to defeat boredom. Not for him the calculated train of reasoning in which his
father delighted. If things went wrong, a scapegoat must be
produced immediately. If things went right, when there was
clapping and cheering and the music of the bands, Bertie shone.
But in the drear classrooms of Windsor and Buckingham Palace,
there were no cheers and no clapping, no hug from his mother or
a whispered 'Well done'. When the day's lessons were over, he
was sent off to physical training under a drill sergeant, just to
make certain that sexual urges did not enter his dreams.

Instead of giving encouragement and sympathy, the parents
poured sarcasm and abuse on his head. Victoria and Albert had
been determined, even certain, that their blessed union would

23

produce a superior, high-minded heir, in marked contrast to the Queen's wicked Uncles' and the weak Dukes of Coburg. Instead they had Bertie! Prince Albert described him as 'the most thorough and cunning lazybones'[1] that he had ever met. Victoria took the strongest exception to his looks. She disliked his small head and large features.[2] 'His nose and mouth are too enormous'. His legs displeased her, for he was knock-kneed. She told this to Lord Clarendon, the Foreign Secretary. Clarendon stuck up for the lad, saying that if the character was all right, the legs did not matter much, 'as people always wear trousers'.[3] Bertie's loud voice almost drove her mad, while his air of superiority, which he assumed when he got the chance – which was not often – infuriated her. She came across him in the children's garden of the Swiss Cottage at Osborne, leaning against the fence and lecturing his brothers and sisters on how to till and sow, while not doing a hand's turn himself. She noted that, while the other children would spend their evenings concocting surprise birthday presents for herself and Albert, Bertie would wait until the last minute and then slip into Windsor and buy some trinket from a shop.

Although Victoria and Albert had planned the marriage of their eldest daughter almost from the day of her birth, plans which had successfully culminated in the fourteen-year old Princess's engagement to Prince Frederick William of Prussia, little consideration had been given to the selection of a wife for Bertie: a wife who one day would be Queen of England. Perhaps his parents found it hard to visualize backward Bertie in the role of husband and father. In foreign Courts, however, the possibilities of a matrimonial alliance were being considered.

Strangely enough, the first feelers came from Denmark. In 1855 the Secretary of the Legation in Copenhagen, anxious to better the relations between Denmark and Britain, wrote to Lord Clarendon suggesting a marriage:

> I know the Glucksburg family well, and one more amiable and excellent does not exist. In the domestic circle admirable, extremely handsome and high-bred, and, although not very clever or brilliant, they possess much of that *esprit de conduite* which in the perpetual storms of life is more to be relied on than the great press of sails.[4]

The Danish Minister in London joined in and sought the help of the Duchess of Cambridge, in whose mind still rankled the thought that her son George should have married Victoria. Planning continued and on 5 July 1858 *The Times* published an article under the heading, 'The Prince of Wales and his Destined Bride'. Out of a list of seven girls, Princess Alexandra was selected as the most suitable candidate. The possibility of the Glucksburg family visiting London came under discussion. Then came a change of Government in Denmark and Baron Blixen-Fineke became Foreign Minister. He was married, morganatically, to Princess Christian's youngest sister. There had been rows, and the Baron was on bad terms with the Hesse-Cassel family. He promptly put a stop to the idea.

Meantime, Bertie's behaviour suggested that he would not only fail to resist feminine temptation, but would welcome it when it came. A healthy young man's chastity record is in direct relation to the amount of temptation which he receives, and none can have received more than the Prince of Wales. This suited Bertie well, though he was constantly foiled by the watch-dogs ever at his heels. But there were slips. Part of the Prince's training consisted of European educational trips and in 1857, at Königswinter, he dined too well, escaped his guards and cornered a pretty girl under the stairs. He was discovered while in the throes of an ecstatic kiss. With unnecessary conscientiousness, the matter was reported to Windsor. It was labelled a 'squalid debauch' and the guards were urged to greater strictness.[5] On his return from Berlin the following year, his parents complained that he talked of nothing but the dances and the parties, and never mentioned any cultural activities. It was with some trepidation that they allowed him to go to Rome in 1859. King Victor Emmanuel's offer to entertain the Prince at Turin was refused, the Queen being fully aware of that monarch's lasciviousness. Count Cavour made caustic comment about '*cette qualité précieuse*' of innocence.[6] So Bertie tramped through the Forum and the Capitol, the Pantheon and St Peter's, and returned to Britain bored but unblemished. He was sent to study at Oxford and later, Cambridge. One afternoon he slipped his keepers and took a train for London and the night spots. He reckoned without the new-fangled electric telegraph. He was met by sombre-clad figures who escorted him to the train leaving shortly for Cambridge.

It was on his tour of Canada and America in 1860 that Bertie found his wings. He was mobbed, he was a triumphant success. The girls were after him in earnest. Martha Haines Butt threatened to kill herself if she did not get a ticket for a ball which he was attending. She got it, and so did many others. Their enthusiasm was so wild that the dance floor collapsed. At a reception given in his honour there were two pretty girls sitting directly behind Bertie. He noticed them, most obviously. Said one pretty girl to the other: 'What lovely hair he has!' The Prince shook with laughter and his escorts scowled. The girl switched to German, which his escorts did not understand but he did. 'How I should love to have a lock of it as a keepsake. Isn't he just lovely? I wonder if I dare cut just a wee bit off. It's rather long – I wonder if he'd mind.' Silence for a while. 'He's such a darling, I don't think he'd mind a bit. Anyway, I'll risk it.' She brought a small pair of scissors from her pocket. Bertie leaned forward as if in prayer, hoping to get out of range. At that moment the welcoming oration came to an end and he was called forward to the stage. A matron in attendance upon him seized the scissors and dealt with the culprit.[7]

When he got home, Bertie was told that his success was due solely to his being the heir of Victoria and Albert. But he had tasted the magic of stardom. He could not long be restrained.

Bertie's attitude to the opposite sex was largely the fault of his parents. He had never been allowed to be alone in a room with a girl – not even with a sister. Prince Albert had a horror of sex, perhaps partly because his rakish brother Ernest contacted venereal disease when he accompanied Albert on the trip to London which culminated in the engagement to the Queen.[8] Victoria, on the other hand, was well aware of her strong sexual appetite and judged others accordingly. Lord Melbourne had had some tricky moments when they were closeted together in the evenings at Windsor.

The Windsor approach to sex was in marked contrast with that prevailing at Bernstorff. The Glucksburg children were not segregated by gender – they were just looked upon as children. They played the same rough games together and gave no quarter. Visiting boys from more restricted families were astounded to be thumped and rolled over by girls.

It was after the kissing incident at Königswinter that Prince Albert realised that his eldest son must marry if he was to be fitted to become King of England. Accordingly, in his calculating manner, he made a list of candidates and then crossed out the unsuitable. His prejudices simplified the task. Thick lines went through the Roman Catholics, Albert abhorring 'the priestly dominion', the rites of which he considered 'perfectly ludicrous'.[9] So no bride could come from Italy or Spain. Russians were out owing to the bitterness caused by the Crimean War. He ended up with six Germans, the same list as *The Times* had put forward, except that he left out Alexandra of Denmark. To Albert, it was natural that there should be no entries from Germany's enemies. He had said before leaving Coburg, 'I shall never cease to be a true *German*'. And he never did.

In January 1858 the Princess Royal, Vicky, married Prince Frederick William of Prussia. Thereafter her mother and father looked upon her as the branch office of Windsor in Berlin, a role of which her in-laws strongly disapproved. It was also very hard on Vicky, fully occupied with learning the ways of a new Court and starting a family. As is the fate with branch offices, she was inundated with memoranda and instructions. One of her tasks was the inspection of the candidates selected as brides for Bertie, and to report on their possibilities and shortcomings. The qualities which Queen Victoria listed as necessary – sound health, good looks, good education, strong character, even temper – could only be found in a paragon. Vicky found no such paragon in Germany. One by one the disappointing reports came in. One girl had bad teeth, another had an objectionable mother. One was too young and sheltered for the marriage bed, and another was plain ugly. In desperation Vicky pleaded that the asset of prettiness be waived, as it was only a 'pleasant ginger-bread'.[10] But prettiness was the virtue which Bertie prized the most. He recoiled in horror from the photograph of one candidate and no one dare risk a repeat of the fate of George III's heir (when introduced to his bride, he had taken to the bottle and spent the bridal night lying in a stupor in the bedroom grate. Only one daughter was the result of that union). Bertie's younger sister,

Alice, watched with disgust as the mating procedure, reminiscent of a cattle show, continued and remarked that she would take strong exception if the same conditions were applied to her. She was told that Bertie was different and quite incapable of making the decision for himself. Meantime Germany was taking it for granted that the Prince of Wales would have a German wife and the Berlin press had been full of speculation at the time of the wedding of the Princess Royal. And no one was more adamant that this should be than Prince Albert's brother, Ernest, Duke of Coburg.

Young Vicky was in a very difficult position. Demands that she renewed her efforts poured in from Windsor. Her loyalty to her adopted country influenced her selection while the Berlin Court, whose attitude to women was limited to bed and kitchen accomplishments, saw nothing wrong with their available candidates. But Vicky was dealing also with the future happiness of her brother and the choice of a British Queen. It was a big problem, and she was only nineteen. So she poured out her troubles to her lady-in-waiting, Countess Walburga von Hothenthal. The Countess, known as Wally, was a very modern young lady, engaged to be married to Augustus Paget, British Minister in Copenhagen. Wally spoke to her fiancé about the 'Princess for Bertie' problem. Paget replied that he knew the very girl – Princess Alexandra of Denmark – and gave her a high rating. Vicky instructed Wally to see the Princess and find out what she could. Wally called upon the Glucksburgs. Alexandra was summoned. 'I was delighted when she came into the room, for I saw in her all the promise of her future loveliness and goodness. She was like a half-open rosebud. . . .'[11] Wally liked everything about the family ànd sent an enthusiastic report to Berlin. Vicky instructed her that she should pass on the information to her parents. Wally sat next to the Prince Consort at dinner at Windsor and, in some trepidation, spoke her piece. Albert listened intently and passed on the news to the Queen, who was sitting on his other side.

Alexandra was no unknown quantity to Victoria and Albert. She had been labelled 'forbidden fruit' and a royal silence was kept about her, for two reasons. The first was the Schleswig-

Holstein question, yearly becoming more acute. The second was the friendship of the Glucksburgs with the Cambridges. The Queen and her husband considered the old Duchess of Cambridge to be a schemer and her brood sexually unstable. Her son George had now married his mistress, the actress Louisa Fairbrother, and they had three sons, but Louisa was ignored by the Court and considered not to exist. Mary, big and bouncy, was far too forward with men. As for Augusta,* she had committed a heinous sin: in 1839 the Queen had become entranced by the Grand Duke Alexander of Russia; 'We had such fun and laughter . . . I never enjoyed myself more'.[12] Then she came across Alexander and Augusta canoodling in the Gallery. There was a 'scene' and Victoria neither forgot nor forgave.

The position was now both grave and urgent, for Bertie was obviously craving for a greater degree of emancipation as a result of his experiences in America, and 'the worst' might happen were he to evade his guards. Accordingly it was decided that the possibilities of the Danish Princess should be explored and a message was sent to branch office, Berlin, to produce a photograph. Vicky obliged, but clearly with some misgivings, for she now warned that such an alliance would be unpopular in Germany. Albert looked at the photograph of Alexandra and was entranced. 'I would marry her at once',[13] he announced.

It was a long and weary winter. The Prince Consort was ill. The old Duchess of Kent died of cancer. Although Victoria had spent her teenage years in battle with her mother, and would do no more than shake hands with her on her wedding day, she was plunged into the deepest gloom. She continually announced that she was going mad and, not unnaturally, the rumour spread around Europe that she was. Frederick William IV of Prussia – who really was mad – died, his death entailing increasing work and responsibility for Vicky and her husband as they became Crown Prince and Princess.

Meantime, in Copenhagen, Princess Christian was considering the future of her elder daughters and she let slip to Germany the information that Emperor Alexander II of Russia was considering Alexandra as wife for his heir. Vicky contacted her mother

* Grand Duchess of Mecklenburg-Strelitz.

– 'it would be dreadful if this pearl was lost to the horrid Russians!'[14] Action was indicated.

It was on 4 June, 1861 that Vicky first met Alexandra, who was on a visit to her relations at Strelitz. Captivated she wrote: 'I never set eyes on a sweeter creature', and penned an 800-word report, giving details of vital statistics, colour, size and features, walk, mental state and character. Alix got top marks in all directions. But she added, somewhat mysteriously, that if the Queen was to think of this perfect creature for Bertie, it would be necessary for her first to be 'initiated'![15] Vicky, hopefully and mistakenly imagining that no one at Strelitz guessed why she was taking such an interest in Alexandra, sent the report by special messenger, since she suspected that mail was being opened at the German borders.

Both the Queen and Prince Consort wrote pages in return, asking for clarification and expansion on certain points and urging secrecy. But someone let the cat out of the bag. The news came to the ears of Duke Ernest of Coburg. Not only did he protest in writing, but he did the one thing that Windsor dreaded – he discussed the matter with Bertie. Furious, Albert wrote to his brother:

> Osborne, July 21, I received your protest against a marriage between Bertie and a Danish Princess. I do not ask, as you will probably expect, 'What is that to you?' or, 'What have you to do with it?' Your position, your relationship and your friendship give you a right to think of Bertie's welfare and the political connections for his future. But what annoys me is, that you spoke to a third person about such delicate and secret affairs, and that you sent me a memorandum which was written by a secretary. . . . We took care not to let Bertie know about the existence of Princess Alexandra, but told him only of the other possibilities. We find it rather strange that just you should tell him about this one princess, and warn him not to marry her, nor allow himself to be induced to marry [her]. I will not waste any words over the fact that we, as his parents, might expect to be told that you wished to warn him. It was wrong to do so behind our backs. Now he has heard from all sides about the beauty of the princess. And he has seen photographs of her in the rooms of the Duchess of Cambridge, at Kew, and they have confirmed what he heard. We explained the political

difficulties such a marriage would bring with it, as well as we could. He understood, as far as a young man of his age and capacities is able to understand them. . . . (It is his wish to marry soon, and it is in his interests, morally, socially and politically). . . . There are *positively no other princesses*, except the sister of Louis.* [This] would connect us for a second time with Darmstadt. All this made it clear to us that Princess Alexandra is the only one to be chosen. . . . We know all the pros and cons, but if we wish to found a happy future for Bertie, we have no other choice.[16]

The principals in the engagement drama began to move around to the positions which they were to occupy when the decisive moment came – the meeting of Alexandra and Bertie. Princess Christian – now known as Princess Louise of Denmark – with her three daughters, left Copenhagen for her old family home at Rumpenheim near Frankfurt, her husband following with the boys when their studies were ended. To Alexandra, this was but a routine summer holiday. The Prince of Wales, who had progressed from Oxford to Cambridge, living at nearby Madingley, had obtained permission to sample military training and was preparing to join the Grenadier Guards at camp at the Curragh. From there he was to journey to Germany to watch military exercises on the Rhine. Victoria and Albert, with their younger children, were to proceed from Osborne to Ireland, to inspect Bertie's progress as a soldier, and then go on to Balmoral. But behind all these moves lay a plan. The Queen dearly loved clandestine operations and she had arranged with Vicky that, while Bertie was in Germany, he should meet, as if by chance, Princess Alexandra of Denmark. The only other people to know of this were Princess Louise of Denmark and Vicky's husband – or so Victoria and Albert hoped and believed.

The charming castle of Rumpenheim on the River Main had been bequeathed by Landgrave Frederick of Hesse-Cassel to his six children on the condition that they and their families should gather there biennially. In this year of 1861 they numbered no less than forty-three. The Hesses *en masse* occupied themselves with outings and sight-seeing, games and picnics, with the emphasis on food. As Mary of Cambridge wrote in her diary: 'At

* Princess Alice had become engaged to Prince Louis of Hesse and the Rhine.

six we had a first-rate repast of trout, potatoes in their skins, stew, ice and cakes. . . . The drive home was delightful.'[17] Political differences there had to be, among so many with loyalties influenced by marriage, but there was a rule at Rumpenheim that contentious subjects were to be avoided.

While the fun continued on the River Main, the Queen and her family departed for Dublin. There they watched a field-day and saw Bertie on parade. His mother thought that he looked well but small. His father considered that he was not taking his military duties seriously enough and hinted that the rein might be tightened.

The Prince Consort was not popular with aristocratic subalterns, and he became even less so when he now condemned the 'idle tendencies of English youth' and deplored that military matters were not allowed to be discussed in the mess. Known as 'the Field Marshal who never went to war', he had been the subject of ridicule in the satirical journals. In fact, he was in direct conflict with the aristocracy, whose members might have liked him more if he had liked money less.

The Queen's party moved off on its stately way to Balmoral. The camp was to end on 12 September. On the evening of the 11th Bertie attended a ball at the Mansion House in Dublin. When he got back to his hut, there was a girl in his bed. Her name was Nellie Clifden and she was experienced. It was a very changed young man who began his journey to Germany on the following day.

On the morning of 24 September Schloss Rumpenheim was early astir, for Prince Christian was taking his family on an expedition to Speyer, some eighty miles away, by train. They were to inspect the wonders of the Cathedral which for three hundred years had been the burial place of the rulers of the Holy Roman Empire. It was regarded by Alexandra as just one more holiday excursion but, to her surprise, her mother fussed around, insisting that she wear her best clothes. As the Danes travelled south by the Rhine, Bertie, his sister Vicky, and Crown Prince Frederick, were making their way from Coblenz, bound for that same Cathedral. The two parties met before the Altar of St Bernard. Bertie was aware that this was going to happen, but Alexandra knew nothing. After introductions were over, the

32

elder folk and the children drifted away, Vicky chatting with Princess Louise, leaving Bishop Nicholaus Weiss to show the young couple the points of interest. Then the Bishop excused himself and the two were alone.

But Crown Prince Frederick, pretending to be entranced with the frescoes, kept his eyes on them. He noted some initial embarrassment. Then Bertie livened up, but Alexandra became 'quieter and more serious'. After lunching, they all went together to Heidelberg. They stayed at the same hotel and next day picnicked in the countryside. As they said their goodbyes, Alexandra and Bertie exchanged photographs. He shook her hand. Then she held out hers for a second shake.[18]

When she got back to Rumpenheim, she told her waiting relations, with a laugh, 'I have got him here!',[19] putting her hand to her bodice where she had put the photograph. Then, seriously, innocently: 'Wasn't it lucky that I was wearing my best bonnet?'[20]

THREE

❦❧

Proposal by Order

Princess Louise of Denmark was a very wise mother. She demanded no categorical statement from Alexandra regarding her feelings for Bertie. When a letter, clearly instigated by Queen Victoria, arrived from Vicky, asking what effect Bertie had had upon her daughter, Princess Louise replied that the matter had not been discussed between them, but that, from what she had observed, the impression had been favourable. Alexandra was only sixteen and she returned, undisturbed, to her lessons and her riding.

Queen Victoria was a very different person. That which she and Albert planned must come to pass. Their wishes must be met. She was trusting that when she next saw her eldest son he would be a changed character, happy, settled in his mind, blessing his dear and clever Papa and Mama for introducing him to such an angel. There would be a nice wedding – stage-managed of course by Papa – and then a house in the country and babies and a fitting preparation for the eventual role of King.

Bertie shuffled into Balmoral on 30 September and talked about anything but Princess Alexandra. He discussed 'the private affairs of Mr this and Mr that'[1] and was much occupied with his projected tour of the Holy Land, doubtless hoping that he would be at the far end of the Mediterranean before his aberration came to light. On being pressed, he gave his opinion that Alexandra's nose was too long and her forehead too low. In despair, the Queen instructed his sister Alice to see if she could wheedle more out of him. She told Vicky: 'As for being in love I don't think he can be, or that he is capable of enthusiasm about anything in the world'.[2] Vicky replied that how the memory of such 'a sweet lovely flower, which would make most men fire and flame', could fade between Baden and Balmoral, was beyond her comprehension. Bertie must be differently constituted 'as regards his head'. Weight was added to this belief when he blurted out to his mother that he had a horror of having children. This Victoria could not understand at all.

The main body of the royal family returned to Windsor, and Bertie to Cambridge, and life became very difficult for Albert. Victoria had a return of gloom over the death of her mother. While the potato crop in Ireland failed, relations between Britain and America worsened and moved towards a crisis. The rain poured down and the drains at Windsor stank. Albert developed a cold with heavy catarrh. On 16 November he learned that Bertie had slept with Nellie Clifden, causing him 'the greatest pain I have yet felt in my life'.[3] The Queen and he retired to their private rooms and debated what was to be done. The scandal was apparently common knowledge in the clubs and the courts of Europe. Would Prince Christian and Princess Louise now refuse to allow Alexandra to see Bertie again? It was while they were in seclusion that the next blow fell – in the form of a letter from Baron Stockmar.

Christian von Stockmar was a doctor, the mentor of the Coburgs, the motivating power which spread the Coburg seed around the palaces of Europe. He was an inhuman man, with a vast knowledge of the world, a man who liked to direct the flow of affairs without involving himself. Stockmar was appointed Leopold's private secretary and political adviser. Later, as King of the Belgians, Leopold placed Stockmar beside the young Queen Victoria when she ascended the throne. It was Stockmar who converted Albert from an insipid, pale-faced student into the opera star with whom Victoria fell in love – Stockmar who extinguished the power which Lord Melbourne and Baroness Lehzen held over the Queen. He was the only person who could arrive at, and leave, the British palaces as he wished and without notice. Each evening, when he was there, Albert would hurry to his room to discuss the problems of the day. But in the 1850s Stockmar, feeling his age, came less often to London. When Albert was in trouble for his supposed Russian sympathies in the Crimean war, he asked help of the Baron, only to be told that he had led a 'garrison life' for too long and that now Albert must stand on his own feet. Accordingly, out of favour, Stockmar had not been informed of the plans for Bertie and Alexandra. But he found out, and also about Nellie Clifden. He was furious and fired a broadside from Coburg.

What he said, loud and clear, was that the Queen and Prince Consort were interfering with the ways of God and nature. They were trying to make good the deficiencies of their heir by buying the strong qualities of Alexandra.

> The main reason for this affair was given to me that it is hoped that the defects of spirit and mind of the one person should be made up by the strength of the other person. How daring would it be to take part in this lottery of possibilities![4]

Stockmar was correct. Victoria and Albert, disappointed with their eldest son, were trying to put matters to rights in the next generation, and were precipitating two young people into marriage without due consideration as to whether they were suitable for one another, without even the privilege of being allowed to make up their own minds. The Baron went on to stress the danger of forcing the Prince of Wales into a union which he might later regret, a union which would make him a prisoner, embittered for life against his parents and his wife. Was it really necessary, he asked, for Bertie to marry early? To him, it appeared that the idea 'seems to be more due to mere opinion than consideration and genuine interest'. This hit hard, for it was the view of Victoria and Albert that they having said so, so it must be. Bertie, they maintained, was unfitted to make up his own mind. The feelings and future of Alexandra did not enter into it. She was poor and came from a family junior in status. She was, therefore, in the Windsor view, exceedingly fortunate to get the chance but the Baron pursued his cold and calculated reasoning:

> Since the affair is based on the condition that one party has the solid features of character that the other party is missing, the certainty of the existence of such features would have to be a *'conditio sine qua non'*.[5]

Thus the indispensable prerequisite of the proposed marriage was that Alexandra had both the character and the health to counterbalance Bertie's deficiencies. But was this so, asked the Baron? He doubted it. 'One of the heads of the family is supposed to be insignificant and imbecile and the other is of lax principles and has the characteristics of an intriguer.' There was a scar on Princess Alexandra's neck. This had been dismissed as the work of a stupid doctor who had experimented upon her when she had a cold. But Stockmar was also a doctor and suspected scrofula (a constitutional state, usually hereditary, tending to the development of consumption). He ended his letter with the warning – 'Not a step further, otherwise a disaster can occur of which the consequences cannot be foreseen.'

As we shall see, the old Baron's words were prophetic. But Albert had reached a stage in life when he no longer believed that he could be wrong in anything. Stockmar, he concluded, must be senile. Victoria, innocent of worries about the health of later generations, assumed that the Baron was inferring that there had been hidden scandals in the Hesse–Cassel family, and there was nothing that she liked better than unearthing wickedness. The suspicion lingered in her mind.

Albert, determined to sort out the Nellie Clifden affair, went to Cambridge to have it out with Bertie. Travelling to and from Madingley while suffering from a heavy cold on a wet November day was an act of sheer stupidity. It would have been simple to summon Bertie to attend on him. He caught typhoid, but instead of being put to bed he was allowed to wander about the draughty Castle, relying on the singing of hymns to cure him. Weaker and weaker he grew, yet Victoria refused to call their eldest son. On her own decision, Princess Alice sent a telegram to Cambridge on 13 December. Next day the Prince Consort died.

In the dark cloud of misery and paranoia into which she retreated, away from the eyes of all but Princess Alice, Queen Victoria developed certain obsessions. One was that Bertie was responsible for the Prince Consort's death, conveniently overlooking her own responsibility in that direction. She shuddered with horror every time that she saw her son and King Leopold found in her 'an antipathy that is quite incurable'.[6] She despatched him on his planned tour of the near east and the Holy

Land. This not only relieved her of the unpleasantness of his presence, but also allowed her time to ensure that he took over no part of his father's mantle. Quite understandably, the British public now expected the heir to play a greater part in State affairs and this had been put forward in the press. The Queen was determined that this should not happen.

Another obsession was that whatever Albert had wished or planned should become her law. He had wished Bertie to marry Alexandra, and so it should be. He had deplored the Danish connection, and so did his widow. Bearing in mind the innuendoes contained in Stockmar's letter, she urged the Crown Princess to ferret out the truth.

Meantime, in Copenhagen, Princess Louise had heard from Cousin George – the Duke of Cambridge – not only all about Nellie Clifden, but also about the antipathy, amounting to hatred, which the Queen harboured against her eldest son. The Princess cried.[7] With three daughters on her hands, and very little money, her position as a mother was difficult indeed owing to the lack of social occasions at the Danish Court and to the enmity between herself and 'the Danner woman'. After the meeting at Speyer, she had regarded an engagement as a foregone conclusion. Now George's revelations, coupled with the death of the Prince Consort, had created a state of flux. It was not Bertie's aberration which upset her unduly, for such initiation was customary for young men in Germany. What she feared most was that his mother's dislike of him would continue and that this dislike would embrace Alexandra. Already there was difficulty enough in the diverging opinions over Schleswig-Holstein. If Queen Victoria carried on with her feud, blaming Bertie for his father's death, Alexandra would be placed in a very difficult situation as daughter-in-law. The Glucksburgs were a tightly knit, united family and the thought of Alexandra's home life being plagued by quarrels with her in-laws worried her. Princess Louise had received advances from Russia on behalf of her eldest daughter, but had repulsed them, preferring the Prince of Wales to the Cesarevitch.

Alexandra was now seventeen and her mother informed her of the negotiations which had been going on, without her knowledge, for a marriage with the Prince of Wales. Her reaction was solely one of anger that she had not been put in the picture, that so many people had been planning for her future behind her back. She wrote a sympathetic and sensible letter to Bertie regarding the death of his father. She had made up her own mind about the future.

Vicky's efforts to unearth failings in the Glucksburg family had surprising results. With the enthusiasm of a reporter on a lurid Sunday newspaper, she interviewed a series of people supposedly in the know, most of whom were anxious to put an end to the romance and, therefore, quite prepared to exaggerate and fabricate. She unearthed stories that Prince Christian was a drunkard and had been involved in a financial scandal; that Princess Louise had had an illegitimate child and that her mother, the 'old' Landgravine, was both a wicked woman and an intriguer; that Alexandra had indulged in a number of flirtations with young officers, one of whom had been removed in consequence; that the scar on her neck was scrofula; and that her aunt Augusta was separated from her husband, Baron Blixen-Fineke, she being not respectable and he an adventurer.

The Queen was appalled. But, there, Albert had suspected such things and said that 'we could not help it'.[8] He had decreed that the marriage should take place and, if Bertie proved obstinate, then she would wash her hands of him and marry Alexandra to her second son. She asked for the rumours to be checked. Vicky investigated. It turned out that Prince Christian had been in financial difficulties in 1856, which was not surprising as he was playing the part of heir to the Throne on a pittance. The family had helped him out. Vicky admitted that she had no idea that the Glucksburgs were so poor – a point of which the Queen made due note when it came to planning for the wedding. The illegitimate child was traced to the bed of Princess Louise's sister, Marie, Princess of Dessau. The 'old' Landgravine had encouraged her in her passion for a groom, with disastrous results. The sum of Alexandra's flirtations was that a young officer had fallen violently in love with her and it had been thought wiser to post him away. That the mark on her neck was scrofula came from a source close to Duke Ernest of Coburg and Baron Stockmar. Vicky commented: 'Really one does not know what to say to prove the contrary to people who are so difficult to convince.'⁹ She was anxious that her brother should marry Alexandra quickly. If he got loose in British society, he simply had not the will-power to resist temptation. She handed out bouquet after bouquet to Alix, saying that her character, strength and sensibility were underestimated – an opinion which was to be voiced over and over again in the years ahead.

The problem which now loomed up was – what would be the Queen's reaction to Bertie when he returned? Would she shudder at the sight of him, or would five months of absence have made her heart grow fonder? The Prince's tour of the near east had proved less restricted and educational than his father had planned. His interest had been more with his guns than with ancient monuments and he had shot at everything that moved, from crocodiles to lizards. His various hosts had entertained him in the way that a young man of twenty liked to be entertained. The royal yacht brought him back along the Mediterranean, calling at Turkey, Greece and Tripoli, and depositing him at Marseilles on 10 June.

The Prince Consort, who had laid out the itinerary, had allowed for only one day in Paris, with an over-night stay at the British Embassy. He had regarded the court of Napoleon III with horror and his widow, despite her triumphant and enjoyable visit to France in 1855, had adopted his view. 'That Sodom and Gomorrah', she labelled Paris (on expounding on the subject at the luncheon table, her youngest daughter, Beatrice, aged five, asked if the salt into which Lot's wife was converted was the same as she put on her chicken). The Queen now sent a message to Sir Charles Phipps, in charge of the Prince, that he should be in bed by eleven and that, naturally, mourning prevented any dinners or parties.

The Empress Eugenie, a great favourite with the royal children, disapproved of Queen Victoria's strong hold on them. Out of mischief, she whisked Bertie off to Fontainebleau. There she deposited him in a ring of attractive young ladies, while she fully occupied, and beguiled, Sir Charles Phipps. Bertie danced until long after his stipulated bedtime. One of his partners, the Princess Jeanne de Sagan, later became his mistress. However, before leaving France, he had the tact to buy presents for Alexandra.

The moment of re-union came at Windsor. To the relief of all, the Queen was pleased with what she saw. She considered that Bertie was 'less coarse looking'. He was more serious, the look in his eyes was better and he was kinder to the younger children. The telling point was that 'he is ready to do everything that I wish'.[10]

Bertie was in fact very much on his best behaviour, quite naturally in view of his mother's bellicose attitude towards him. He found her grief for his father overpowering – throughout his life he could not tolerate long mourning. He longed for the day when he would be loosed from her apron strings, when, at twenty-one, he would have his own establishment in London and the country home at Sandringham in Norfolk which the Prince Consort had arranged should be bought for him. Marriage was a means of escape from dreary Windsor. He had realised, and accepted, that his bride would be chosen for him, but, on the plus side, out of the seven candidates, he had been able to choose by far the prettiest. Already the public were taking the engagement for granted. Pictures of, and articles about, Alexandra were appearing in the magazines. One review had posed the awkward question – if the choice was restricted to only seven young ladies, what were the chances of finding perfect love?

The Queen planned on. She was making a nostalgic journey to Coburg in September and she arranged with King Leopold of the Belgians that, on her way there, she should meet Princess Alexandra and her parents at his palace of Laeken near Brussels. At the end of August the announcement came from Copenhagen: 'The Prince and Princess of Denmark, accompanied by the greater part of their family, have left for Ostend where it is the intention of Their Royal Highnesses to remain for some weeks for the benefit of the sea-bathing.'[11] On 2 September the Queen travelled to Brussels, and the Glucksburgs came there from Ostend. Next day she met her future daughter-in-law. She wrote: 'She looked lovely, in a black dress, nothing in her hair, and curls on either side, which hung over her shoulders, her hair turned back off her beautiful forehead. Her whole appearance was one of the greatest charm, combined with simplicity and perfect dignity.'[12]

The Queen had next to clear the situation with Prince Christian and Princess Louise, and she dreaded it.

> Now came the terribly trying moment for me. I had *alone* to say and do what, under other, former happy circumstances, had devolved on us both together. It was not without much emotion that I was able to express what I did to the Princess: my belief that they knew what we wished and hoped, which was terrible for me to say *alone*. I said that I trusted their dear daughter would feel, should she accept our son, that she was doing so with her whole heart and will. They assured me that Bertie *might hope* she would do so, and that they trusted *he* also felt a real inclination, adding that they hoped God would give their dear child strength to do what she ought, and that she might be able to pour some comfort into my poor heart, that they were sure she would become quickly attached to me, and be a good wife to Bertie. I replied I would do all I could to be a *real* mother. . . .[13]

There was a fitting accompaniment of tears and Queen Victoria then moved on to Coburg – there to shed more tears as she stirred up reminiscences of Albert's boyhood.

Coincidentally, the Prince of Wales travelled from Windsor to Ostend. He was accompanied by Sir Charles Phipps and Sir William Knollys, his Comptroller. He walked by the sea with Alexandra. She was better dressed than when he had seen her at Speyer – Wally Paget had seen to that, despite the order of Queen Victoria that pretty frocks were not to be used as an enticement. Phipps and Knollys, observing from a diplomatic distance, noted that Bertie was carefree and happy, she completely natural. It was also noted that there was no sign of the Prince being in love, though, having only met once before, what signs were envisaged it is difficult to assess. They were seventeen and twenty, granted a few minutes out of the parental orbit, walking by the water's edge, leaving their footprints in the sand, listening to the music of the waves.

The Prince and his party proceeded to Brussels, putting up at an hotel. On the following morning Bertie drove to Laeken to listen to the advice and instructions of King Leopold. On the 8 September *les Danois,* as they were now labelled, arrived at the same Brussels hotel. Bertie spoke with Prince Christian and Princess Louise and told them of his wish to marry their daughter. He later commented: 'I don't think I ever saw anybody so much pleased as Prince Christian was.'[14] They all dined together and it was agreed that action should be taken on the morrow. Bertie told Wally Paget, who was much of his age and whom he had come to know well through Vicky: 'I shall take a walk in the garden with Princess Alexandra for three-quarters of an hour. Then I shall take her into the grotto and propose to her, and I hope everything will turn out to everybody's satisfaction.'[15] Wally was somewhat taken aback by the exactness of the time-table and the calculated approach.

Next morning the Prince and the Danes drove to Laeken Palace where they were received by King Leopold. Smiling, he played out the charade, inviting his guests to walk with him around the gardens and admire the autumnal flowers. It was all worked out to a step. The older folk proceeded on their way, chatting together. The young couple slowed, until there was a suitable gap between them. Then Bertie took Alexandra's arm and led her into the grotto. There they became engaged. His lines had been well rehearsed. She did not say much – but her 'Yes' was firm. They went back to the palace where the older folk were awaiting them, ready to register the requisite degree of surprise. The Prince asked parental permission to make Alexandra his bride. Granted. 'We then went to luncheon . . .'

The Prince's next assignment was to write to his mother. It was a most detailed piece of reporting, tactfully put together. 'May God grant that *our* happiness may throw a ray of light on your once so happy and now so desolate home. You may be sure that we shall both strive to be a comfort to you.'[16] It may be fairly deduced that either Phipps or Knollys was in the editorial chair.

There was a plethora of expressions of overpowering love in his engagement communiqué. 'I did not think it possible to love a person as I do her. . . . I am in a dream. . . . I do not know whether I am on my head or my heels. . . . ' Yet, to the observers, he still showed no outward signs of love, though Alexandra did. Perhaps in love with love – and knowing nothing of it – her eyes were nevertheless always on him. She listened with wonder to a gay young man who had seen Niagara Falls and the White House in Washington, who had shot crocodiles on the Nile and spoken with the Pope in Rome, a prince who would inherit an empire upon which the sun never set. She had never had a smart dress, nor danced all night, nor travelled further afield than Rumpenheim and Strelitz. The stars were in her eyes.

They had a week together in Brussels. There were outings, to the field of Waterloo, to the Flanders woods, to the Abbey Villers.[17] They rode together. She played the piano and sang to him. There was a court ball. Tactfully, Alexandra made up to old King Leopold, ever addicted to flattery. He liked it, but noted how simple and unformed she was, in marked contrast to Vicky at the same age. There was only one restraining influence. By firm order of Queen Victoria, the engaged couple were not allowed to be alone. The permitted limit of intimacy was a short time together in a room of which the door was open, Princess Louise on duty outside.[18]

Les Danois departed for Rumpenheim, Bertie for Coburg. He came into his mother's presence holding in his hands, as if it were a piece of delicate china, a twelve-page letter from Alexandra – his first love-letter. It was a most successful gesture. Sadly, the sweet scent of romance was soured by news which had reached the Queen that her second son, Affie the sailor, had disgraced himself sexually, his aberration being 'far worse than Bertie's'.[19] She immediately sent off for full details.

Although the engagement had taken place on 9 September, it was not until the 16th that it was made public and then only in a half-hearted way. A paragraph, obviously activated by the Queen, appeared in the Press:

> We understand that the marriage of the Prince of Wales to the Princess Alexandra of Denmark has been privately settled at Brussels, and that it is based entirely on mutual affection and the personal merit of the young Princess, and is in no way connected with political consideration. The late Prince Consort, whose sole object was the welfare and happiness of his children, had long been convinced that this was a most suitable marriage. The knowledge of this is in itself a sense of deep gratification to the Queen, and will be as such satisfactory to the country.

The Times printed it, without comment, in an obscure corner. Although the royal marriage act created no problem, in the event it was not until 5 November that the Queen's formal assent to the marriage was officially announced. There were many reasons for this, hidden away in the passages of the Queen's labyrinthine mind, German reaction being one of them.

The news was received with elation in Denmark. Copenhagen was decorated for the return of Prince Christian and his family. When Alexandra appeared at the opera, the audience rose and roared approval and congratulations.[20]

Britain was delighted. Lady Palmerston summed up the feeling when she said: 'I like the Danish connection. We have had too much of Germany and Berlin and Coburg.'[21] But the Germans were furious and inflamed. Baron Stockmar banged the table in anger. Duke Ernest of Coburg denounced the engagement as 'a thunder-clap for Germany'. In Berlin the Crown Prince and Princess became unpopular for the part which they had played. Fortunately for them, they had already planned a long tour of the Mediterranean countries, thus avoiding unpleasantness at court.

Alexandra and her family were anxious that Bertie should visit them, so that he might become acquainted with Denmark and that they might get to know him better on their own ground. Alexandra wanted him to meet her young friends, see Bernstorff and her horses and dogs. A perfectly normal situation. So Bertie informed his mother that he wished to visit Copenhagen before his wedding. But the tortuous depths of her mind were unfathomable. From that moment she altered course completely, turning directly against Alexandra's parents. Prince Christian she described as 'stupid' and Princess Louise as 'wicked' and 'mischievous', looking upon her relations with horror. It was all rather odd, for there were no real grounds for this horror, and she raised no objection when later a grand-daughter married into the Hesse-Cassels. She was in fact waiting for this chance to show her superior powers, to make clear that what she said counted. She, not *les Danois*, would dictate the movements of the young people. Bertie was refused his request on the grounds of the critical position in Schleswig-Holstein. Instead he would accompany his sister and the Crown Prince on their Mediterranean tour – thus being away when the official announcement of his engagement was made and, worse, away for his twenty-first birthday on 9 November, an occasion which called for national

45

rejoicing. The Queen was making it obvious – there were to be no spot-lights for Bertie.

The Queen was also seemingly at cross purposes. While she backed the Prussian claim for Schleswig-Holstein, she was aligning Britain and Denmark by agreeing to the marriage of her heir. The only course of action open to her was to eliminate the Danish influence in Alexandra and to play down the role of Denmark in the wedding. She wrote to Vicky: '. . . the German element is the one I wish to be cherished . . . now more than ever. . . . Alix's parents are inclined to encourage the English and merge the Germany into Danish and English and this would be a dreadful sorrow to me: the very thing dear Papa and I disliked so much in the connexion is the Danish element.'[22] This latter she certainly discouraged. When King Frederick of Denmark wrote to her saying how pleased he was at the engagement and that he wished the wedding to take place in England, Queen Victoria commented: 'How impertinent!!! No answer will be given.'[23] Neither was an invitation sent.

On the personal side, Bertie was instructed that he must write to Alexandra in German. Prince Christian was instructed that his daughter would attend upon the Queen for five weeks from the beginning of November. He was to bring her and return for her at the end of her stay. No hospitality was offered and no mention made of Princess Louise. It was further stipulated that Alexandra should bring with her neither Danish lady-in-waiting nor Danish maid. King Leopold did his best to stop this idea, fearing what might happen to the sweet girl while alone in the folds of the 'black widow', but for once his advice was ignored. Princess Louise, however, made her first stand and showed her strength. She insisted that Alexandra be back in Copenhagen for her birthday on 1st December. Despite pressure, she remained adamant. Victoria, who hated being crossed, put in an unexpected blow. She recruited Bertie on her side. Not entirely to his credit, he backed the stronger of the opponents, writing to Copenhagen that, if the Princess wished to marry her daughter to the Prince of Wales, she must learn to put up with small inconveniences.[24] Princess Louise repeated – either Alexandra was back for her birthday or she did not go. She won that round.

Prince Christian and his daughter arrived at Osborne on 5

46

November.. Alexandra was terrified when her father left, but, as it proved, without grounds, for Queen Victoria unpredictably proved to be kindness itself. Admittedly Alexandra, well briefed, was an ideal guest. She made great fuss of the Queen's younger children, she read the approved religious books, she took lessons in English, writing and drawing and she went to bed regularly at ten o'clock. Most important of all, she sat attentively by the Queen as she listened to reminiscences of life with Albert. One night she burst into tears, thus earning a special diploma. She was simple and straightforward. She always came to breakfast in a jacket. 'My dear,' said the Queen to her one day, 'you seem very fond of jackets. How is it you *always* wear a jacket?' 'Well,' said Alexandra, 'I like them; and then, you see a jacket is *so economical*! You can wear different skirts with it, and I have very few gowns, having to make them all myself. My sisters and I have no lady's maid, and have been brought up to make all our own clothes. I made my own bonnet.'[25]

In her letters to Vicky the Queen opened the flood gates of laudation. Alexandra, she wrote, was 'kind, loving, sweet, sensible, gentle, good, simple, unspoilt, honest, affectionate, intelligent, cheerful, merry.' 'She is so affectionately attached to me! It is a great blessing and I do thank God for it – that in our misery He has permitted this.' 'She is one of those sweet creatures who seem to come from the skies to help and bless poor mortals and brighten for a time their path!'[26] It seemed as if the future was to be all roses for Alexandra of Denmark. She was deservedly pleased with herself, although in after years she would laugh at the time when she was sent 'on approval' to Osborne, as if she was a package of soft furnishings from Gorringes.

FOUR

The Wedding

As Alexandra returned to Copenhagen to prepare her trousseau, Queen Victoria underwent one of her sudden changes of front. The forthcoming wedding became a nightmare to her. 'I dread the whole thing awfully . . . it is for me far worse than a funeral to witness.'[1] Bertie, back from his Mediterranean tour, got on her nerves. He insisted on arguing and this always gave her headaches. She became anxious as to his performance as a husband and confided in King Leopold: 'I am *very* anxious for the result. I fear dear Alexandra is under a complete delusion.'[2] She down-graded the wedding, giving priority to three other dates on her calendar – the first anniversary of the death of the Prince Consort and the movement of his remains to the mausoleum at Frogmore in the middle of December, the anniversary of her mother's death on 12 March and the arrival of Princess Alice for the birth of her first child in April. For three troubled months battle was waged over the matrimonial arrangements: there were disagreements over the date of the wedding, the place of the wedding, the colours of the dresses, who was to be invited, who was to stay at Windsor, when the bride was to arrive. The only person who could stand up to the tide was Alexandra's mother, Princess Louise.

The finalised date of 10 March 1863 fell in Lent. Understandably, the Church protested. The Queen demolished the argument by saying that she was staging a religious ceremony and not a variety performance. The choice of St George's Chapel, Windsor, for the service was universally condemned. Londoners considered that they were being robbed of a 'day off' and a chance to see the bride – they had expected St Paul's or Westminster Abbey. Under the heading, 'A Quiet Affair', *Punch* castigated the arrangement:

> As it is now finally settled that the marriage of the Prince of Wales is not to take place in London, but in an obscure village in Berkshire, remarkable only for an old castle and non-sanitary arrangements, Mr Punch ventures to suggest that the secrecy of the proceeding should be carried out to the utmost, and that all the intimation the nation should have that the Heir Apparent is wedded should be the following advertisement among the Marriages in *The Times* of March 13th:—
>
> > 'On the 12th instant, at Windsor, by Dr Longley, assisted by Dr Thomson, Albert Edward England, K.G., to Alexandra Denmark. No cards.'*

As the capacity of St George's limited the guest list to nine hundred, there was bitterness amongst those who had expected to be asked and now were not. This feeling was most apparent among politicians and Duchesses. 'There was no intention to invite Dizzy (Disraeli) but Palmerston remonstrated strongly against the omission of a man who had been twice leader of the House of Commons.'³ The Duke of Cambridge's sister, Augusta, at whose home Vicky had first met Alexandra, ordered a lavish new outfit of wedding and travelling clothes but waited in vain for her invitation. Those who were lucky enough to be chosen complained bitterly about the inconvenience of travelling to Windsor in their splendour. At the time the railway only ran as far as Slough, carriages were cold and uncomfortable, while the risk of damage to *grandes toilettes* by smuts from the engine was considerable. There were mutterings of discontent from within the Castle. The princesses and the Ladies of the Household had hoped for a lightening of the mourning arrangements for the Prince Consort, but no, the order came that they must limit themselves to grey, lilac or mauve.⁴

But it was in Denmark that the most bitter resentment was felt. The Danes considered, and with grounds, that their country was being dismissed as of no consequence – their King had not even received a formal request for the hand of Princess Alex-

---

* Printed on 31 January 1863. It is apparent that even by then the final date had not been announced.

49

andra. Invitations were sent most sparingly and only the closest relations of Prince Christian and Princess Louise were asked. However, when it was suggested that Alexandra should leave home in January and spend five or six weeks with King Leopold at Brussels before reaching London – Queen Victoria having in mind a period of quarantine to ensure that the bride was free of the 'Danish influence' – Princess Louise dug her toes in. She was determined to keep her daughter with her for as long as possible. In any case it was essential that she should be in Copenhagen so that she might be fitted for her trousseau, which was being beautifully embroidered with hand-sewing by Danish seamstresses.

Finance was a curb on the independence of the Danes, the wedding expenses being on a scale beyond their vision and experience. The Prince of Wales sent Alexandra £3,000 for her trousseau and £15,000 in jewels.[5] These included a complete set of diamonds and pearls, comprising diadem, necklace, stomacher and bracelet, and a beautiful waist-clasp, formed of two large turquoises inlaid with Arabic characters and mounted in gold. The wedding ring was set with six precious stones – a beryl, an emerald, a ruby, a turquoise, a jacinth and a second emerald, the initials of the six gems spelling 'Bertie'.[6] Alexandra was relieved of the task of providing the wedding dress. King Leopold wished to play his part in this and sent an exquisite creation in Brussels lace. But at the last moment it was decided that the bride should wear a national product. It consisted of a white satin skirt, trimmed with garlands of orange blossom and puffings of tulle and Honiton lace, the bodice being draped with the same lace, worked in a pattern of roses, shamrocks and thistles.

The Prince could well afford his gift, Parliament having granted him £40,000 per year, bringing his annual income up to around £105,000. At the same time Alexandra had been granted £10,000 as 'pin money' and £30,000 in the event of her becoming a widow. On hearing this Prince Christian remarked caustically that, despite the small 'rise' he had recently received, his daughter's 'pin money' would exceed by £8,000 the sum upon which he was supposed to support a large family and keep up his position as heir.

The Wedding

Queen Victoria undertook to pay the travelling expenses of *les Danois*. Augustus Paget, Minister in Copenhagen, was appointed royal courier and to accompany the party. In February he received instructions from the Foreign Office:

> The Queen has been pleased that the expenses to be incurred for the journey of Their Royal Highnesses should be defrayed by this Country and you will accordingly draw upon the Chief Clerk of the Foreign Office for such sums as you may require. Her Majesty has selected Lt General Grey and Colonel F. Seymour to meet Their Royal Highnesses at Brussels as Her Majesty's personal Attendants, and to make the further arrangements for the embarkation on the Royal Yacht, as those who had the honour of being sent in 1840 to bring the beloved Prince to England for his Marriage.[7]

The Queen was determined that, not only should the ghost of dear Albert walk beside the bride, but that there should be no excessive expenses on the part of the Danes. She raised a question – as Prince Christian and his party would be travelling on Danish railways and a Danish royal steamer as far as the frontier, was she expected to pay for that part of the journey? Paget saw the danger light and was careful. Before he spent £70 on illuminating the British legation, he cleared the cost with London.

Denmark cared well for their Princess. She was presented with 100,000 kroner, known as 'the People's Dowry'. She put part of this aside for distribution to poor Danish girls to be married at the same time, and this increased her popularity even more. King Frederick excelled himself. His present was a necklace containing 2,000 brilliants and 118 pearls, the two largest of which had been exhibited at the International Exhibition at the Crystal Palace. From it hung a facsimile of the famous Dagmar Cross, in which was set a fragment reputed to belong to the True Cross, with a piece of silk taken from the grave of King Canute.[8] And, although tired and ill, the King came to Copenhagen to see her off.

At three o'clock on the afternoon of 26 February 1863 the gates of the Yellow Palace opened, salutes were fired and Princess Alexandra and her family began their journey to England. She was wearing a brown costume with white stripes, topped with a chic little bonnet which she had made herself. Although

51

the crowds to see her were dense, her progress through Denmark was orderly and picturesque, in marked contrast with the near riot conditions which she was to meet in London. There were flowers, and massed schoolchildren and loyal addresses. At Korsor, where the party left the railway for the steamer, the Burgomaster said:

> The Royal House of England, of which you are about to become a member, is one of the most exalted in Europe, and Great Britain. . . . is the greatest nation in the world, while Denmark is, as our own poet has admitted, but a small, poor country. But, and we say it with just pride, for all its insignificance we have been important enough for the son of England to come to us for a bride. Fully conscious of the value of the pearl we give away, we send greetings to our kindred, the great English people. . . .[9]

And yet Alexandra was quiet and sad as she watched her country fading behind her and left it to her sister Dagmar to do the waving and the smiling and the chatting. There came to her the echo of the words of Queen Victoria, saying that, when she quit Denmark, she left her loyalties and her memories behind. Fortunately she was surrounded by her brothers and sisters, Frederick, William and Waldemar, Dagmar and Thyra, for whom the trip was one huge frolic. They pulled the leg of their eldest sister mercilessly. Germany, somewhat surprisingly, produced an enthusiastic reception, the people of Altona, Hamburg, Hanover and Cologne roaring their approval of the beauty of the bride. Laeken Palace at Brussels was reached on 2 March. There Alexandra retired to bed with a cold.

On the morning of the 5th the Danish party boarded the royal yacht, *Victoria and Albert*, picking up a British squadron of ironclads off Flushing. The barometer fell rapidly, a storm blew up and that evening the yacht and her escort anchored in Margate Roads. Next morning the corporation of the seaside resort presented Princess Alexandra with the first address of welcome to be received from an English civic authority. The ceremony proved too much for the sense of humour of her family. As the yacht sailed away towards the Nore, they collapsed into fits of laughter. Brother Willy having given an imitation of his sister receiving the civic gentlemen, Alexandra pushed him down upon a chair and belaboured his head with the loyal address of the mayor and corporation.[10]

Nine o'clock, Saturday morning, 7 March 1863. The royal yacht nosed her way slowly up London's river. Shore batteries fired, steamers hooted and small craft of all varieties crowded the water from shore to shore. Ships were dressed over-all, church bells were ringing and flags and bunting bedecked the bankside houses. Alexandra turned to her mother and asked: 'Are all these things for me?'[11]

At Gravesend there was tumult. The Princess was dressed all in white, a white shawl around her shoulders, and her hair was parted in the middle in the fashion of the Empress Eugenie. When they saw her at the taffrail, the lightermen and the stevedores and all manner of seafaring folk roared their delight. She bowed and waved and then, turning towards her mother for guidance, ran from side to side.

The special train which brought the Prince of Wales from Windsor was late. He was wearing a blue frock-coat and grey trousers and was obviously pleased with himself. He ran down the pier and jumped into a rowing boat. Alexandra was waiting to greet him on *Victoria and Albert*. To the crowd's delight he kissed her before their eyes. As they walked together towards the train that was to take them to Bricklayers' Arms Station, Southwark, sixty 'comely' maidens, dressed in white skirts and red cloaks – the red and white of Denmark – strewed violets and primroses in their path. And so, in a special saloon-carriage, they proceeded slowly, along a crowded line, to the Old Kent Road.[12]

There were many reasons why this Saturday proved to be one of the most extraordinary days in the long history of London. The crowd scenes have seldom been rivalled and the authorities were caught unprepared. An obvious reason for the vast influx to the ceremonial route was the recent increase in the railway network, with improvements to rolling stock and timetables – many of those who made the trip had never been to the metropolis before. A second cause was the lack of royal occasions in past years. There had been the Great International Exhibition in Hyde Park in 1851 and the state visit of Emperor Napoleon III and Empress Eugenie in 1855, but little else. The Prince Consort had never encouraged 'gilt and gingerbread' and

53

displays of enthusiasm, and since his death the pall of mourning had been unrelieved. And in those days when holidays were few, a royal procession meant permission to take a few hours away from dull routine, a chance for 'larks' and a glimpse of the other side of life.

A third cause was relief that, at long last, a royal marriage partner was arriving from a country other than Germany. For the past century they had come, with relentless monotony, from Mecklenburg and Brunswick, Hesse and Prussia, Coburg and Leiningen – the women lacking in beauty and the men with their hands outstretched for money. Furthermore, the new processes in photography now made it possible for pictures of Alexandra to be in the shops. They had sold by tens of thousands and reached every corner of the country. This contrasted strongly with the position when Prince Albert arrived in 1840, when no likeness of him was available.

The Corporation of London was determined that Alexandra should have an unforgettable reception, (a view not shared by the Queen, the Master of the Horse or the Metropolitan Police) and spent £40,000 on decorations and illuminations. The result was that arrangements for controlling the vast crowds were hopelessly inadequate, cordons were repeatedly broken and it took nearly four hours for the procession to reach Paddington station. The carriages looked drab, the horses carried no rosettes, and there were no outriders.

The first hitch came at London Bridge. Here there was a hold up lasting half-an-hour. It began to snow. The cause of the delay was that the Lord Mayor and the Aldermen had lingered too long over their lunch at the Guildhall and, underestimating the density of the crowds, were unable to get through. Only the Lord Mayor succeeded and, his wife having presented flowers to the Princess, the procession was free to continue. But by this time the streets were solid with people and cavalry troopers with drawn sabres were called upon to clear the way.[13]

There were many frightening moments for Alexandra. The charger of an officer in the Blues caught a foreleg in the wheel of her carriage. She jumped out and, accustomed to caring for her own horses, seized the hoof and released it. She won a fan for life that day. Another horse and rider fell near her, both lucky to escape unhurt. A mother, propelled forward by pressure from behind, threw her baby into one of the carriages to save it from being crushed. A boy was pulled from under the wheels.

St Paul's was festooned with the new fangled electric lights and there were stands for ten thousand there. Lord Ronald Gower was in Piccadilly:

> St James's Street was densely thronged by nine o'clock; all about Pall Mall was bright with red cloth, banners, and bunting, and garlanded with flowers. All the shops were transformed into places with benches and seats . . . At two in the afternoon this part of London was hardly passable . . . Piccadilly was a singular sight, an innumerable throng stretching on both sides of the street out of sight; every window and corner full of humanity, up to the chimneys and the trees in the Green Park . . . At last, and it was time, for it was past four, a carriage appeared coming from out St James's Street – first one, then a second, and a third all full of the most uninteresting folk who might well have been spared; they were certainly not ornamental. But now trot by a handful of Life Guards escorting an open carriage and four – the postillions in dark blue jackets, and within, the Princess Alexandra, with her affianced husband. There is a general rising, the mob cheer lustily, and hats and handkerchiefs are waved as, at a slow trot, they pass by. The Princess's lovely face has won all hearts . . .[14]

The concluding thrill of the journey came with the special train which took them from Paddington to Slough. The engine was in the charge of the Earl of Caithness, a leading amateur driver who satisfied his craving for speed on the footplate.

At Windsor the Widow waited. All through the day reports had reached her of the tumultuous reception that was being given to her eldest son and his bride to be. The Queen was pleased and gratified, but little of the credit went to the chief participants. She whiled away the time by writing her journal:

> . . . The preparations in London and all over the country are quite wonderful, and people are very anxious it should be known that it is meant out of love and affection to us both! . . . Lord Clarendon yesterday so truly said that, when *I* married, I had only reigned two years, and dearest Albert was not known, and could not be, though everyone had heard the highest praise of his character and talents. Still, no

one knew or dreamt of his becoming such a wonderful *great* man! There was great rejoicing at my marriage, but on this occasion, as on that of my dreadful loss, there are outbursts of depth of feeling, which are most touching and gratifying, testifying to the appreciation of *our* domestic life of twenty-two years, and all my beloved one did![15]

At a quarter-to-six news came that the special train had left Paddington. The Ladies and Gentlemen gathered in the Corridor. The bells began to ring. Rain poured down. As the escort and carriages showed in the twilight the younger members of the royal family rushed to the door. The Queen moved slowly down the stairs. There she greeted her future daughter-in-law, who looked, as she said, 'like a rose'. But only for a few minutes did the Queen chat with her guests before retiring 'desolate and sad' to her room. Vicky and Alice followed, to try and cheer her up. Then came a knock on the door and Alix peeped in. It was fortunate indeed that Bertie was marrying such an understanding young woman.

Later the young people of both families gathered upstairs. It was the first time that they had met *en masse*. They numbered fourteen, ranging from Vicky aged twenty-two to her son William four, and Waldemar and Beatrice five. The Queen's children were vexed because they had not been allowed to go to London to see the decorations and the procession. They were not accustomed to meeting other children or young people of their own age, and were apt to be bellicose when they did. Having been well trained by their Coburg father, they were very conscious of the value of money. One of them made a snide remark to the effect that Alexandra was marrying Bertie for his rank and worldly goods. She snapped back: 'You perhaps think that I like marrying your brother for his position. But if he was a cowboy I should love him just the same and would marry no one else.'[16]

On request, she turned a cartwheel – the first occasion that such a feat had been accomplished in the stately rooms of Windsor. When she performed the same manoeuvre at Sandringham some years later, she explained that speed was the secret of propriety.

Paddington Station, Tuesday morning, 10 March 1863. The

platforms were packed and special trains were leaving in quick succession. Newspaper boys were shouting, 'Royal wedding, read all about it', 'Framed and glazed, here's the Prince and Princess both for a penny'. For this particular occasion, class distinction had been swept aside. 'Lords and ladies in magnificent attire seemed to be esquired by corduroy and fustian, while waving plumes and travelling caps, silk and satin and railway rugs, were for the moment on most friendly terms.'[17] The Duchess of Westminster was wearing half a million pounds worth of jewels. Garter King of Arms was surrounded by his suite and heralds. The robes of the Maharajah Dhuleep Singh were sewn broadcast with precious stones and embroidered with the birds of the east. If the 10.40 Special had crashed, half the red book and the peerage would have had to be re-written.

In London there was a touch of fog and frost but by the time the guests and the sightseers reached Windsor the sun was brilliant and the Castle looked a picture outlined against the blue sky. There had not been a royal wedding there since that of Henry I in 1122. For the chosen in St George's Chapel there was much to hold the interest until the service began. Ninety-year-old Field Marshal Viscount Combermere came slowly in – he had served in the Peninsula and commanded Wellington's cavalry in Portugal. There was whisper of wonder when Lady Spencer made her entrance in a spectacular dress once worn by Marie Antoinette. Lord Palmerston countered by taking out an ivory comb and tidying his hair. Benjamin Disraeli had managed not only to obtain a ticket for himself, but one for his wife also, although many wives had been disappointed. He was crowing about his success. The Duchess of Marlborough was furious and the Duchess of Manchester cut him for months afterwards.[18]

There were four carriage processions from the Castle to the chapel, those of the royal guests, the royal family and household, the bridegroom and the bride. The Queen made her independent way, via the Deanery and the leads, to the Royal Closet. She was wearing her weeds, with a long veil to her cap, her only adornments being the ribbon, star and badge of the Order of the Garter. It was so long since many of those present had seen her that they stared at her as if she was a great actress peeping out from retirement. In her turn, she thought that they looked like players on a mighty stage.

Then 'our boy', as the Queen called him, began his journey towards the altar, stepping over the black stone slab that marks the grave of King Charles I. He halted at the chancel steps and bowed to the Queen. And there he waited. And there he waited for more than ten, long, seemingly endless minutes. He always hated waiting. Looking down, his mother noted: 'Bertie looking pale and nervous . . . During the long wait for his Bride he kept constantly looking up at me, with an anxious, clinging look, which touched me much.'[19] The guests fidgetted and whispered. Lord Clarendon commented: 'People began to wonder if the Bride was coy and to hope she had not changed her mind.'[20] At last she came, her father on one side of her and the Duke of Cambridge on the other, her long train held up by eight bridesmaids, titled ladies all. Her eyes and the tip of her nose were 'a tiny bit red',[21] because she had been crying at the thought of leaving her mother, but only those very near to her could see this. To the mass of those waiting for her in St George's she was a vision. From her tiny waist spread the bouffant skirt of white satin, with silver embroidery and Honiton lace. Orange blossom was all about her and ringing her soft brown hair. Her head was bent and her face was pale and she moved with a slow grace, gliding with almost imperceptible movement. Thackeray was reminded of a fairy tale featuring swans.

Jenny Lind, the Swedish nightingale, began to sing the *Chorale* for which the Prince Consort had composed the music – 'This day, with joyful heart and voice . . .' The Queen raised her eyes to Heaven. Dr Norman Macleod, the Scottish divine, was watching her and afterwards said: 'She seemed to be alone with him before the Throne of God.'[22] As the first verse ended, she burst into tears.

In one of the pews below her a very different feeling prevailed, taking the form of an outburst of Prussian hostility. Vicky, Crown Princess of Prussia, had been worried that her son William would make a nuisance of himself and had accordingly placed him between his two young uncles, Arthur and Leopold, in the hope that they would be able to restrain him. Her suspicions were correct, but the boy had a certain reason for his bad behaviour. William was ever particular about his dress. For the wedding a miniature German military uniform had been made for him, and of this he was inordinately proud. One of the Queen's sons (unspecified) cut off the tails of the jacket.[23] William was, therefore, allotted a Scottish outfit. This riled him considerably and, when driving round Windsor to see the decorations, he threw his aunt Beatrice's hat into the road.[24] During the service he showed signs of restiveness and his mother reprimanded him. He then began fiddling with the cairngorm in his dirk. Having loosened it, he threw it across the choir. Leopold, similarly dressed, took him by the shoulder, whereat William bit his bare leg.[25]

The clear voice of the Archbishop of Canterbury filled St George's:

> Alexandra Caroline Mary, wilt thou have this man to thy wedded husband, to live together after God's ordinance in the holy estate of matrimony? Wilt thou obey him, and serve him, love, honour, and keep him in sickness and in health; and, forsaking all other, keep thee only unto him, so long as ye both shall live?

Soon the united procession of the bride and groom was formed and the Princess of Wales, on the arm of her husband, moved through the nave and the curtain dropped behind them. Then the silver trumpets blared, the cannons sounded, the bells rang and the electric telegraph clicked out the news. Within seconds guns were firing and church bells peeling in every corner of the British Isles.

Back at the Castle, the Register signed, there were three separate luncheons – a large one for the company in St George's Hall, a second for thirty-eight Royalties in the Dining-room, and a third, with places set for two – Queen Victoria and Princess Beatrice – in the Queen's private room.

It was shortly before four o'clock when Bertie and Alix said their goodbyes, she 'much agitated and affected' and all her family in tears. The Queen watched them go down the crowded staircase and then hurried to the corridor to see them drive away in an open carriage. 'They stopped for a moment under the window, Bertie standing up, and both looked up lovingly at me.'[26]

As the couple, Alexandra in ermine, set off for their week's honeymoon at Osborne in the Isle of Wight, Windsor went mad. The kernel of the enthusiasm lay in the boys of Eton. Among them was Lord Randolph Churchill, father of Sir Winston, and he thus wrote home to tell of his exploits:

> Nothing stood before us. The policemen charged in a body, but they were knocked down. There was a chain put across the road, but we broke that. Several old *genteel* ladies tried to stop me, but I snapped my fingers in their face and cried, 'Hurrah!' and 'What larks!' I frightened some of them horribly. There was a wooden palisade put up at the station but we broke it down . . . I got right down to the door of the carriage where the Prince of Wales was, wildly shouting 'Hurrah!'. He bowed to me, I am perfectly certain; but I shrieked louder. I am sure, if the Princess did not possess very strong nerves, she would have been frightened. But all she did was to smile. . . .[27]

As the honeymoon train pulled out the guests and the sightseers in their thousands found it was each for himself, no quarter given. The ordered plan for the departure of the 'specials' collapsed and the officials were swept aside by the human tide. Families became separated. The Duchess of Westminster forced her way into a third class compartment, dragging Lady Palmerston after her. Disraeli sat on his wife's knee. The Archbishop of Canterbury, bruised and buffeted, demanded of a policeman how he could be saved. The harrassed constable replied that his only hope of salvation was to grab a seat in the next train.[28]

The platform gates were closed and a crowd piled up against them. In desperation, the staff shut the doors of the station building. Amongst those trapped within was Mary Stanley, sister of the Dean. After enduring for half an hour conditions resembling those in the black hole of Calcutta, she wriggled her way into a waiting-room, opened the window and, with other conspirators, climbed through and gained the platform. A train came slowly in and was full before it had stopped. She eventually reached home at ten o'clock, for London proved to be as chaotic as Windsor.[29] The illuminations were on, the shops decorated and the theatres open and free to all. The streets were packed until three in the morning. In the crush at Ludgate Hill, to see St Paul's lit by electricity, six people were killed and a hundred injured taken to hospital.[30]

The Wedding

It was late when Bertie and Alix reached Osborne, for there had been welcoming committees and loyal addresses at stops along the way. But finally they were alone, in the vast and silent Italianate mansion which had been fashioned out of the Prince Consort's dreams. Or were they? A tall hat lying on a stand filled with walking sticks and umbrellas; papers beside a despatch box from the Fine Arts Commission, a pen ready for use, ink in the wells. It was as if someone had recently been at work there – just as the Queen wished it. Everything that belonged to Albert remained as it had been when he left the island for the last time. Shyly and hand in hand, Bertie and Alix moved across the cold, mosaic floor to the window, looking out over the park and along the white ribbon of path which led down to the sea, and at the lights of the ships in the Channel beyond.

FIVE

Spring Love

Into the first year of Alexandra's married life there stampeded an astonishing sequence of events. By March 1864 she was the mother of a two-month child, her father had become King of Denmark, her brother William was King of Greece, her sister Dagmar was set on the way to becoming Empress of Russia and her beloved Denmark was at war with Prussia and Austria.

Europe was at a cross-road. In Prussia Bismarck was laying the foundations of the German Empire with blood and iron. In Austria, Emperor Francis Joseph had been weakened from his defeats by French and Sardinian troops at the battles of Magenta and Solferino. In Italy, King Victor Emmanuel and Garibaldi were struggling to form a united nation. In France Napoleon III, having embarked upon his ill-fated attempt to found an empire in Mexico under Archduke Maximilian of Austria, had passed his zenith and was concentrating on liberal reforms rather than on military gains. In Britain the austerity of Albert the Consort and the gloom which followed his death, were being swept away by the Prince of Wales and replaced by the merry social round-about which was to whirl on until his death in 1910.

The London Season of 1863 was fantastic, glittering occasion piling up on glittering occasion, as money, accrued from the boom caused by the Crimean War, from coal, the railways, and the high price of wheat, was lavished on social junketing and competition. Society needed a leader and now they found one in Bertie who, freed from his mother's apron strings, with two establishments of his own, had the desire as well as the capacity to dance and adventure into the early hours, all the nights of the week.

It soon became clear – to Queen Victoria amongst others – that sex and late nights did not suit Alexandra. Only three months past her eighteenth birthday when she was married, she came to England from a close knit family, reared on a diet of plain food, early to bed, routines, out-of-door exercise and no greater excitement than simple card games. By the late summer of 1863 she had become little more than a skeleton and the deafness which was soon to afflict her seriously was daily becoming more obvious.

Yet the honeymoon had given no indication of the excitements which lay ahead. The weather was kind, snowdrops, primroses and daffodils graced the lawns and Osborne was in its greatest beauty. Vicky, on her way back to Berlin with her husband and son, was one of the few visitors. She reported to the Queen that Bertie looked blissful, Alix lovely and 'all breathes peace and happiness . . . Love has certainly shed its sunshine on these two dear young hearts . . .'[1]

Meantime, in London, Prince Christian and his family were enjoying themselves immensely. Victoria, relenting somewhat from her chilly attitude, had arranged for them to stay in an hotel and had dropped a hint that she would like them to be entertained. The hint was taken. Lady Spencer gave a ball, Lady Stanley followed suit and Lord and Lady Palmerston asked them to dinner. Lord Clarendon met *les Danois* and formed a favourable impression of Alexandra's mother. She told him that the point she feared about the marriage was that the Queen would not give her heir sufficient occupation, a shortcoming which she could easily, and with advantage, rectify. 'In short,' Clarendon wrote of Princess Louise, 'if she were to let out half of what is in her mind, she would run the chance of a precious good snubbing at Windsor.'[2]

But 'Eliza' – as Society called the Queen – had a keen nose for scenting out the thoughts of women. She guessed well enough what was in the mind of Princess Louise and put this gifted lady on her danger list. Pointedly, Victoria never visited Denmark. When it was suggested to her that a brother of Alexandra would do well as a husband for one of her younger daughters, she replied that one of *that* family was quite enough.[3]

Bertie and Alix had hoped that, when their honeymoon was

over, they would be able to move into their London home, Marlborough House in the Mall. It had been granted to the Prince of Wales on his eighteenth birthday, having been previously occupied by Queen Adelaide, widow of William IV. Parliament had allowed £15,000 for refurbishing and workmen were still busy in the reception rooms.[4] So the young couple had to divide their time between Windsor Castle and Buckingham Palace.

The farewell party given by Bertie to his in-laws on the evening of their departure was far removed from the style of royal festivities approved and practised by the Prince Consort. The children ran races along the corridors of Buckingham Palace and there was a competition to see who could make the most noise on a 'piano organ'.[5]

Easter was spent at Sandringham. The railway was not yet complete to Wolferton and they drove from King's Lynn. Alexandra looked about at the woods, the wide fields, the villages and the churches, the flat lands running down to the sea, and fell in love.

> A characteristic reception was given them by the country gentry and peasantry, huntsmen gathering in their scarlet uniforms, while some two hundred school-children, strewing flowers and bearing flags, appeared to hail the Princess.[6]

Sandringham Hall, as the house was then called, was little more than a hunting lodge. The previous owner, Mr Spencer Cowper, had added an Elizabethan porch and gables, which made it look rather ridiculous. The interior was plain. The walls were decorated with Italian panels, painted with festoons of flowers. The Prince Consort had arranged the purchase and the price paid for the house and 8,000 acres was £220,000. This was the cause of local comment as, when the estate had been auctioned in 1836, it had only fetched £76,000.[7] But Albert was to be proved right in the end. As a dealer in property, he made no mistakes.

There were those among the entourage who did not approve of the new royal acquisition by the Wash. Alexandra's Lady of the Bedchamber, Lady Macclesfield, was among them. She announced that it would be difficult to find 'a more ugly or desolate looking place',[8] and finding the north-east winds blow-

Princess Alexandra at the time of her marriage. From a painting by R. Lauchert

Sandringham as it was on coming into the possession of the Prince of Wales in 1862

The Prince and Princess of Wales riding in Windsor Great Park in the year of their marriage

favourite ghillie at Balmoral, John Brown, should report for duty at Osborne. Brown soon became her Personal Servant and, from that day until his death in 1883, never left the side of his mistress, taking neither days-off nor holidays. There were no further demands that Vicky and Alice should visit England.

This arrangement had its effect on Alexandra. Bertie could not abide John Brown and was incensed at his mother's relationship. He was at heart a snob, while the Queen was more at her ease with the lower classes. The result was that the Queen did not visit Sandringham, for she would not go without Brown, and Bertie would not accord him the treatment and status upon which the Queen insisted.

At heart the Queen objected to Alexandra because her presence meant that Albert's planning had gone astray. As the curator of her husband's wisdom, she deplored any sign that his judgement had been faulty. But, as the years past, she was forced to the conclusion that Baron Stockmar had been right when he had urged the ending of the romance between Bertie and Alix, and that it would have been better if Bertie had married Princess Elizabeth of Wied, who was stronger and cleverer than Alexandra.[3] Thus, throughout the first eight years of Alexandra's marriage the pen of Queen Victoria inscribed her faults.

In the spring of 1864 she wrote that Alexandra would never again be as beautiful as she was before her marriage. 'Her face is like a knife and she is as flat as a board.'[4] Although the Queen did not believe in mothers feeding their children, she was strongly in favour of an ample bosom. Alexandra, she said, was stiff at Drawing Rooms, a task which the Princess was undertaking as the Queen did not yet feel able to face public occasions. She had become 'haughty and frivolous' and went out too much in society where she met the wrong type of people. 'Alix and I never will or can be intimate'.[5] There was a clash over fox hunting. The Queen forbade her daughter-in-law to ride to hounds at Sandringham. The Princess adored hunting, or rather the riding side, as she admitted that 'she hoped the poor fox would get away'.[6] When out with the West Norfolk she was a magnet which drew a field of five hundred and roads choked with carriages. She did not query the order. She retreated inside herself and became, as the Queen said, somewhat grand and chilly. For a month Alexandra obeyed. Then, mounted on her mare *Viva*, she re-joined the field. Nothing further was said.

A further row between mother and daughter-in-law blew up when the Queen's third daughter, Helena, became engaged to Prince Christian of Schleswig-Holstein★ in 1865. Alexandra was furious, regarding the match as an insult to her family and herself. There was a danger that the Wales would absent themselves from the wedding. But the Queen was taking other considerations into account and these, for the sake of palace peace, were explained to Bertie by his brothers and sisters. Helena was possessed of little charm and no beauty and, if this suitor was to be turned away, it would be most difficult to find another. Christian was certainly not a romantic figure. Thirty-five, fat, balding and lazy, the pipe which he smoked continually was fuelled with a pungent tobacco. He was ignorant of the plans for his future and, when summoned to Windsor, imagined that it was to assume the role of second husband to Victoria.[7] When Christian lost an eye in a shooting accident, he had a series of glass substitutes made, of varying expression to suit differing moods and occasions. At the dinner table he would show them off, changing them around between courses, so putting his guests off their pudding. When Alexandra realised that Helena might remain a spinster if her marriage plans were thwarted, she calmed down and withdrew her opposition. But the Queen did not forget that opposition and said of Alexandra, 'It will be long, if ever, before she regains my confidence'.[8]

Queen Victoria placed squarely on the beautiful shoulders of Alexandra the blame for the premature births and weaknesses of the Wales children. She chose to forget the physical handicaps which had plagued Albert and taken him to his grave at forty-two, the haemorrhages of his mother and the plethora of diseases which had riddled the Coburgs and the Gothas. Although her own mother, the Duchess of Kent, had planted the seed of haemophilia in her, Victoria herself was strong and therefore concluded that there had been no legacy passed down either from George III, or from his odd children. Even the problems of Bertie's health as a child were ignored. It was, she concluded, all

★ Younger brother of the Duke Frederick who had claimed Holstein when Christian IX became King of Denmark and thus precipitating the 1864 war.

the fault of that Hesse-Cassel tribe – sinners all, vulgarly display-
ing themselves at their annual Rumpenheim junketings.

Yet the fear harboured by Queen Louise that Queen Victoria's hatred for Bertie, freely expressed at the time of the Prince
Consort's death, would continue, proved wrong. As the years
passed her natural love increased and she stood by him in times of
trouble. True, she objected to his wild life, but took to the ploy
of sending reprimands via her cousin George, Duke of Cambridge. George, who was very fond of Bertie and Alix, hummed
and ha-ed, in the way all Cambridges did, and passed on only a
watered down version of the original. True, also, Victoria did
not show her love by delegating authority to her heir, but here
she was adhering to Albert's theory that Bertie was incapable of
taking responsibility. There were grounds for this. As a test, an
item of 'secret' information was passed to him. It was all around
London by the following morning. Then there was the risk of
indiscretion during Bertie's sexual interludes, for he amused
himself with all manner of women, especially in France. Fresh in
the memory was the example of Napoleon III and Virginie,
Contessa di Castiglione, the beautiful spy planted in the Imperial
bed by King Victor Emmanuel and Cavour.

The Queen's agitation at the premature birth of Alexandra's
children was due in part to fear and in part to annoyance, fear that
her successor in the second generation would be weak,
annoyance that she could not be 'in at the birth'. She dearly loved
to be beside the natal bed, letting loose the flood gates of her
emotions, organising all and sundry, giving advice gained from
long experience. Sadly she told Bertie that it was apparently fated
that she could not be there in time. So annoyed did the Queen
become that when the second daughter, Victoria, was born she
commented that the event was 'a very uninteresting thing',[9]
comparing it with the breeding habits of the rabbits in Windsor
Park.

When the Wales' children went to see her, which was not
often, she was anything but complimentary about them. She
found them backward and delicate compared with her other
grandchildren. She noted that they were pigeon-breasted, while
her own brood had fine chests. In 1868 she wrote: 'They are such
miserable, puny little children (each weaker than the preceding

one) that it is quite a misfortune. I can't tell you how these poor, frail, little fairies distress me for the honour of the family and the country. Darling Papa would have been in perfect despair.'[10] When the Wales children were staying with her at Osborne the following year, she thought that they looked most wretched, with the exception of Georgie. It was ever to be the same. George, despite his knock-knees, was her favourite. He was also the merriest; becoming too bumptious at luncheon, his grandmother condemned him to a session under the table; on being released, he appeared stark naked.[11]

There had to be a trial of strength between Windsor and Sandringham and it came in September 1864. The war in Denmark had ended in July and Alexandra dearly wanted to visit her homeland, introduce her husband to it, comfort her parents and show them her baby boy. The Prince was looking forward to making an excursion to Sweden and to staying in Paris on the way back.

The Queen did not like the idea of the trip at all, fearing that Bertie would make some provocative remarks in Copenhagen. She compromised but stipulated that the visit to Stockholm must be strictly incognito, that baby Albert be returned to England when Bertie and Alix left for Sweden, that Germany should be visited on the return journey and that Bertie was never to take decisions about his child's movements without consulting her.

The Wales were received with delight by King Christian and Queen Louise. The Danes roared their approval of Alexandra, both in the streets and at receptions, for they had heard how she had championed their cause in London. There had been doubts about how the Prince would be received, for the feeling in Denmark was strongly anti-British, but he had a natural gift for overcoming animosity (as he was later to show in Ireland and France) and found it a challenge. He walked with Crown Prince Frederick unescorted through the streets, laughed, joked and said the right things, and soon he was sharing the ovations with his wife.

Yet everything Danish did not appeal to Bertie. The tempo was too slow, the bond of family was too strong for one whose home life had, in the main, been a continuous battle royal. One whole evening at Bernstorff was passed in discussing the illness of an elderly lady-in-waiting. There were no gay nights and no racing. When taken out shooting, he discovered that the prey was the fox. Although realising that he would be castigated at home, he bagged two. Better a fox to shoot than nothing at all.

The party moved to Fredensborg, the King's summer palace. Here were beautiful grounds, but life was hardly exciting, with little to do except stroll down the long path to the lake. One evening an equerry, who had newly joined the suite, remarked to the Prince, after a long silence: 'There is no place in the world, sir, more boring than Fredensborg.'

Bertie swung round and snapped: 'How dare you say such a thing?'

The equerry subsided. There was another silence. After some minutes the Prince added, with feeling: 'Obviously you don't know Bernstorff!'[12]

But there was one subject of strong personal and international interest. The Cesarevitch, the Grand-duke Nicholas of Russia, was also a guest of King Christian. He was courting Dagmar, then seventeen. Their engagement was announced on 28 December. Nicholas was suffering from tuberculosis, but Queen Louise did not worry about health matters, even about the premature babies of her eldest daughter. She trusted that all would come out well in the end.[13]

In the spring of 1865 the Cesarevitch became seriously ill while on a visit to his mother in the South of France. Dagmar hurried to his side. As she knelt by the bedside of her dying fiancé, he took her hand and placed it in that of his brother. 'She is worthy of your love and of you,' he whispered, 'and you will make her happy.' Dagmar married the brother in 1866 and on the assassination of Alexander II in 1881, they became Emperor Alexander III and Empress Marie Feodorovna.

The Prince and Princess sailed for Sweden, leaving baby 'Eddy'* at Bernstorff in the care of 'Apapa' and 'Amama'. They ignored the order that they were to travel incognito and stayed with King Charles XV at the Royal Palace in Stockholm. Bertie enjoyed himself and, when he joined the King in an elk hunt, Europe blazed with publicity. The Queen's anger boiled over.

* The family name for their first-born.

She despatched a strongly-worded telegram. Fortunately for Anglo-Danish relations, there was an error in the cipher and the message was not fully understood.[14] Three letters followed in quick succession from Balmoral. On 7 October Bertie gave in and the baby began his journey home. With him went a letter from the Prince pointing out that Alexandra hated parting with 'her little treasure',.that the hotels in Stockholm were squalid and the British Legation overcrowded, and that the King would have been annoyed if his invitation to stay in the palace had been turned down. He ended: 'If I am not allowed to use my own discretion, we had better give up travelling altogether.'[15]

This incensed the Queen even further and she issued an order that the Wales were not to visit France on the final leg of their journey but travel through Belgium. Now Bertie had been very much looking forward to meeting his friends, Emperor Napoleon and Empress Eugenie, and to showing Alexandra the Paris shops, Compiègne and Fontainebleau. The couple were therefore in a rebellious mood as they approached the German shore. At Kiel, on entering Prussian waters, the captain of the royal yacht ran up the Prussian flag. Alexandra saw it and demanded the reason. She was told that it was a courtesy. White with anger, she said: 'Tell the captain that I refuse to move one inch from where I stand until that flag comes down.' It came down.[16]

They were in no mood to cope with Berlin and their visits were restricted to short stays with the King of Hanover and sister Alice at Darmstadt. On the way home they were met at Cologne by Vicky and her husband Fritz. It proved a chilly interlude as Crown Prince Frederick, with a complete lack of tact, was wearing a decoration awarded to him for valour in the Schleswig-Holstein war.

Alexandra's second baby was expected in July 1865. It arrived on 3 June. It was a boy and was named George Frederick Ernest Albert. Queen Louise wrote to Bertie: 'How proud you must be, two boys, don't you grow more attached to Alix at every present thus brought to you in pain and anguish? What will your dear Mama say? Will she not say it is all weakness in Alix?'[17] It was a comparatively easy birth and in strong contrast with the experience which lay in store for the Princess in 1867.

Owing to that third pregnancy she was unable to travel to Russia for Dagmar's wedding on 9 November 1866 and the Prince of Wales went alone to St Petersburg. Disturbing stories filtered back of his behaviour there, at Moscow and at stops en route.

Alexandra's baby was due in March. On 15 February, while at Marlborough House, she developed rheumatic fever. Bertie did not realise the seriousness of her illness and went off to a race meeting. A covey of telegrams brought him back. Five days later a daughter was born. The doctors considered it unwise to give chloroform, resisting the pleas of the mother that her pain should be relieved. 'White leg'* followed.[18] Often Lady Macclesfield would find her crying from the pain in her hip and knee. And it was only the beloved Lady of the Bedchamber who seemed to appreciate the danger in which the Princess lay. The doctors appeared confused and Bertie, while issuing optimistic reports, was out nightly on the prowl. Lady Macclesfield reported: 'The Princess had another bad night, *chiefly* owing to the Prince promising to come in at 1 a.m. and keeping her in a perpetual fret, refusing to take her opiate for fear she should be asleep when he came! And he never came till 3 a.m.!' It was not until a week after the birth that Queen Victoria arrived at Marlborough House and saw at once how serious the condition was, describing the sight as 'heart-rending'.[19] Alexandra, whose mouth was so swollen and sore that she could scarcely eat, leaned her head on the Queen's shoulder and whispered, 'Will it ever get better?' The Queen later spoke with Sir William Jenner. Sir William considered by some to be a more accomplished courtier than physician, confided in her that there were symptoms which he disliked. 'Altogether he is most anxious, and was very gloomy,' she wrote in her diary.[20] The Queen sent a telegram to Copenhagen and on 18 March Queen Louise appeared by the bedside, followed two days later by King Christian.

But the public did not share the confidence of the Prince or the doctors. The arrival of the parents and the guarded bulletins led people to believe that the situation was more serious than they were being told. Day long, crowds waited outside Marl-

* A condition arising after childbirth, in which thrombosis extends from the uterine sinuses into the iliac veins.

borough House, letters and gifts of medical stores poured in, and the word spread that the Princess was dying. The demand for more news grew strong and noisy and the Prince sent an equerry out into the street to assure the waiting crowd that there were no grounds for anxiety. The doctors backed him up, saying that it was only a matter of time before the Princess regained her health. The anxiety was the first sincere expression of the love which the British people felt for the Princess of Wales.

No sooner had these announcements been made than Alexandra had a serious relapse. On 15 April *The Times* reported the opinion of the doctors that 'the inflammation was baffling to the last degree'. One of them, Sir James Paget, later said that, but for the soothing presence of Queen Louise, the Princess would have died.[21] The recovery was slow and it was not until 10 May that the christening could take place – in Alexandra's room, where she still lay in bed.[22] The names given were Louise Victoria Alexandra Dagmar.

A strange side to Bertie's character appeared during his wife's illness. So addicted had he become to the fast life, each night seeking a new thrill, that he seemed incapable of allowing any circumstances to interfere with the routine. He would make a show of emotion when beside his wife's bed, but he could not face the evenings in a quiet house, alone with elderly ladies-in-waiting concerned only with the patient's welfare. He convinced himself that Alexandra was suffering from nothing more serious than post-natal depression and that it would cure itself. Off he would hurry to dine with his friends. Men such as the Duke of Cambridge and General Knollys became very angry.

Fever, 'white leg' and rheumatism in the knee joint were not the sum of Alexandra's troubles. Her pregnancy and illness brought out in her the otosclerosis inherited from her mother. With each passing week she became more deaf. She was adult now, had endured long agony and been near to death. The deafness came down as a curtain between her and those who did not know her well. No longer could she keep pace with the smart chatter at social gatherings. She retreated into the small world which she knew best and loved the most, the world of her children and family, of her home and her animals. Her interest also turned to the care of those who had suffered as she had done, to the help of those in trouble, to a love which covered all in need. She fought to stop the curtain falling between herself and Bertie, but she was hard pressed.

On the evening of the day on which Louise was christened, he left for Paris. He was to represent Queen Victoria at the Great International Exhibition staged by Emperor Napoleon III. Although on this occasion he had a valid reason for going, he no longer made excuses or gave grounds for his expeditions to France. By twenty-five he was part of the Parisian scene. Each spring he crossed the Channel *en garçon*. He reserved an apartment at the Hotel Bristol and was a member of the Jockey Club. When he entered the Maison Dorée, the diners respected his privacy. Princess Jeanne de Sagan was his mistress and it was whispered that he had had a child by her. On this occasion of May 1867 he flirted with Hortense Schneider, then starring at the *Variétés* in Offenbach's *La Grande Duchesse de Gerolstein* and he brought home a suitcase packed with pictures of her. Lord Clarendon commented: 'The Prince of Wales is leading a very dissolute life in Paris and so far from concealing it, his wish seems to be to earn for himself the reputation of a roué. '[23]

In August the Wales, complete with brood, journeyed to Wiesbaden in the hope that the baths there would alleviate the rheumatism. As a holiday, the trip was not a success. Bertie was for ever disappearing, to the races at Baden or on shooting expeditions, while his wife rebuffed, in spirited fashion, all attempts of the Prussian royalties to make their peace with her. In November they were the guests of the Queen at Windsor. Alexandra hobbled about with the aid of two sticks and only managed with great effort to get in and out of carriages. 'The poor leg,' the Queen wrote, 'is completely stiff and it remains to be seen whether it will ever get quite right again. I much fear not. '[24]

It never did. But Alexandra, with superb courage, fought the twin disadvantages of lameness and deafness. She was determined once more to dance and skate and ride. When she hunted, the pommel of her saddle was switched to the right, allowing her the full use of her good leg. Life must continue as before. By the end of the year, frail as she was, she was pregnant again. In the spring she accompanied her husband to Ireland, ignoring the menace of Fenianism. The Irish loved her, not only for her beauty and charm, but also because she was not English. On 6 July 1868 her fourth child, Victoria, was born.

By this stage of her life Queen Victoria had turned against large families, considering four to be ample, although she herself had had nine. She was becoming somewhat bored with the flood of grandchildren enveloping her. Yet she and Alexandra had the same basic reason for multiple births – the retention of the love of their husbands. But there was a difference. Victoria had noticed that Albert was much more attentive and easy to live with when she was pregnant. To him, sex was solely for the procreation of children and, in the intervals between their arrival, tempers grew frayed, there were scenes and knockings at locked doors. Victoria needed sex. When she was told after the birth of Princess Beatrice that she was to have no more babies, she asked: 'Oh, doctor, can I have no more fun in bed?'[25]

Alexandra was frigid and had no overpowering demands. She had children not only because she loved them but also to hold Bertie's interest and to keep him away from other women. She would, in the event, have been happier with Albert, who confessed that the mere thought of extra marital relationships made him feel sick. She looked at life from the Danish standpoint, by which family life was all encompassing. She failed to understand that children meant little to Bertie. He treated them like puppies, letting them crawl over him and brushing them aside when he was bored. There was a likeness to him in Napoleon III, a victim of hypo-pituitarism, who sought love constantly but never captured the essentials of romance and emotion. In his strange, twilight way, the nearest that Bertie approached to true love was with Alexandra, but her love for him he stretched to the limit.

A third daughter, Maud, arrived on 26 November 1869. One to come. The last pregnancy of Alexandra was the worst that she had yet endured. She was deeply worried when her husband was subpoenaed to appear as a witness in the Mordaunt divorce case. Although Bertie was innocent of active involvement, he had shown an imprudence sadly unfitting to an heir to the Throne. She had good reason to be hurt and the public took her side, the rumour spreading that, after a visit to her parents in Copenhagen, she would not return. But this was far from her intention and she redoubled her efforts to hold her husband, appearing by his side whenever possible – no easy task, for throughout the summer of 1870 he was hissed on a number of public occasions. Then France fell, 'the Republic of England' was declared at a mass meeting in Trafalgar Square and the abuse of everything royal poured from press and the platform.

On 4 April 1871 the Prince and Princess left Marlborough House to spend Easter at Sandringham. Two days later Alexandra gave birth to a son. Despite her previous experiences, nothing was ready – no nurse, no specialists, no medical stores and no baby clothes. The local physician, Dr Farre, hurried to Sandringham House in the early hours of the morning and, after the delivery, despatched a telegram to Osborne to inform the Queen that the Princess and the infant were 'going on quite well'.[26] Then Dr Rendall arrived and, after a conference, the conclusion was reached that the child had but very little time to live. In the evening the Rector of Sandringham christened him Alexander John Charles Albert. When Alexandra awoke next morning it was to be told that he was dead.

At Windsor and Osborne the cold wheels of officialdom began to turn. What was the burial procedure for infant royal children? It was recalled that, when the same tragedy had occurred in the families of George III and his sons, the funerals had been in semi-state at Windsor; it was decided, and the Queen concurred, that the same procedure should now be followed.

The thought of standing on show in her grief in St George's Chapel filled Alexandra with both horror and revulsion. She begged that the service be private and at Sandringham. Bertie despatched a pleading letter to his mother, who gave in on the point of the Windsor funeral but refused to cancel the court mourning which, she said, would last for ten days.[27]

Neither the Prince nor Princess wished for such mourning, but the Queen had decided and nothing could be done. The result was tragic. The republican press seized upon the chance to further damage the royal image, describing the baby's death as 'a wretched abortion' and the mourning and funeral arrangements as 'sickening mummery at Sandringham'.[28]

The Prince held the dead child in his arms and placed it in the tiny coffin, the white pall about it. From her bed, drawn to the window, Alexandra watched the sad little procession make its way along the path, amid the lawns and the greening trees, towards the church. Through her tears she saw her husband, holding to either side of him the black gloved hands of Eddy and Georgie. Instead of 'dust and ashes' a blaze of spring flowers quilted the coffin.[29] Then the tenants and the villagers piled high the grave with their wreaths and posies. Alexander John lies to the right of the path leading to the porch of St Mary Magdalene.

SEVEN

Winter Sunshine

The devoted friend of Alexandra was the Hon. Oliver George Montagu, fourth son of the seventh Earl of Sandwich. His grandfather commanded the united British, Hanoverian and Belgian horse at the Battle of Waterloo. He was standing by the Duke of Wellington when a round-shot hit his right knee. 'By God, sir,' he remarked, 'I have lost my leg.' 'By God, I believe you have,' replied the Duke laconically.

Oliver was in the Royal Horse Guards, rose to be the Colonel commanding and served with them in Egypt before becoming equerry to the Prince of Wales. The same age as Alexandra, he was described by a contemporary diarist as 'the most delightful and popular of men',[1] but, like so many officers of the Blues, he was addicted to gambling. 'That wicked boy',[2] the Prince called him, overlooking, in his intimitable way, his own penchant for a wager. Oliver Montagu was not of the marrying kind, a trait which ran in his family as only one of the four brothers married. But he fell in love with the Princess of Wales and loved and served her until his death at the early age of forty-eight.

Oliver and Alexandra adored and understood one another, being the exception to the French rule that true friendship between man and woman cannot come until *'après'*. There was never a hint of scandal and they played their parts of knight and fairy princess to perfection. He was ever ready to come to her aid, showing a strength and steadfastness lacking in her husband. Bertie would never allow his wife to be slighted or a word spoken against her, but his way of life was such that Alexandra could not be spared bitter moments. Coming out onto the dance floor she could sense the eyes of the professional beauties upon

87

her; beauties who were possessive, whispering, sardonic, sure of themselves. She knew well that, if they had not already slept with her husband, they most probably would.

Oliver Montagu was one of the most eligible bachelors in Britain, looked upon with awe by debutantes and their escorts. He would saunter into the ballroom regardless of anyone but his Princess, who always danced the after-supper waltz with him.[3] She would move towards him with her fascinating 'Alexandra limp', find strength and radiance in his arms and for a while feel safe, encircled by his love.

Yet there was an underlying sadness in this unfulfilled love, a sadness hurting him more than it hurt her. Oliver had to put before the world the picture of a rock-hard officer of the Blues, proof against the emotional weaknesses of men, ever loyal to the Prince. But he carried within, firmly controlled by military discipline, feelings of a very different nature. He wrote to his father, referring to himself in the third person, a letter which revealed the truth: 'Outwardly he is a noisy crowing brute but if everyone knew what his inward feelings are and what he had to go through inwardly they would not envy him his existence. I know not . . . of anyone put into the unfortunate position that I have been and yet, thank God, to have got through the worst without much damage to others.'[4]

A consolation for Oliver Montagu was the love which the Wales' children had for him. They looked upon him as a favourite uncle and called him 'Tut-Tut'. It was he who shielded them, at their mother's request, when they got into scrapes, which was often. One autumn when the family was staying at Abergeldie on Deeside, Sir Francis Knollys, Private Secretary to the Prince and known to the children as 'Fooks', drove over from Birkhall, four miles away. He was in a four-wheel shay and driving himself. While Sir Francis was talking to their father, Eddy and Georgie unbuckled the reins from the bridle. Sir Francis said his goodbyes, mounted the shay and called 'gee up'. The pony, finding no controlling feel from the reins, set off at full gallop. A wheel of the shay hit a boulder at the turn to the Lodge and Sir Francis became airborne, but fortunately landed in long grass and was unhurt. The shay was severely damaged and when the pony, towing the wreck, was recaptured, the truth about the reins was discovered.

The Prince of Wales roared in Hanoverian fury and swore that he would have the hide off his sons. The boys, recognizing the roar as one indicating great danger, streaked for safety into the woods and were lost to sight. Alexandra, busy comforting Sir Francis and placating her husband, gave signal, by head and eye, to Oliver Montagu. He also disappeared into the woods. Having located the culprits, he persuaded them to return to the Castle where they hid until the paternal ire had subsided.[5]

The longest period that Alexandra and Oliver ever spent together came in the winter of 1868–9, the Prince of Wales inviting Montagu to join him and his wife on their trip to Egypt and Greece. It was certainly the happiest holiday of Alexandra's life. Much of the time was spent at sea or sailing up and down the Nile. The Prince was a man who always had to be occupied and he soon became bored sitting on deck after dinner, watching the sun go down. Off he would rush to play cards and gamble with his cronies, leaving Alexandra and Oliver to relax in their long chairs, uninterrupted and content with their own company. It was then that the two really came to know – and love – each other.

To indulge in a vacation of six months' duration did not meet with the approval of Queen Victoria to whom it savoured of 'junketing', an expression which she applied to most forms of light-hearted pleasure. She herself enjoyed Continental touring, but her excursions were of a stately nature, the original 'package' tour de luxe, with the emphasis on sightseeing. She was conservative in her locations, remaining faithful to Aix-les-Bains, Florence, Coburg, Darmstadt and Nice. She kept a seven-coach private train at the Gare du Nord at Brussels and restricted its speed to twenty-five miles per hour by night and thirty-five by day. Her attendants numbered over one hundred and she took with her her bed and chair, ponies and donkeys, chefs and grooms. These regal processions were in strong contrast with the proposed itinerary of the Prince of Wales, which took in Paris, Copenhagen, Stockholm, Berlin, Vienna, Trieste, Alexandria, Cairo, the Nile, the almost finished Suez Canal, Constantinople, the Crimea, Athens, Corfu and Italy.

In giving her consent, the Queen was influenced by two

main considerations. First, the doctors had advised that it would be beneficial to Alexandra's health to spend the winter in the sunshine. In the second place, the Prince's gambling and adventures with women had attracted much public criticism and it was deemed advisable that he should be absent from the scene for a while. But the Queen laid down strict regulations: (1) no alteration should be made in the itinerary without previous consultation with her, (2) a strict incognito should be observed, the Prince and Princess to travel as Lord and Lady Renfrew, (3) a rigorous eye should be kept on expenses, (4) invitations should only be accepted from the courts of near relatives, and (5) Sunday should be kept as a day of rest, with no amusements.[6]

The Prince agreed, but a further stipulation made by his mother nearly led to the cancellation of the trip. Alexandra wished to take with her the three eldest children, enjoy Christmas in Denmark and then return to England. The Queen said that the boys could go, but not the girl. Alexandra despatched a pleading letter to Osborne, only to be told that she was selfish and that her children belonged 'to the country'. Alexandra then announced that, if she could not take Louise, she would rather not go. Bertie, incensed and seeing his holiday in danger, attacked his mother with unusual vigour. 'She certainly is not selfish,'[7] he wrote, and pointed out that his sisters, Vicky and Alice, brought their small children from Germany to England. The Queen gave in and switched her criticism to the friends Bertie was taking with him.

On the evening of 17 November 1868 the Wales' family left Charing Cross, travelling in a state saloon attached to the 8.30 Continental express. In Paris they stayed at the Hotel Bristol, but not for long. Emperor Napoleon and Empress Eugenie whisked them away to Compiègne, their palace set in the woods some fifty miles north of the capital. Here was staged a spectacular stag-hunt – '*la chasse à courre*' – during which Bertie was thrown from his horse. Queen Victoria, reading this in the newspapers, realized that two of the stipulations which she had laid down had already been broken. She also read that there had been a state ball. That was Alexandra's night and France proclaimed it. For fifteen years Eugenie had been the fashion plate of Europe, a strikingly beautiful woman who had introduced the crinoline and the wide brimmed hat. Now she was forty-two and inclined to *embonpoint*, and the time had come for her to hand on the torch to the twenty-four-year-old wife of the British heir.

On they went to Denmark, to be greeted with a rousing reception in Copenhagen, where they stayed for six weeks, spending Christmas at Fredensborg. The children were the stars, and altogether the baby worship, the family conversation, the games and the Yuletide festivities bored Bertie and he slipped away with his crony, Crown Prince Frederick, to Stockholm, having earlier noted the attractions of Swedish beauties. King Charles XV initiated him into the Order of Freemasons, which earned him a wigging from his mother who had a horror of secret societies.

In Denmark Alexandra was joined by the Hon. Mrs William Grey, who was to be her lady-in-waiting for the rest of the tour. Mrs Grey was Swedish, a merry widow and to Alexandra's relief she spoke Danish. On 15 January the great adventure began. The Wales' children accompanied their parents as far as Hamburg and then returned to England and the care of Queen Victoria. The Prince and Princess headed for Berlin.

Saddened by this parting, Alexandra now had to face up to the ordeal of meeting the Prussian Court. Her husband had persuaded her to be pleasant and she tried very hard, but it was not easy to smile at Bismarck, especially when he sported Danish decorations. King William was easier to handle, as he had an eye for the ladies. He was a tough and simple soldier, although with some odd ideas about the divine right of kings. He slept on a truckle bed and enjoyed cold baths. When his guests requested the warm variety, he would order a gas jet to be lit under an iron tub. King Leopold of the Belgians sat down at the wrong end, right on the spot where the jet was focussed. His agonised scream was long remembered in Berlin. Alexandra managed well enough with the King, but failed miserably with Queen Augusta, an austere and bitter woman, estranged from her husband. On saying goodbye at the end of the visit, Alexandra said: 'I thank Your Majesty for all your kindness and friendship.' The Queen froze and demanded why she had not been addressed as 'Aunt Augusta'. 'It is very impolite of you,' she said. 'By the way, you may call me as you wish, it does not make any difference to me.' She turned her back and walked away.[8]

On to Vienna, with the temperature twelve degrees below freezing and the countryside blanketed in snow. Two years had passed since Prussia had checked the might of Austria at the battle of Koniggratz and Emperor Francis Joseph was determined to outshine the welcome which the couple had received in Berlin. He would have nothing of incognito and staged a state welcome. When the train drew into Vienna station there was a guard of honour, bands were playing and twenty-seven archducal families lined the platform.

In the hall of the Hofburg the Empress Elizabeth, all in white and sparkling with diamonds, was waiting to receive them. It was the first time that she and Alexandra had met. In character they were poles apart, the Wittelsbach Empress being intelligent, sad and introspective. But they had two loves in common: horses – and clothes, Elizabeth announcing that only she and Alexandra among the Royals of Europe knew how to dress. There were five hundred horses in the Imperial stables and the two women spent hours together appraising them. A diplomat who saw them side by side said that such beauty would never be seen again and this despite the fact that they were both thin, which went against the prevailing fashion for curves.

Throughout the week of the visit it was Strauss all the way. Johann conducted at the State banquet given by the Emperor, his music floated over the ice at the skating carnival given by Princess Schwarzenberg and at a party given by Prince Hohenlohe. The Strauss brothers gave a piano recital of their best loved tunes, including *An der schönen blauen Donau*.[9] 'The Blue Danube' had been first played at a ball given by Prince and Princess Metternich during the Paris Exhibition of 1867 and had become the rage. The lilting tunes of the waltzes were in Alexandra's ears as the party travelled south to Trieste and the Adriatic.

Waiting in the harbour was HMS *Ariadne*, attended by the paddle yacht *Psyche*. *Ariadne* was a ten-year-old frigate which had been refitted at Malta, her 32-pounders having been taken out and cabins built in their place, the gun ports becoming windows. On board were those who were to accompany the Prince and Princess up the Nile, including a marine artist, a taxidermist, the Revd Onslow from Sandringham and Peter

Robertson, a ghillie from Balmoral. There also arrived by train from Darmstadt a slim boy of fourteen, the trip being his introduction to nautical life. Then a cadet, this was Prince Louis of Battenberg, son of Prince Alexander of Hesse. Prince Alice had used her influence to introduce him to the British navy, and had also spoken to Bertie, who had agreed to take the boy with him in the role of ADC.

Louis had never been to sea in a warship and hardly knew port from starboard. The Prince and Princess took an immediate liking to him, forming a friendship which was to last throughout their lives. But the favoured treatment which Louis received was ill advised. One day he would dine off caviare and champagne at the royal table, the next struggle to digest 'the weevil-ridden biscuits and tough grisly salt beef'[10] served up below. In any event, initiation into the navy was a grim ordeal for anyone, but here was a titled foreigner, completely inexperienced, receiving royal favours. His fellow cadets made Louis' life hell, so much so that he considered resigning – in which case Britain would have lost one of her ablest sailors. He learned the hard way and was terrified when sent aloft. The danger was indeed very real for, before the voyage was over, one boy fell from the rigging and was drowned, an event which wrung Alexandra's heart as she watched the rescue boat searching for the body.[11]

Alexandra had her first impact with the East on the morning of 3 February at Alexandria. The harbour was packed with assorted craft decorated with bunting and flags, Egyptian music clashed with that of the band of *Ariadne* and the crowds were dense and excited. A special train took them to Cairo, country folk all along the line, some scantily dressed, some not dressed at all, but all sporting brightly coloured hats.

The Khedive Ismail had assigned the Esbekieh Palace to the royal party. This was an architectural folie de grandeur which recalled Second Empire Paris. Mrs Grey wrote:

> The Prince and Princess have an immense bedroom, full of rich French furniture. The beds are very beautiful, made of massive silver and cost, I believe, £3,000 each! My room is so large that, even when the candles are lit, there might be somebody sitting at the other end of it without you knowing it. You could not even hear people speaking from

one end to the other! . . . It is more like a State drawing-room at Windsor than a bedroom.[12]

But sleeping was not easy. There was a menagerie in the gardens and many tents, packed with acrobats and dancers. Flood-lit fountains played throughout the night.

The big excitement for Alexandra in Cairo was an invitation to dine at the Harem of '*La Grande Princesse*', the Khedive's mother. In the middle of the dining-room was a round silver table, about a foot high, and around it cushions on which the visitors sat cross-legged. Alexandra was never a big eater and she now faced the ordeal of tackling twenty courses – chicken broth, a huge piece of mutton, omelette, sausages full of garlic, vermicelli and sugar, fried fish, a gummy mixture of rosewater and tapioca, hashed meat and onions, mince made of sage rolled in a cabbage leaf, pastries, sweetmeats, jelly, sour cream and, to round off the meal, a tureen of boiled rice. Most of the eating was done with the fingers straight into the mouth and Alexandra was complimented by '*La Grande Princesse*' on doing this in the accepted fashion, using only the thumb and two fingers.

Poor Mrs Grey was in trouble:

> I must confess that I never in my life was more disgusted or felt more inclined to be sick. The taste of these extraordinary dishes as well as the sight of all those fingers dipped into the dishes of thick sour cream and the next moment tearing off a bit of meat or sausage from which I felt myself in duty bound to eat, was really too nasty. I did refuse once or twice, but the hostess took that for shyness, and each time took a bit of the dish herself and put it into my hand – once a large onion dipped in gravy![13]

There had been no liquid refreshment served with the meal and, when at last a cup was handed to her, she swigged the contents. It was spiced vinegar. Her expression of horror and suffering tickled the sense of humour of the Egyptian ladies and they rocked with laughter.

There was after-dinner entertainment in the drawing-room. The band was female, the uniform consisting of trousers and yellow frockcoats with gold buttons; strange music indeed was produced by flute, cornet, violin and guitar. On came a troupe of

ing over the Wash 'unendurable'. Why, with the whole of England to choose from, this spot had to be chosen, was beyond her. For Bertie the attractions were obvious – the shooting and the remoteness from Windsor. For Alexandra, the root of her devotion was that at Sandringham she breathed the air of home. Cold winds and flat lands were no strangers to her. Across the heath the cathedral-like pines became a blaze of glory when the sun set in the sea behind them and the magnificent scenery in the sky was the same as in Zealand while the villages on the estate reminded her of Gentofte. Then there was the little church of St Mary Magdalene . She could walk to it across the park, in much the same way as she had walked with her family along the path from Bernstorff when the bells began to ring. It was there, on Easter Sunday, that she took communion, having sat up late the night before, familiarising herself with the form of the English service.

The Norfolk stay was a second honeymoon and life was simple. Alexandra came into dinner with her knitting and afterwards they played a card game called Chow-Chow, the stakes being token fish at a penny the dozen. They took picnic lunches to the cliffs at Hunstanton, a servant laying out a cloth on the rocks.[9] Silent, Alexandra stared out across the North Sea towards the coast of Denmark, homesick still, while Bertie dreamed of the fine new house which he would build at Sandringham and of the great shoots which he would stage when the game shelters grew up and pheasants filled the sky. Two young people alone, but leagues apart in their dreaming.

One subject, however, was of intense interest to both of them. Alexandra's seventeen year old brother, Prince William George, a midshipman, had been invited to become King of the Hellenes. After King Otho had been expelled from Greece in the October revolution of 1862, the throne had been offered to Queen Victoria's second son, Prince Alfred. But he was in line to succeed in Coburg, and in any case the powers would not tolerate a British Prince in charge of Hellenic affairs, so the offer was refused. Albert's brother, Ernest of Coburg, was then approached. He considered the matter but made certain stipulations which put him out of the running, to the great relief of most of Europe. So a Greek deputation visited Denmark and sug-

C

gested to King Frederick that Prince William George should have the Crown.

Flattered, King Frederick was enthusiastic but reckoned without Prince Christian and Princess Louise. Both parents considered it unwise to send a seventeen-year-old boy into the turmoils of Greece, fearing that the crown would be one of thorns. They insisted on guarantees regarding his income and security. Matters became most heated and Prince Christian challenged one critic of his actions to a duel. But the parents did not mention the matter to the boy. He learned about the negotiations in a strange way. He told of it himself:

> One morning when I was a naval cadet I left the Yellow Palace as usual with a packet of sandwiches for my lunch. One of the sandwiches had sardines in it and was wrapped in an extra piece of newspaper to prevent the oil from leaking out. I glanced at the paper and read to my delighted amazement that I was King of the Hellenes. I had just been hoping, though, that something exciting would happen.[10]

One of his reasons for accepting with enthusiasm was that, by doing so, he would escape the ordeal of taking the naval examinations. He won the day and in the autumn became King George I of the Hellenes. Britain backed him, his income was assured and he went to Athens bearing the gift of the Ionian Isles, previously garrisoned by British troops and long coveted by the Greeks. Alexandra had shared her parents' fears and only accepted her favourite brother's new position when she concluded that he would be safe under the protection of Britain.

On 7 April she moved into her London home, Marlborough House and, without time to settle down or even arrange the rooms, she was launched into the unbroken programme of state and social events which was to last until the autumn.

London was full of Germans, making the journey to attend the christening of Princess Alice's baby daughter, Victoria. Among them was Prince Alexander of Hesse. He wrote of the Prince and Princess of Wales:

> This Danish Princess, whom all call Alix, is perfectly lovely, very natural and charming, as beautiful as her husband is plain. Bertie is a funny little man . . . he is so broad for his height that he looks shorter than his wife . . .[11]

While the emphasis at Marlborough House was on the social round, at Windsor the Queen's attention was firmly focussed upon babies. She had been beside her daughter throughout the labour and the birth, Alice wearing the shift that the Queen had worn at all her lyings-in. 'Oh,' cried Victoria, 'if it could be I who was to wear that shift, that it could be I who was to undergo the trial, that I could be giving another child to Albert.'[12] In Germany Vicky was having milk problems with her baby son, Henry, and had asked her mother for a donkey. 'The nurse is of no use to poor Baby and the milk does not seem to agree with him, so we shall wean him as soon as the donkey comes'.[13] In addition, although early in the day, the Queen was concerned about a baby for Alexandra.

As a husband, Bertie was in marked contrast to his father, who, as the Queen said, had adopted a motherly role from the start. Now she saw her son chasing around like a schoolboy let out of class and Alexandra taking no care of herself. She decided to speak sternly to them or there would be 'mishaps'. Before April was out she was confiding in Vicky that Bertie's bad manners had returned and wondering how Alix stood it. A few weeks later she was stressing her daughter-in-law's thinness, adding – 'and hopes there cannot be!!!' Night after night of excitement filled Alexandra's diary: her first dinner party at Marlborough House – the banquet and ball given by the City of London at the Guildhall, of which *The Spectator* wrote, 'The Princess was in more than usual radiance. . . . No wonder the worthy aldermen flopped themselves about in an agony of delight, and basked in her smiles like their own turtles in the sun'; the Marlborough House ball; the famous Guards ball held in the picture gallery of the International Exhibition building; the fête staged by the Duke of Northumberland, and the visit to Oxford, where the undergraduates gave the Prince and Princess a reception which has probably never been rivalled for enthusiasm and rowdiness. But the day which Alexandra was never to forget was 16 May when she held her first Drawing-Room. Lady St Helier was there:

> The crowds in the streets were enormous, but were nothing in comparison to the multitude of ladies who attended the Drawing-Room. Many people started at 9 o'clock in the

morning and waited in their carriages in the streets till the Palace doors were opened at 12 . . . The hustling and pressure were so great that many gowns were almost entirely destroyed before the wearers reached the Presence Chamber where the Princess of Wales stood . . . Every scrap and Vestige of trimming on some of the dresses and trains was destroyed . . .[14]

This was the male, American view from Benjamin Moran:

The Princess has a pretty, amiable, kindly face, large expressive blue eyes, regular classical features, and a finely shaped head, indicative of talents and natural ability. But her complexion is not good, and as de Bille, the Danish Minister, said to me, she wants some of the roast beef and ale of England to give her flesh and more development . . . Nearly three thousand ladies paid their respects or were presented and it was long after 5 o'clock before the ceremony was over. So trying was it at one time that the doors had to be closed . . . the poor girl was absolutely exhausted; I may say that it was barbarous to impose so much upon her and none but the English people would have done it.[15]

The Queen became more and more worried about Bertie and Alix. She deplored their social whirl, likening them to two puppets putting on a show twice nightly. 'I fear she will never be what she would be had she a clever, sensible and well-informed husband, instead of a very weak and terribly frivolous one! Oh! what will become of the poor country when I die!'[16] She waited in vain for news of a pregnancy. And she perceived yet another danger ahead. Prince Alfred was obviously 'smitten' with his sister-in-law and was haunting Marlborough House. Physically more tough than Bertie, Affie was in the navy and had already blotted his copybook with one sexual extravaganza. As is often the way with a younger brother, he coveted the possessions of the elder. The Queen wrote to Vicky: 'In confidence I may tell you that we do all we can to keep him from Marlborough House as he is far too much 'épris' with Alix to be allowed to be much there without possibly ruining the happiness of all three . . .'[17] She went on to recite Albert's views on temptation, that while feelings of admiration and even love were not in themselves sinful, it was one's duty to resist. And Affie was obviously making no effort to resist. She despatched him to Germany to inspect a selection of ducal virgins, in the hope that his attention would be diverted.

To her great relief, as September dawned the Queen learned that Alexandra was with child and three weeks later noted that she was getting broad at the waist and that her clothes were being let out. An edict was issued that engagements were to be strictly limited henceforth, and Alexandra had a holiday at Abergeldie, relaxing in the peaceful autumnal air of Deeside. The Wales returned to maternal favour – for a while.

Soon the beat of events speeded up once more. On 15 November Frederick VII of Denmark died, leaving unsigned a Joint Constitution which incorporated Schleswig with Denmark. Alexandra's father succeeded as Christian IX and, reluctantly, he signed the Constitution, realising the trouble which lay ahead. The Duke of Augustenburg claimed the Duchies of Schleswig and Holstein, through male descent, and pro-claimed himself their king. The German Confederation sent troops to the border and occupied Holstein. But, behind the scenes, Bismarck, who had become Minister-President in 1862, was determined that the troubled territories should belong to Prussia. He dreamed of the Kiel Canal linking the Baltic with the North Sea and wanted a trial war to test his troops and gain experience of the movement of men and supplies by rail. Neither Sweden nor Russia would support Denmark. The mass of British opinion was pro-Danish, but the Queen, although pro-German, was for neutrality – as were certain of her advisers. The Queen was hearing the ghost voice of Albert calling from the mausoleum, 'Germany, ever Germany . . .' Together France and England could have halted the trend of affairs, but Albert's hostility to France was causing Napoleon III to keep aloof. Instead the German forces marched unopposed over a tiny nation – setting the scene for the Seven Weeks War, the Franco-German War, and finally World War I.

The War resulted in a family schism. Alexandra, throwing overboard all the instructions she had received that she must leave behind all her native loyalties when she married Bertie, campaigned, and noisily, for her father and her country. Her husband backed her up and became most incensed. He gave vent to some very bellicose remarks and urged that the British fleet should be sent to the Baltic. This was 'the only occasion during his life on which the Prince displayed any disposition to imitate former Princes of Wales by becoming entangled with the Parliamentary Opposition',[18] and he was backed by the press and public opinion.

On the opposite side were the Queen and her outspoken daughter, Vicky, Crown Princess of Prussia, whose husband was at the front. The Queen was following faithfully the creed of Albert while at the same time trying to cool matters, telling Vicky that it was not a woman's mission on earth to urge violent measures. But she was, without doubt, acting against the wishes of her people in favouring a situation which allowed Denmark to go to the wall and it was the last time that politicians permitted her to influence affairs to this extent.

Worry over a war which in the end caused her father to lose a third of his kingdom, was detrimental to Alexandra in her advanced state of pregnancy and night after night she cried herself to sleep. She cut the Prussian Ambassador dead. 'The Duchies belong to Papa', she shouted at the dinner table at Windsor. She became so outspoken that the Queen forbade the very mention of Schleswig-Holstein in her presence. Bertie called his sister Vicky 'a thorough Prussian' and poured scorn on her husband's 'deeds of valour' against the outnumbered Danes. Alexandra was also somewhat naughty. When a visitor to Windsor asked Princess Beatrice what she would like as a present, the six-year-old girl turned to her sister-in-law for advice. After a whispered conference, Beatrice announced that she would like Bismarck's head on a charger.[19]

Alexandra's baby was expected in early March, 1864.[20] At the new year she and the Prince were staying at Frogmore House, Windsor, and the Queen was at Osborne. The weather was very cold and each day there was skating. On the 8th the Wales and their guests drove to Virginia Water where Bertie organised a game of ice hockey while Alexandra was pushed about the ice in a chair fitted with runners. There was a gay picnic lunch on the bank, the sun was shining and a band played. In the afternoon Alexandra complained of slight pains and said that she was returning to the house. Lady Macclesfield looked worried, but Bertie pooh-poohed her fears and went on with his game. It was four o'clock when the two reached Frogmore. No sooner had Alexandra reached the hall than the pains became serious and Lady Macclesfield helped her to her bed. Fortunate indeed was it that the Princess's Lady of the Bedchamber was there, for she had already had twelve children, there were three to come and she was herself pregnant at this time, so there was no lack of experience. In addition Alexandra loved her.

Lady Macclesfield moved quickly. She sent a servant to fetch Dr Brown, the Windsor town doctor who had attended Queen Victoria since 1838, and another to the local draper to buy flannel, wadding and other necessities, for there was nothing available at Frogmore. She telegraphed to London for the specialist doctors who would, in normal circumstances, attend the birth, for nurses, and for the Home Secretary, whose presence was necessary to witness that the child was not supposititious. She prepared one of her own petticoats for use as a receiving flannel.

Bertie returned as darkness fell and was thrown into a state of rare excitement but managed to control his feelings as he sat by his wife's bed, holding her hand. There was difficulty in locating Dr Brown, and guests and servants joined in the search. He galloped up to the house just in time. The baby was born at a quarter to nine on January the 8th, the doctor and Lady Macclesfield managing affairs efficiently between them. In fact the doctor was only at the bedside for twenty minutes.[21] The baby boy weighed three and three-quarter pounds. Luckily Lord Granville, the Lord President, was shooting at Windsor and his word was taken as to the true origins of the royal baby. Too late, six famous doctors arrived from London and, when they marched into her room, Alexandra was highly amused.[22]

The news was telegraphed to Osborne. The Queen was flabbergasted and at first concluded that Bertie and Alix, in their inexperience, had made a mistake with the date. When she learned the truth she was displeased, for she liked regularity in all things, although her own last child had arrived a fortnight late. Better late, she thought, than early. She decided that the premature birth was due to all the gallivanting to which Bertie was addicted. The next day she set out for Windsor to take command. There she peeped at a tiny morsel of humanity wrapped in cotton wool, lying in a basket close to a big fire to keep it warm.

At the Castle Bertie met his young sister, Beatrice. Brightly, she informed him that her new nephew was to be called 'Albert Victor'. This was news to the proud father and he was duly incensed. He protested, but nevertheless on 10 March, at Buckingham Palace, the child was christened Albert Victor Christian Edward.

Society, ever keen on a royal pun to raise a party laugh, labelled him *'All-but on the ice'*.[23]

SIX

Of Babies and the Mother-in-Law

Alexandra had six children – three boys and three girls. Albert Victor was followed, in 1865, by George. Louise arrived two years later, then Victoria in 1868 and Maud in 1869. The third boy, Alexander John, was born in 1871 and lived only long enough to be christened – one day. Life for the Princess was made difficult by the constant infidelities of her husband. They pained her, and during her pregnancies she lost much sleep awaiting his return from numerous nocturnal adventures. Thereafter, Alexandra absented herself from the marital bed. She loved her babies overwhelmingly, but it was a relief, both for body and mind, when child-bearing was over. The experience left her deaf, lame and condemned to wear a dog-collar which hid a blemish on her neck. All the children were born prematurely and none of them inherited half the strength of Queen Victoria.

One of the main problems Alexandra had to face was the relationship with her mother-in-law. At this time the Queen was critical of her on three points. The first was that Alexandra did not make Bertie's life more comfortable and so keep him by the home fire, instead of letting him wander round the pleasure haunts of London until the early hours. A black mark against Alexandra was that she did not get up until eleven o'clock and Bertie had his breakfast alone, a thing which Albert would never have done. The second was that Alexandra's babies were premature, weak and puny. The third was that she did not bring her children up on the stern lines which Victoria and Albert had followed for their brood.

73

The Queen and Alexandra also clashed on two subjects which, by common consent, did not enter the conversation when they met, a stumbling block to any degree of intimacy between them. The Queen backed everything German – as late as 1870 when the Franco-German war began, she wrote to the King of Prussia, 'Dear Brother, As an old friend, I cannot see you go to war without crying, "God save you and bless you" with my whole heart.'[1] As we have seen, Alexandra loathed the Prussians, always continued to do so and was rude to them whenever she had the chance. Then there was the Queen's animosity towards the Danish royals, and Queen Louise in particular, whom she described as odious, mischievous and ambitious. In fact Queen Louise, an understanding and talented woman who was most popular in Denmark, was merely doing the same as Queen Victoria had done, and was still doing – attempting to make good marriages for her children. But Queen Victoria was a law unto herself and she could not tolerate opposition. The struggle between the families of Coburg and Glucksburg to populate the palaces of Europe continued.

Alexandra was not afraid of Queen Victoria, but she *was* her daughter-in-law, twenty-five years younger and in a strange country. She could not have been expected to stand four square to this majestic barrel of a woman whose cold, steely eyes and storms of anger were so fierce that experienced ministers stumbled from her presence. No one in Europe would enter the ring with her. When Bismarck tried, he lost on points.

Victoria was at an awkward age. Lips wet with tears are ripe for kissing and she sorely missed the presence of a man in her life. When Vicky, tactfully, advised that her gloom and mourning should be put aside, the Queen fired back that it was all very well for her to talk, but Vicky had a man in her bed while she only had an old red dressing-gown to clasp. A clerical gentleman, trying to be helpful, suggested that she should regard herself as a bride of Christ, an idea which the Queen dismissed with the words – 'That is what I call twaddle!'[2] To fill the gap of loneliness, she made increasing demands on her married daughters to spend more time with her, but they had homes and duties in Germany, and children to bring up. So Alice, who was a forward-thinking young woman, arranged, in December 1864, that her mother's

dancing girls, shaking their heads and bodies separately, as if no one limb belonged to another. After two hours of this Alexandra, out of a mixture of pity and boredom, remarked that the girls must be tired, only to be told that they could easily carry on for five hours.

The evening ended with a tour of the upstairs rooms which housed five hundred 'wives', and hardly a pretty face among them. Alexandra was perplexed as to the purpose of a large silver divan, covered with cushions, which stood in the centre of an otherwise empty room. It was, in fact, the focal point of the establishment.

On the 6th the flotilla of blue and gold steamers, towing barges, began its journey up the Nile. At its head was the *Federabanee*, in which was the main dining-room and quarters for Oliver Montagu, Lord Carrington, Louis of Battenberg and the equerries. On tow was the *dahabeah Alexandra*, fitted out with every luxury as the sleeping quarters of the Prince and Princess. Next came the kitchen steamer towing a barge loaded with a multitude of birds and animals condemned to be killed and eaten. This was followed by the provision steamer, carrying amongst its stores 3,000 bottles of champagne, 4,000 of claret and 10,000 of beer, and behind it a barge carrying a French laundrywoman and a variety of riding horses, mules and a milk-white, and very noisy, donkey for the exclusive use of the Princess. Next came the craft of the attendant experts, navigators, engineers, naturalists, gamehunters, antiquarians, and Mr W. H. Russell, 'the man from *The Times*'. The last steamer was *The Ornament of Two Seas*, bearing the Duke of Sutherland and his private party who, at the invitation of the Prince, had joined the expedition.

Queen Victoria took exception to the Duke's participation, writing in a letter to Vicky that Bertie 'has invited quantities of extraordinary people to meet him out in the East, which is very wrong and will be very expensive'.[14] She took particular exception to Sir Samuel Baker, the explorer of the upper reaches of the Nile, whom she considered 'unprincipled'. But Bertie was greatly in favour of the presence of *The Ornament of Two Seas*, as it provided him with 'somewhere to go' in the evenings. There he would retreat to gamble and play cards, leaving his wife and Oliver Montagu in their lounge chairs on the deck of the *dahabeah*, content with themselves and the moonlight silver on the sand.

The Prince's principal interest lay in shooting. Anything that moved, from owls to doves, was his target – with one shot from his punt-gun he killed twenty-eight flamingoes, which Louis of Battenberg described as being mere slaughter. Bertie's ambition was to get a crocodile and at last he killed one, a nine-foot female, using an explosive bullet which blew off a front leg. But the hyenas were too clever for him. He sat up half a moonlight night by a newly-killed kid but only saw a swift-moving shadow; in the end it was the vultures who devoured the bait.

Apart from visits to the antiquities and the sights on her milk-white ass, Alexandra's favourite pastime was the distribution of *baksheesh*. It was no use warning her. The more the children crowded round her shouting '*Baksheesh! Baksheesh!*', the more she gave. From the deck of the *dahabeah* she threw them oranges and bread, and discovered that empty bottles were treasured possessions, being hung as decorations from the roofs of the native huts. The sellers of 'antique' and 'historic' trinkets quickly realised that she had a kind heart and was an easy 'touch'. 'De most lubly dings in Egypt. Cleopatra's neglace! *Je vous prie, altesse,* I find her myself.' The mementoes and bric-a-brac piled up and at the First Cataract Alexandra's currency reserve was considerably depleted. Here naked men rode the water on logs. As they scrambled from the river a French correspondent described them as, '*Ils n'etaient vetus que de la main droite*'*, the left hand holding the log on the shoulder. But as the Princess held out a coin, the right hand quickly shot out to grasp it.

The most discussed subject on the steamers concerned the possibility of attack by tourists. Mr Cook, of London, had chartered steamers and was tempting tourists with the prospect of seeing royals besporting themselves on the Nile. The British Press was indignant, and in particular the *Morning Post:*

> Mr Cook doubtless thinks he and his forty British Toms and Tabbies are quite entitled to gaze on Royalty at the First Cataract. Imagine Thebes, the hundred-gated city, with a tourist at each portal to intercept the royal visitors! Picture

---

* Clothed only by the right hand.

A rare etching of Edward and Alexandra *en famille*

The King and Queen of Denmark and the Princess of Wales (*seated*) with (*standing*) the Prince of Wales and Princess Dagmar, at Osborne Cottage, where they stayed for the Cowes Regatta, August 1876

the most enterprising of Cook's party perched among the ruins of Luxor and Karnak, armed with the newest binoculars!

From the sterns of the steamers watchful eyes scanned down-river. When a plume of smoke was spotted on the horizon, the cry went from craft to craft, 'The tourists are coming!' But each time it turned out to be a false alarm, proving to be a local boat or a merchant vessel from Cairo. In fact the boats of Cook were being plagued with troubles, running short of coal and being stranded on sand banks. But it was a close run thing. As the Prince and Princess left Assouan and headed for the Second Cataract, the tourist force raced up. W. H. Russell wrote:

> Their steamers are just below us in the stream! The tourists are all over the place. Some are bathing off the banks; others, with eccentric head-dresses, are toiling through the deep sand. They are just beaten by a head in the race! Another day, and the Prince and Princess would have been at their mercy.[15]

For the journey up to the Second Cataract the flotilla was restricted to one small steamer and two *dahabeahs*. This upset Alexandra considerably, for by this time she regarded those in attendance as part of one great family. She had taken everyone of them to a picnic in the ruins of Karnak, she at the head of a gay crowd of two hundred – all the suite, Egyptian *valetaille*, French cooks, sailors from *Ariadne* roaring with laughter as they urged on their donkeys, Peter Robertson the ghillie, with his kilt adjusted to suit the latitude, and the French laundrywoman. 'No, no,' cried Alexandra, 'You must all come with us up the river.' But that was impossible.

At the beginning of March the depleted party reached Wadi Halfa, 220 miles from Assouan and nearly a thousand from Cairo. Alexandra rode high above the cataract and looked south towards the heart of Africa and a mountain range forty miles away. Then the journey downstream began.

It was at Wadi Halfa that she collected perhaps the strangest item in the collection of mementoes which she was to send back to Sandringham. This was a ten-year-old boy of Abyssinian origin. Alexandra saw his face in the light of the torches which lit the bank and was intrigued by his ivory teeth and broad smile.

When questioned, he said that his name was Selim, that his father was dead and that his mother had re-married and was not interested in him. He had become a donkey-boy, relying on the tourists for a living. He knew a few essential words of English and French. Alexandra coveted him. Her sister-in-law, Princess Alice, had a Malay boy as her attendant. Why should she not have an Abyssinian? Selim appeared to be delighted with the idea of going to England, saying that he had nobody to whom he wished to say goodbye.

Another acquisition was a black sheep with a long tail. Intended for the next day's luncheon, it had gnawed its way through the tethering rope and wandered along the steamer's deck on the scrounge. It came across the Princess lying in a long chair and put its cold nose on her knee. It ate out of her hand and the two became friends. When an irate cook informed her that she was fraternising with the morrow's lunch, she announced that under no circumstances would she partake of the meal. It was labelled to accompany Selim to Norfolk.

On 16 March they were back at Cairo and an invitation came to the Princess to again visit *La Grande Princesse*. Alexandra and Mrs Grey had now been accepted as intimate friends of the ladies of the Harem and a joke was indulged in, jokes being a rarity in that establishment.

Would it not be fun if the two esteemed ladies were to be returned to HRH the Prince dressed in native style, so that he would believe that his wife and her lady had been kept in the harem and two 'slaves' sent in their place? Many giggles. So the eyebrows of the Princess and Mrs Grey were painted, thin veils put over the upper and lower parts of their faces and the disguise completed with burnouses which concealed the rest of them. They returned to the Esbekieh Palace. Bertie was still out, dining and enjoying himself with the Khedive, but Mr Kanne, the royal courier and travel organizer, received a considerable shock.

A trip which was conducted personally by the Khedive, was to see the Suez Canal. Nearing completion, it was due to be opened by the Empress Eugenie, with great pomp and circumstance, later in the year. Ferdinand de Lesseps, the French designer, was there to greet them and the Prince opened the sluice of a completed dam, allowing the waters of the Mediterranean to flow into an empty basin connecting the canal with the Bitter Lakes.

The journey from Port Said to Alexandria was made on board the Khedive's yacht, *Mahrousse*. She was more like a palace than a ship, fitted out with every luxury, for example, marble stairs led down to the dining saloon where there was a long table, laden with Sèvres china, huge dessert dishes and silver candelabra. The royal party of thirty took their places. Prince Louis of Battenberg described what happened a few minutes later:

> As we rounded the breakwater, the ship gave two or three heavy rolls. The gilt chairs on one side slid away to leeward, complete with their occupants, along the parquet floor to the ship's side, while the candelabra and fruit dishes fell over with a great clatter. At the next roll, the chairs on the other side slid away, leaving the bare table deserted. At the same time piles of plates, which stood on marble consoles along each wall, crashed down in two avalanches. Most of the lights went out. The Khedive's French *Maîtres d'hôtel* and powdered footmen were sprawling on the floor, mixed up with the guests and the general wreckage. The scene was indescribable. A few minutes later the ship was once more as steady as a church.[16]

Next stop Constantinople, and Alexandra stood at the rail of *Ariadne* watching the shore line of Egypt fade into the haze, sad at the ending of an adventure which she was always to remember. But there were thrills and splendour awaiting her in Turkey. She became the first woman to sit down to dinner with the Sultan. Dressed in blue satin and diamonds, she sat on the right of Abdul Aziz. There was another break with tradition that night: for the first time the Sultan's ministers were allowed to sit down in his presence. Then on to the Crimean battlefields, deserted now, little disturbed since 1856 – Sebastopol, Alma, Balaclava and Inkerman (the Prince galloped through the Valley of Death where the Light Brigade had charged and fallen). And so to Greece where Alexandra's brother George reigned. In 1867 he had married fifteen year old Olga, Grand Duchess of Russia and niece of Emperor Alexander II; they had two sons, Constantine ('Tino') born in 1868 and George, who had been born during the tour of the Prince and Princess. Mother and sons were now in Corfu.

King George, now twenty-three, was a most democratic young man and wandered about the streets chatting to all and sundry. Although he was popular, he kept a portmanteau packed in case the Greek people should ask him to go. No such request came. He lived simply and, if he and Olga wished to go to the seaside, they hired a cab in the square. They lived in a monstrous white palace, cold and draughty, at the end of Kifissia Road. Alexandra and her brother behaved towards one another as they had done in childhood. A British equerry, resting in the palace garden, was disturbed by the sound of laughter and shouting. Into sight came the King, dribbling before him a woman's hat. Behind ran Alexandra protesting noisily. Seeing the equerry, the King stopped and explained himself.

'She had an ugly hat and I did not like it. So I took it off and kicked it.'

His sister interrupted: 'It was my hat and it was so rude of him, and now I can never wear it any more.'[17]

Corfu was one of the highlights of Alexandra's long holiday. There she met her sister-in-law and her two nephews. She also fell in love with the island. While the suite stayed in the King's Palace, Bertie, Alexandra and their attendants, as well as the Greek Royal Family occupied the villa of *Mon Repos*,* situated on a promontory two miles away. The gardens, full of olives, magnolias, cypresses, eucalyptus, oranges and lemons, swept down to the sea, and their fragrance stayed for ever with those who had sat in them. On one occasion during the visit the peace was disturbed by a duel between the King of the Hellenes and the Prince of Wales, over-ripe oranges and other fruit being used as ammunition. But Bertie was every quick to tire of the high spirited games of the Glucksburg family and he soon slipped over to Albania to kill some boar.

There were still new sights and experiences ahead for Alexandra. At noon on 2 May *Ariadne* dropped anchor inside the old fort in the harbour of Brindisi. After saying their goodbyes to the crew, the Prince and Princess boarded a special train and began the long haul through Italy. Two days later they stepped out on to the

* Prince Philip, Duke of Edinburgh, was born there in 1921.

platform at Susa and joined the Mont Cenis 'ascending' railway. The vista over glaciers and snow-clad mountains was in strong contrast to the flat banks of the Nile and the desert.

Six days in Paris was the tour's grand finale; they stayed at the Hotel Bristol – *cette vieille boite* as Mr Ritz was later to call it. Once again they were within striking distance of Queen Victoria and a bundle of black-edged envelopes awaited them. She announced that the holiday must have proved very expensive, but, if Bertie thought that the country would contribute towards it, he could guess again. She ended: 'I hope dear Alix will not spend much on dress in Paris'. To which her son replied that he had bought her two simple dresses, 'as they make them here better than in London'.[18]

So at last Alexandra travelled back to Osborne to collect her family, a moment of wild delight for both mother and children, the latter having found the stay with their grandmother a depressing and restricting experience. But the Queen, proud of the job she had done as custodian, poured out advice and instructions as to the future procedure. Regular habits, early to bed and early to rise, and only one child at a time to come down to the drawing-room in the evenings.

Back at last at Sandringham, the cargo of mementoes brought home in *Ariadne* was unloaded, among them Selim and the long-tailed sheep. If the young Abyssinian did not prove a success, at least he provided interest and excitement. The job of pipe-cleaner, which was allotted to him, did not fully occupy his time and so the Devil provided mischief for his idle hands. His delight was to hide behind bushes and leap out on unsuspecting tenantry. As many of the Norfolk country folk had never seen a coloured skin before, the effect was strong, and embraced both horses and humans. Developing a taste for the good life as a result of his surroundings, one morning he wandered out of Marlborough House into the streets of St James's. Entering an exclusive hosiery establishment, he ordered forty gaily coloured ties and put them down to the account of the Prince of Wales. The Prince did not like this at all and suggested that, as a cure for such wickedness, Selim should be baptized into the Church of England, the introduction to take place at Sandringham church. But Selim somehow got the Rector's message wrong and strut-

ted round the house declaring, 'There is no other God but me'.
The climax came on a cold November afternoon. Preparations
were being made for the Prince's birthday shoot, an annual event
and the most important day in the year for him. The sound of
shots came from the Sandringham woods. An army of keepers in
Germanic dress, tense with military zeal, set off at the trot.
Further shots followed but at length the keepers returned, having
failed to find the culprit.

The shoot began and the Prince raised his Purdy and pulled
the trigger. Nothing happened. Examination showed that the
firing mechanism was broken. The Prince roared with anger and
demanded the head of the offender upon a charger. After detailed
detection, the crime was traced to Selim. It was too much to bear
and the entreaties of Alexandra were in vain. Selim was sent off
to a clergyman who specialized in exorcizing 'devils', and
nothing more was heard of Selim, the donkey-boy of the Nile.[19]

The black sheep, on the other hand, proved a great success,
became the pet of the local children and lived happily ever
afterwards in the Elysian fields of Sandringham.

EIGHT

❦❧

Dark December

Throughout the eight years during which Alexandra was bearing children, she was continually plagued by builders who swarmed over her country home of Sandringham. She liked the old Hall to which she had been introduced on her honeymoon, and in particular her upstairs sitting-room with its stucco decorations, but the place was not grand enough for Bertie and there was insufficient accommodation for the guests who were essential to his way of life. Inexperienced as he was in property management, he poured money into the house which, in reality, did not merit the expense. In his careful reckoning the Prince Consort had allowed a sum of £60,000 for improvements. His son spent over £300,000. Each year until the combination of international financiers and winning horses put him to rights, the Prince was some £20,000 in the red, and the chief cause of this was Sandringham – that 'voracious white elephant',[1] as Edward VIII was later to call it. The development of the estate and its acres vindicated Albert's selection, but the vast amount spent on the house itself was never financially justifiable.

The Prince's first step was to build Park House and Batchelors' Cottage to accommodate guests and senior members of the household. Then he added a new kitchen and servants' quarters, and planned a new wing. But he could not obtain a satisfactory design for this wing and in 1865 he impetuously decided that the only answer was to sweep the lot away and start again. He engaged A. J. Humbert as architect and two years later work began. Sandringham took on the likeness of a battle-field and the holiday in Egypt was a blessed escape from the rubble. At the end of 1869 the Prince rented Gunton Hall, Lord Suffield's place near

103

Cromer, and moved in with his family. He was thus able to keep an eye on the re-building and improvements which were being made to the estate. An ornamental lake was considered to be too close to the house and a landscape gardener, Mr W. B. Thomas, was called in to make two new ones, using the spoil from them to fill in the original lake. While engaged in this work, Mr Thomas broke a leg. Alexandra was much upset by this and tended him with such loving care that he sent her white roses on her birthday for the rest of his life.[2]

In April 1870 the Prince escorted his wife over the threshold of the new house and inspected the progress made within. He was far from pleased. Over the porch had been inscribed the words, 'This house was built by Albert Edward and Alexandra his wife in the year of Our Lord 1870', but he was in doubt whether this promise would be fulfilled. He demanded more speed. When he came back in September and found heaps of rubble still about and unfinished ceilings, he threatened that he would cancel the customary labourers' dinner held on his birthday, if the house was not finished by then. It was.[3]

The new house was much more impressive than its predecessor, but had lost much of its matured charm. In Jacobean style, with gabled roofs, it was built of brick with stone dressings. The only part retained was the conservatory, which was converted into a billiard-room. The Prince was very proud of his gas plant and wrote to his mother: 'I now have gas everywhere, which is a great improvement (of course, not in the living rooms!)'.[4]

The occupation of Sandringham House* was a fitting excuse for a series of house-warming parties. Outstanding among them was the birthday ball for the Princess on 2 December. Three hundred guests arrived by brougham and coach, driving up under the gas lights which turned darkness into day. There was dancing to Coot and Tinneys band which played in the gallery throughout the night, but the toasts and good wishes which greeted the christening of Sandringham House proved to be of little avail. 1871 was a sad year for the Wales family. In April their baby son died. The Republican movement was gaining strength and Republican clubs flourished in Cambridge and Norwich.

* It had previously been called Sandringham Hall. It was now known locally as 'the Big House', to distinguish it from Park House and Batchelors' Cottage.

There were fears that Sandringham might become a target for agitators and police protection was offered to those living nearby. Criticism of the Prince increased and when, after he had taken the Princess to Kissingen for the cure, he went on to Bad Homburg to gamble, *Reynolds Newspaper* commented that 'he was staking his gold upon the chances of a card or the roll of a ball – gold, be it remembered, that he obtained from the toil and sweat of the British working-man, without himself producing the value of a halfpenny . . .'[5]

In October a visit was paid to Lord and Lady Londesborough at Londesborough Lodge near Scarborough. The Prince celebrated his birthday at Sandringham and a few days later became ill. Two others who had been at Londesborough Lodge were also suffering – the Earl of Chesterfield and Charles Blegg, a groom from Sandringham. In Newcastle the fiery Sir Charles Dilke urged his audience to have done with Queen Victoria and set up a Republic. Finally, on 23 November came the announcement that the illness of the Prince of Wales had been diagnosed as typhoid.

No magnet drew large Victorian families to one place more strongly than the imminence of death. At times when quiet, peace and maximum efficiency were demanded, relations, near and distant, arrived to occupy every spare bedroom, overburden the kitchen, harrass the servants, and pour out advice from a minimum of medical knowledge. It was as if the 'star' of the piece was departing on a long train journey and it was fitting that all those who knew him should gather on a dismal platform as he steamed out into the winter's twilight. That is what happened at Sandringham in December 1871.

Fortunately for Bertie, though perhaps not for his household, his sister Alice and her children were staying at Sandringham as the disease developed. Taking after her father, Princess Alice was intelligent and perceptive. Her life had not been easy. At seventeen, when very much in love, she had been called upon to nurse the Prince Consort through his last illness and then to support her mother during the mourning. Married in 1862 in funereal gloom to Prince Louis of Hesse and the Rhine, she went to a German court which savoured of the eighteenth century. The Grand Duke of Hesse, an old recluse who had married his housemaid, did nothing for himself – if he wanted to blow his nose he rang a bell and a servant brought a handkerchief on a tray. Alice felt stifled by the dreary court, with its strange etiquette and endless heavy meals. Then came war: in 1866 the Prussians overran Hesse, trains stopped and there were no newspapers or mail. A great convoy of wounded came back to Darmstadt and Princess Alice improvised hospitals and worked in them. She saw suffering and sights which she kept from the knowledge of her mother. Four years later France and Germany went to war. The Princess turned her home into a hospital and daily supervised at four others. She built for herself, in Hesse and in England, a reputation bordering on that of Florence Nightingale, whose friend she was. The strain through which Alice had passed changed her appreciation of life. She was consumed with a desire to improve hospital conditions, help sick children and the aged and further the emancipation of women. She began to doubt the creed of orthodox Christianity. Her husband was of little help to her. His preoccupations were shooting, ordering suits from London and drinking sherry. She turned to David Friederich Strauss, theologian and critic of the Bible, and he became a frequent visitor to her Darmstadt home. He dedicated a book to her and the antisemitic Berlin court were furious at her friendship with a Jew. The Empress Augusta dubbed her 'a complete atheist'.[6] Conflict between such contrasting women as Alice and Alexandra was inevitable.

To ease the accommodation problem and to avoid the risk of infection, the Wales and Hesse children were sent to Windsor. Bertie's condition worsened and on 29 November the Queen was summoned. This was against the advice of Alice, who had bitter experience of what a handicap her mother could prove in a sickroom, but Alexandra insisted. The Queen was not impressed by Norfolk – 'wild-looking, flat, bleak country' she thought it – but she was on her best behaviour.

> I went to Bertie's room, and was allowed to step in from behind a screen to see him sleeping or dozing. The room was dark and only one lamp burning, so that I could not see him well. He was lying flat on his back, breathing very rapidly and loudly. Of course the watching is constant, and dear Alix does a great deal herself.[7]

As there was a slight improvement, two days later she returned to

Windsor. On 8 December she was back again, in answer to an urgent telegram from the doctors. Deep hard-crusted snow lay over the fields and park of Sandringham. The light went early and, as the night froze into silence, the terrible thought seized Victoria that on the 14th – the tenth anniversary of the death of her husband – her eldest son, the heir to the throne, would also die.

The same thought had come to the British people and caught their imagination to the exclusion of all other subjects, even Republicanism. Long queues waited for the bulletins. The Queen's journey to Norfolk was the signal for fierce competition between the newspapers to be first with the news. Reporters arrived at Sandringham by the score, every available gig and trap was hired and waited at the Norwich Gates to race to the telegraph office at Dersingham. Artists captured the arrival of doctors and notabilities. Remote Sandringham, quite unused to being the centre of momentous news, became known in those dramatic weeks to every home in Britain.

There was plenty to report. The royal family arrived in force – Princes Alfred, Arthur and Leopold, Princesses Helena, Louise and Beatrice. The Duke of Cambridge chartered a special train to rush him to Wolferton. Prince Louis of Hesse came from Germany and the royal yacht stood by to carry the Crown Princess of Prussia across the Channel. John Brown received particular attention from the artists.

Within the walls of Sandringham family skirmishes and fracas were frequent. Princess Alice was the first to clash with the established way of life at the 'Big House'. Lady Macclesfield, who regarded herself as the shield and guardian of the Princess of Wales, seethed with anger. She wrote: 'How Princess Alice is to be rooted out it is not easy to see . . . Suffice it to say for the moment that she is the most awful story-teller I have ever encountered, meddling, jealous and mischief-making.'[8] The struggle for power between sister and wife continued. When someone remarked that Bertie's recovery depended on 'divine providence', Alice exploded: *'Providence*! There is no Providence, no nothing, and I can't think how anyone can talk such rubbish.'[9] This deeply upset Alexandra, for her strength depended upon her faith in God.

Another disturbing influence was the Queen. Now that it was clear she would have to be in residence for some time she assumed her customary role of being head of the clan and the people of Sandringham soon learned the meaning of the expression, 'one-ness', understood so well at Windsor and Osborne. Orders were issued through her 'sergeant-major', John Brown: there was to be no smoking; windows, which had been kept firmly closed owing to the intense cold, were opened while the clocks, which Bertie kept half-an-hour fast in order to gain more daylight for shooting, were returned to Greenwich standard, the Queen denouncing the practice as a lie. She inspected stables, kennels, schools and cottages. If the condition of her son allowed it, she went on excursions to the coast and to local places of interest. If it did not she trudged round the grounds in the slush and the snow. Although Sandringham was bulging to the seams with guests, the gardens were empty when she was there. She was held in awe and she walked alone.

The two visitors most welcomed by Alexandra were Princess Louise, fourth daughter of the Queen, and Prince Leopold, her youngest son. The rebels of the Royal Family, both light-hearted, Louise was a talented artist and sculptor while Leopold was highly intelligent. Although he was an epileptic and a haemophiliac, he had insisted upon coming to Sandringham, knowing that his presence would help Alix. Louise was the Princess's confidante. It had been hoped that she would marry Alexandra's brother, Crown Prince Frederick of Denmark, and the Danish Press had announced that the engagement had taken place,[11] but Queen Victoria decided that one Glucksburg in the family was enough. So in 1870 Louise had married the Marquess of Lorne, the heir of the Duke of Argyll, a marriage which was to prove unhappy. The Queen's interference in such matters too often led to tragedy.

Despite her inexperience, Alexandra proved a born nurse. Lady Augusta Stanley heard from Lady Macclesfield:

> The dear Princess keeps up with unshaken patience and courage. She is with the Prince all day long, and does *everything* for him – the fact of being able to do so, and of his preferring her ministrations to those of all others, has been

her *best comfort* – or in her own words 'my only comfort' . . .[12]

She slept in his dressing-room and was on instant call. Yet she had another victim of typhoid to watch over and care for – Charles Blegg, the groom. He lay in his uncarpeted, sparsely furnished room above the stable and each day the Princess climbed the steep steps to see him, taking him such luxuries as she thought might tempt his appetite and ensuring that he received the same medical attention as her husband.[13]

Now Bertie became delirious. He switched from abuse of his wife to frantic demands for her presence. Already deeply hurt by the Lady Mordaunt affair and her husband's aberrations with Hortense Schneider and others, Alexandra now learned much more beside, 'all sorts of revelations and names of people mentioned'. For thirty-six hours he talked incessantly in many languages, sang, swore, whistled and poured out the secrets of his sexual ecstasies. His strength was that of a maniac. Prince Alfred described how 'he suddenly took all his pillows and threw them about the room – one at the Princess!!'[14] Next time Alexandra entered the room she did so on all fours, but, when she rose, Bertie floored her with a direct hit. There were five doctors in attendance upon him, Sir William Jenner and Doctors Gull, Marshall, Clayton and Lowe. 'That's right *old Gull*,' the Prince shouted, 'that's good, two or three more spoonsful, old Gull.'[15] Short, sharp words seldom heard in royal establishments came like bullets from the bed. The Princess was led away. In moments of returning normality, Bertie was obsessed with the idea that Alexandra would leave him. He addressed her, strangely, as 'my good boy'. She told him that she was his wife. He answered: 'That was once but is no more. You have broken your vows.'[16] The words were bouncing back from the mirror of time. 'My good boy' pointed out that these were words which she had previously spoken to him. In some row, she must have told him clearly that her days as physical wife were ended. The words had become deeply implanted in his mind and strangely now came forth unbidden.

Sunday the 10th was a day of national prayer for the recovery of the Prince. *The Times* prepared its readers for the worst. Poets struggled to find inspiration:

The royal Prince is sick and weak,
His wife is watching by his bed,
His mother looks so anxious there
And sister Alice props his head.[17]

Flash'd from his bed, the electric tidings came,
He is not better; he is much the same.[18]

The crisis came on the 13th. In the morning Dr Gull suggested to Prince Alfred that an extra bulletin should be issued saying that 'the strength was failing'.[19] But the country would have taken this as confirmation that the Prince was dying and Alfred insisted that he wait a little longer. In the evening there was a sudden deterioration and Alexandra rushed from the room, calling for the doctors. At 7 p.m. the Queen went to the bedside. Bertie looked up at her wildly and shouted, 'Who are you?' Then quietly, 'It's Mama. It is so kind of you to come.' The Queen was terrified when she saw him clutching at the bed-clothes 'and seeming to feel for things which were not there'.[20] Alice said: 'There can be no hope. It is the death rattle – I have heard it before.' Alexandra was near to the limit of her endurance. Bertie appeared to be actually *in extremis* when one of the doctors made an urgent call for two bottles of 'old champagne brandy'. When they arrived, he stripped the patient and began to rub him briskly with the spirit. At last returning animation rewarded his efforts.[21]

Alexandra sat by the bed. Slowly the hours ticked away toward the 14th. Midnight passed and still Bertie lived. At 4 a.m. he fell asleep. He awoke at 8 o'clock and signalled that he wanted a drink. Prince Alfred suggested ale.[22] Bertie drank a glass quickly, asked for another – and went back to sleep. He was round the corner. But Charles Blegg was not; he died in the room above the stable. Alexandra comforted his parents and attended his funeral. She placed over his grave a tombstone bearing the words: 'One is taken, and the other left.'[23]

The bulletins remained optimistic and the tide of relatives ebbed from Sandringham. To the public, convinced that Bertie would die as his father had, it seemed as if a miracle had taken place and the relief was immense. The story of the glasses of ale, coupled with the escape from death on the dreaded 14 December, filled the news; talk of a new Republic faded. The cloud had been lifted from the Christmas celebrations and on Boxing day at Drury Lane a packed audience insisted on singing 'God Save the Prince of Wales' three times. But, in fact, Bertie was still far from being out of danger and twice more Alexandra summoned the Queen to Norfolk. His pulse was 112 and his temperature stayed over 100. Breathing was difficult and a deep seated chest inflammation was suspected. His hair came out. There was trouble with a hip, which caused violent spasms of pain in the leg. 'His leg,' wrote the Queen, 'is swelled from a stoppage and thickening of the veins – and he must not walk . . .'[24] In his blue and white bedroom there long remained the mark on the ceiling left by the pulley-hook from which he hoisted himself out of bed.[25] It was not until mid-February that anxiety was over.

But a miracle had taken place at Sandringham, a miracle concerning the relationship between Bertie and Alexandra. When at last they were alone together, free of the Queen's presence and Alice's carping and lecturing, a great love came to them. Drained of sexual desires and the energy or taste for wordly pleasures, he was a changed man. He had walked in the darkest shadow and was frightened; he clung to the woman who had held his hand in his moments of fear and treasured the lovely face which came to him out of the mist as consciousness returned. She was his insurance policy against the fear of death and, propelled by the germ of self-preservation, he worshipped her. It is dangerous to love a man who is only in part his natural self, but Alexandra gave that love, part out of pity, part out of possessiveness, part out of maternal feeling. Purged from her mind was the bitterness which she had endured at his straying. Forgotten were the endless nights when she had lain sleepless, awaiting his return. The Duchess of Westminster seeing them together wrote: 'The Princess, looking thin and worn, but so affectionate, tears in her eyes talking of him, and his manner to her so gentle'.[26] Alexandra wrote to Lady Macclesfield: 'This quiet time we two have spent here together now has been the happiest days of my life . . . It has been our second honeymoon and we are both so happy to be left alone by ourselves.' And to Princess Louise: 'You would hardly know me now in my happiness. We are never apart and are enjoying our second honeymoon.'[27] Queen Victoria saw the change when the pair joined

111

her at Osborne early in February. After noting that Bertie still looked very delicate and worn, she went on: 'There is something different which I can't exactly express. It is like a new life – all the trees and flowers give him pleasure as they never used to do – and he was quite pathetic over his small wheelbarrow and little tools at the Swiss cottage. He is constantly with Alix and they seem hardly ever apart!'[28]

A thanksgiving service for the recovery of the Prince was planned for 27 February 1872 at St Paul's Cathedral. The Queen did not like the idea, referring to it as 'a dreadful affair', but on the 28th she was writing of it as 'a day of triumph'.[29] It most certainly was. There had not been such vast crowds since Londoners had greeted Alexandra for her wedding. But this time the authorities made no mistakes – the decorations were superb and the traffic arrangements excellent. The outward journey from Buckingham Palace was via the Strand and Fleet Street, the return through Holborn and along Oxford Street. Alexandra and Bertie rode with the Queen in a state landau drawn by six horses, and a Sovereign's escort was mounted. At Temple Bar the procession of nine carriages was met by the Lord Mayor, who, in a red velvet cloak and mounted on a white horse, rode before the Queen to the Cathedral. Thirteen thousand people were somehow packed into St Paul's and the names of those invited filled ten big volumes. Among the crowd the police picked up a French anarchist who had been sent over to England by a powerful revolutionary committee on the continent to assess the course of political feeling. The notes that he had made that day were found on him. An excerpt read: 'The people are all mad with joy, and will probably all be drunk tonight. There is no chance of a revolution here for the next fifty years.'[30]

Only six months before, a notice – 'To Let' – had been hung on the gates of Buckingham Palace and during the autumn speakers throughout the country had been urging the overthrow of the Sovereign and the setting up of a Republic. What had brought about the transformation? There was, certainly, the eternal attraction of carriages and cavalry, decorations and illuminations, uniforms and bands. Also, the Queen had a rarity value, for few people had seen her since her husband died. There was interest in the state of health of the Prince and, though his

112

way of life was disapproved of by many, he always merited star rating on public occasions. But the magnet which drew the thousands to the streets was Alexandra, Princess of Wales, pale, angelically beautiful in dark blue velvet and ermine. Their coming was a tribute to her and a recognition that she had stood by her errant husband and nursed him back to health. The legend of Alexandra was born and was to grow in strength in the thirty years before her coronation. She had introduced to the royal family an element which had been sadly missing – the element of love. Tales of her good works were reaching the family magazines. Church and reformers struggling for better conditions for the British people found in her the example which they sought. As Bernal Osborne, the Liberal politician, said of her: 'It is the Princess who keeps the Throne for her husband'.[31]

NINE

The Next Generation

Americans adored Alexandra. While they found the British society hostesses, bound to the code of the stately homes, forbidding, hard and difficult to approach, the Princess was democratic, friendly and ever anxious to help on points of etiquette.
Visitors from the United States viewed with horror the way
British parents brought up their children, or perhaps, more
accurately, did not bring up their children, leaving them in
isolation in the nursery and schoolroom and throwing their boys
into sadistic schools at the age of eight. An American newspaper
commented that the most beautiful point in the beautiful life of
the Princess of Wales was the way she cared for her family.

There has been criticism of Alexandra for 'smothering' her
offspring with love and treating them as children when others of
their age were independent in the adult world. But this was the
custom of the Glucksburgs. King Christian and Queen Louise
set the example. They treated Alexandra on her visits to
Denmark as if she was still a girl and King George did the same in
Greece. The treatment may have retarded realization of the
responsibilities and seriousness of adult royal life, but it kept
alive the freshness and fun of youth and it conserved the love of
the family.

Alexandra's belief in happiness, love and freedom came in
strong contrast to the nursery and schoolroom regime of previous generations of British royal children. In this she was backed
by her husband, whose aim it was to be regarded as an elder
brother by his sons, rather than the hectoring and bullying Papa
who had caused misery and suffering in his own childhood.
George III had brought up his vast brood on regimental lines and

114

every minute of the day was ordered. Life was so spartan that one son died. Up at six in the morning, no carpets or fires in the bedrooms, baths every alternate week and no supper on Mondays. The children had to stand to attention in the presence of their parents. Queen Victoria's childhood had also been closely ordered. Isolated from children of her own age, she was never alone for a moment and her governess held her hand every time she went up or down stairs. The educational curriculum was so severe that at the age of twelve she was on the edge of a nervous breakdown. Prince Albert followed in the same mould. He held the key of the nursery quarters on his chain and oversaw every hour of the working day, setting standards in education which his eldest son could never attain. There were no holidays, no encouragement and no contact with other children. Sloth and sex were the evils which must be avoided at any cost, hence, after a long day of mental effort, the boys were handed over to a physical training instructor to ensure their complete exhaustion.

Alexandra and Bertie went to the other extreme. Their children climbed over and around them like puppies. Queen Victoria commented with disapproval that Alix had all five infants in the room while she was writing letters, and no nurse in attendance. 'She was in her glory,' said the head nurse, Mrs Blackburn, 'when she could run up to the nursery, put on a flannel apron, wash the children herself and see them asleep in their little beds.'[1]

Alexandra deeply wished to feed her children herself, but was prevented by her duties and the views of her mother-in-law. Queen Victoria did not approve of this natural function and it was left to her determined daughter, Princess Alice, to break the rule. Vicky, Crown Princess of Prussia, followed suit, and on one occasion Alice fed a child of Vicky's. Their mother dubbed them 'cows' and named heifers on the Balmoral farm after them. Once again the Queen's veto – this time on breast-feeding – led to tragedy. Vicky never had the same understanding of, and affection for, the three elder children whom she did not feed, as she had for the younger ones whom she did.

Despite their frailty, pigeon-chests and knock knees, the Wales children were mischievous and wild. 'They are such ill-bred, ill-trained children, I can't fancy them at all,' was the verdict of Queen Victoria. 'Wild as hawks,' was the opinion of Lady Geraldine Somerset, 'rampaging little girls' and the boys 'past all management'.[2] In days when children were seen but not heard, the Wales tribe would play havoc with a grown-up game of croquet and interject remarks as their elders conversed at tea. The boys used strong language which they had picked up in the stables. The Queen feared that her grandchildren might be adversely affected by the fast people whom Bertie entertained at Sandringham, but there was no danger of that, for their friends were the grooms and the servants, the tenant farmers and the village schoomaster. Their toys were simple, bows and arrows made by a gardener, boats fashioned by a footman. When they visited the schoolrooms of young relatives, expensive and complicated toys were locked away to save them from being smashed. At a children's tea party the young Wales' decided that the woven flowers on the carpet looked somewhat faded, so they procured cans from the bedrooms and began to water them in an attempt at revival. The game came to an abrupt end when water dripped upon the adults gathered in the room below.[3]

The girls were every bit as mischievous as the boys. At an afternoon reception at Chiswick House, the Princess was walking with a distinguished male guest in earnest conversation, when the two elder children crept up behind them and lifted the long train of their mother's dress, revealing ankles and apparel not customarily exposed.[4] On one occasion they coaxed their pony up the stairs of Sandringham and into their mother's sitting room.[5] Alexandra shrugged her shoulders and said, 'I was just as bad myself.'[6]

Louise, whose birth had brought such agony to her mother, was the quiet one among the girls, looking somewhat sad with her long face and 'listless eyes'.[7] Victoria, known as 'Toria', was the most intelligent and musical – and a spitfire to boot; she clouted her cousin, Nicholas of Greece, with a bag of beans and, when he retaliated, she sneaked to her father.[8] Maud was the best looking and the toughest. She wished that she had been born a boy and named Harry, in compliment to her father's friend, Admiral Keppel, the famous sailor.

Eddy and Georgie were a contrast. The elder boy was lethargic and serious. He had the long Coburg nose and weak chin and leaned on his mother for support. He would stand beside her while her long tresses were being combed in the mornings and would attempt to hold her hand or put his arm round her waist when being photographed. She was the centre of his world. When they were parted, he would carry one of her letters in his pocket and periodically take it out and kiss it. George's nose was shorter, his eyes set further apart and he had a healthy complexion and bounding energy. But he too had a fixation on his mother. The competition for affection and attention led to frequent fights between the brothers. George said: 'Eddy and I often have awful rows and we go for each other like two turkey-cocks . . . He's a much better boy than I am and my mother worships him. Isn't my mother beautiful?'[9] When driving with her two sons in the Park, Alexandra sat between them, allowing them the comfort of the corner seats of the barouche. When asked why this was so, she replied that the occasion demanded a buffer state between two warring elements.[10]

The favourites of the Prince of Wales were George and Maud, both, when young, inclined to be extroverts like himself. As a father his moods were variable. Although overindulgent with his children at times, they held him in great respect owing to his sudden and frightening outbursts of temper. This trait he inherited from his mother but, while the Queen was slow to anger and slow to forget, Bertie blazed up into fury, the storm abating as quickly as it had come. At such moments his offspring learned to make themselves scarce. They were all frightened of him, particularly George, who, when he himself became a father, said that, as he had feared his father, so would his sons now fear him. The result was disastrous.

Bertie was quick to take advantage of the propaganda value of parenthood. When in February 1873 he left the House of Lords in the middle of a debate, he sent the following note of apology to Lord Granville: 'The Princess and I are going to take four of the children to the circus at 7.15, and it is now 6.30. I have not a moment left.'[11] It was gratifying to their lordships to learn that he was bound on such a happy, domestic engagement, rather than a *cinq à sept* tryst with an actress. Alexandra did everything in her power to keep tight the bond between father and child and each year on his birthday she composed verses for recitation.

Thus on 9 November 1869 Eddy was led to the study to stammer out, with maternal prompting:

> Day of pleasure brightly dawning,
> Take the gift on this sweet morning.
> Our best hopes and wishes blending,
> Must yield joy that's never ending.[12]

The children moved around with their parents, to Marlborough House, Chiswick House, Osborne Cottage in the Isle of Wight and Abergeldie Castle on Deeside, but Sandringham meant home to them. Although they looked forward to visiting Apapa and Amama in Denmark, who spoiled them outrageously, they dreaded staying with Queen Victoria. Once, being prepared to join her at Balmoral, the girls burst into floods of tears and Maud stamped her foot and shouted, 'I won't go'.[13]

At Sandringham were their friends on the estate, their ponies and goat, their dogs and gardens. For fifty years prior to the advent of the Prince of Wales, the Norfolk estate had deteriorated under an absentee landlord. Farms were run down, buildings in poor repair and housing for the workers primitive. Sandringham badly needed the injection of money and interest that it received from the Prince. Farms were re-planned, cottages and schools, stables and kennels were built. There was work for inside staff, gardeners, keepers, grooms, carpenters, plumbers and bricklayers, and many a local industry benefitted from the fillip. The result was gratitude, affection and respect for the Prince, adoration for his wife, and the sunshine of good feeling extended to their children. The usual prefix 'Your Royal Highness' was barred. The village children joined in the games of cricket and often cadged lifts home from school in the Princess's carriage when she took her young out for an afternoon drive.

Morning service at St Mary Magdalene was a big event in the week, the attraction being to see the Princess – 'our Missus' as the village women called her – surrounded by her children. As a prize for the one who had worked hardest and behaved best, Alexandra, with the full cooperation of the rector, allowed the winner to choose a hymn. No. 126 was a favourite.

> From Greenland's icy mountains
> From India's coral strand . . .

The sunlight poured through the stained glass window, the patchwork of colours stirred by the blown leaves and clouds. The rays caught the white bonnet, flower-trimmed, and made radiant Alexandra's beautiful face.

> Where Afric's sunny fountains
> Roll down their golden sand . . .

The three girls were in competition to see which could sing the loudest. Eddy was beside his mother, staring up at her. Georgie was restive and looking about for some mischief to enliven the proceedings. His mother's eyes were on him and she shook her head. A member of the congregation described her thus: 'Some exquisite little being wafted straight from fairyland, to say and to do the kindest and prettiest things all the days of her life . . .'[14]

The Princess took her children to tea at houses on the estate with a complete lack of royal procedure. A particular friend of hers was Mrs Louise Cresswell, a widow who farmed at Appleton. Mrs Cresswell had a son in the same age group as the Wales' children and the six youngsters would scamper off together to climb stacks, find eggs, talk to horses, chase rats. Tea was in the big living room, crowded with seedsmen's catalogues and prizes won at cattle shows, in the light of a brass oil lamp and a blazing wood fire. There were muffins and home-made strawberry jam, buns in paper cases and a great plum cake. No wonder that, with such memories, George when he became King was to say that Sandringham was the place that he loved the best.

In the early 1870's the entourage of the Prince and Princess of Wales was strengthened by the arrival of faithful servants who were to serve them through to the twentieth century. Two of them remained with the widowed Queen Alexandra into her old age. Francis Knollys, son of General Sir William Knollys, became the Prince's Private Secretary, and his sister, Charlotte, the Princess's Woman of the Bedchamber. Colonel Sir Dighton Probyn, V.C. joined the Household as Comptroller and Treasurer and the Rev. J. N. Dalton was appointed tutor to Princes Albert Victor and George.

Education did not receive high priority in the family considerations of Bertie and Alix. But Queen Victoria, imbued with the creed of Albert and Stockmar, had her eyes on her grandsons and in 1871 a tudor arrived. Dalton, thirty-two, early discovered

119

that Albert Victor was so dim and lethargic that he had to be written off as 'incapable of being educated'.[15] The receptive powers of George were little better. And there were further problems with the younger boy – bad temper, contrariness and conceit. Dalton, who made endless progress reports for the benefit of himself, the parents and the Queen, commented: 'Self-approbation enormously strong, being almost the only motive power in Prince George.'[16] Yet Dalton won the respect and liking of the boys and remained in his post for fourteen years. He did his best to widen their focus beyond the boundaries of Sandringham and in London took them on conducted tours of cathedrals, historic buildings, museums and galleries. It was not easy. In Westminster Abbey George disappeared. He was found on the top of Queen Elizabeth's tomb. On being told to come down immediately, he looked at her effigy and remarked: 'What an ugly old woman!'[17]

By 1876 the time had come for decisions about the princes' education. The Queen wished them to go to Wellington College, in which the Prince Consort had taken a lively interest. But Mr Dalton raised objection, pointing out that the educational standard of the princes, in particular the elder, was far below that demanded by a public school. It would be most unsuitable if the heir was proclaimed a dunce. Alexandra and Bertie now had to face the truth that their brood was below average. They planned that Eddy and George be entered as naval cadets on the *Britannia* training ship at Dartmouth, but overlooked Prince Louis of Battenberg's warning that the lot of princes in the British Navy was grim.

Queen Victoria did not agree with the idea, remembering only too clearly the scrapes in which her son Alfred had got himself into during his early days at sea. She wrote:

> The very rough sort of life to which boys are exposed on board ship is the very thing not calculated to make a refined and amiable Prince, who in after years (if God spares him) is to ascend the throne. It would give him a very one-sided view of life which is not desirable . . .[18]

Why should not the elder boy go to Wellington and the younger to *Britannia*? Mr Dalton gave the answer:

> Prince Albert Victor requires the stimulus of Prince

120.

George's company to induce him to work at all . . . The
mutual influence of their characters on one another (totally
different as they are in many ways) is very beneficial . . .
Difficult as the education of Prince Albert Victor is now, it
would be doubly or trebly so if Prince George were to leave
him . . .[19]

He talked with the Queen and she understood and gave in.
Already with little confidence in her heir, she now had even less
in the son who would succeed him. The dream which she and
Albert had shared of providing paragons to guide the future of
Britain faded away and she was forced to conclude that the
monarchy would not long survive her.

So Eddy and George went to Dartmouth and, despite the
presence of Mr Dalton, Prince Louis' experience was repeated.
Their messmates kicked them around on the excuse that they
might as well assert themselves now as they would not be able to
later. According to custom, the princes had to fight all boys
bigger than themselves, a practice which was ended by the ship's
doctor when blue blood poured from a royal nose. Advantage
was taken of their privileged position to use them as a channel for
smuggling forbidden tuck on board. Usually they were discovered and lost their pocket money, which was only a shilling a
week. It was a great shock after Sandringham.

Two years passed. George progressed, and it was decided to
make the Navy his career; it was planned that he should go on an
extended world cruise. But what about Eddy? He was as
lethargic as ever. If he was sent on his own to an educational
establishment his backwardness would be discovered. So it was
decided that the brothers should sail together, and Mr Dalton
went too; at Spithead they boarded HMS *Bacchante*, an unar-
moured corvette of some 4,000 tons, and left for the Mediterranean on 17 September 1879.

Some ministers were amazed and appalled. Here were the
only two sons of the Prince of Wales departing on a three-year
cruise, in a vessel the sea-worthiness of which was suspect. What
would happen if *Bacchante* was to founder? Would Britain be
ruled by long-faced, listless Louise, now hiding away in her
shyness in the schoolroom at Sandringham? The protest reached
Queen Victoria. She had also not approved but, having been told

the sad truth, had acquiesced. She told the ministers to mind their own business as it was a domestic matter. But how nearly were the fears of the ministers justified! In a violent storm 400 miles off the coast of Australia, the steering gear of *Bacchante* was smashed and for five days she drifted rudderless and out of touch with the escorting squadron. The calculated risk taken by the Queen and the Prince of Wales shows beyond doubt that they had accepted the handicaps and weakness of Albert Victor. They may have had hopes that he would prove a late developer, but for the moment he was best well out of sight. Alexandra could not see it that way. The link with her first-born, a mite who had arrived two months early, was so strong that she was blind to the truth.

At each port of call the boys awaited eagerly letters from 'Motherdear'. Being parted from them, it was hard for her to realize that they were growing up. Her letters were always newsy and full of fun. A story appeared in the newspapers that the princes had been tattooed on the nose. Alexandra wrote to George:

> How could you have your impudent snout tattooed? What an *object* you must look, and won't everybody stare at the ridiculous boy with an anchor on his nose! Why on earth not have it put somewhere else?[20]

It turned out that their noses were undecorated. They had visited the Botannical Gardens in Barbados, sniffed the large lilies there and returned to *Bacchante* with yellow pollen on their faces. But they took a tip from their mother and were, later, tattooed on their arms.[21]

They came home in August 1882 and Alexandra and their sisters met them at Cowes. Eddy was eighteen and George just seventeen. They were young for their age and George was so short that he was labelled a dwarf by his mother.

The following year the ways of the princes parted. George returned to sea and Eddy, aided by a battery of tutors, attempted to imbibe enough knowledge to allow him to go to Cambridge and then on into the Army. He shared language tutors with his sisters. They also were a problem. As they passed through the barrier of puberty they became deeply shy, without sparkle or beauty. Socially, they were unnoticeable and only livened up when the ladies retired at Sandringham, leaving the men down-stairs to their bridge, the bowling alley and their brandy. Then there would be gossip in the corridors, secrets exchanged and surprises prepared for the men, such as apple-pie beds and jugs of water balanced on half-open doors. It was all innocent fun for Bertie would allow no 'corridor creeping' in his own establish-ment.

The lack of attraction was a disappointment for their father, for he would have dearly loved to parade at Ascot or Henley with a ravishing daughter on his arm. If only the princesses had been more beautiful than his ladies, if only they could have cheeked him, teased him about an elderly gentleman's loves, and put him in his parental place! But there was no sign of this. The girls became known as 'Their Royal Shynesses' and, by an unkind few, 'The Hags'.[22] The truth was that they had no chance against their mother, whose beauty could outshine all but that of Lady Dudley. The story went the rounds that a foreigner, seeing the Princess of Wales and her daughters standing together, asked Alexandra which of them was her mother. Bertie was very touchy on the point of their looks. At a review at Aldershot a woman remarked to Mrs Phoebe Jeffcock that Princesses Vic-toria and Maud were plain. Mrs Jeffcock replied that they were certainly not as beautiful as their mother. The man standing in front of them swung round and fixed them with a furious and icy stare.[23] He turned on his heel and strode away. It was the Prince of Wales.

Princess Louise, the eldest daughter, was the first to marry. When she was twenty-two she fell in love and was determined to marry the man of her choice, for she remembered the problems which had attended the engagement of her aunt Louise and fully expected opposition. She bearded her grandmother saying that, if permission was refused, she would die an old maid.[24] She threatened her parents that if they stood in her way, she would put her head into one of those new fangled gas ovens.[25] But in fact the engagement was welcomed both by the Queen and her parents. Yet this was surprising as her fiancé was eighteen years older than herself, a commoner and a business man. However, Alexander William George Duff, sixth Earl of Fife, to his friends

'Macduff' was a Scot who hailed from the banks of the Dee – and a very, very rich one, a fact duly noted in the German duchies. Queen Victoria bordered on the facetious in sending him her congratulations:

> WINDSOR CASTLE, 27 June 1889. – I have received the announcement of your intended engagement to my dear granddaughter, Louise of Wales, with the greatest pleasure, and I most readily and gladly give my consent to it. I love my dear granddaughters dearly and they are like my own children: their happiness is very near my heart. Dear Louise will, I am sure, be happy with you, whom I have known and liked from your childhood. That my beloved grand-child should have her home in dear Scotland and in the dear Highlands is an additional satisfaction to me! As I hope to see you to-night, I will say no more, but that I remain, my dear Fife, your very affectionate future Grandma, VICTORIA R.I.[26]

The British public was also delighted, the main reason being that the Princess was not marrying a German, a relief also felt by her mother. The interest in the marriage was widespread, the magazines bringing out special wedding numbers.

> At that time it appeared by no means impossible that the Princess herself or one of her children might one day sit on the British Throne. In those circumstances, a foreign marriage of the particular kind which then seemed intrinsically probable would have been frankly unpopular with the British people, who would have pictured themselves as being one day reduced to bringing back their Queen now wholly Germanised, from some obscure grand duchy.[27]

Certainly by this time Alexandra had almost resigned herself to the fact that Albert Victor would never marry, while sailor George was showing little serious addiction to the ladies, his worst slip to date being when his father discovered him kissing a girl under the stairs.

Macduff was born in the year that Victoria and Albert moved into old Balmoral Castle and his father was the Queen's close friend. He was one of the few people who could pull her leg and get away with it. At dinner at Windsor, when he was noisily mopping up his soup, he paused, looked up and said in his broad

Scottish accent: 'Yer Majesty will be pleased to hear that I've given up brandy and sodas.' 'I'm glad to hear it, Lord Fife,' said the Queen. 'I'm sure you'll be the better for it.' 'Thank you, Ma'am, I think I shall; besides I find Scotch whisky and Seltzer an excellent substitute.'[28]

Macduff inherited 257,657 acres in Scotland with an annual rental of £78,000,[29] was a partner in the banking firm of Sir Samuel Scott and Co. and vice-president of the Chartered Company of South Africa. As with other members of his line, since Queen Anne handed the British Monarchy over to the Hanoverians, he stayed close to the royals. It was not only in Scotland that he could offer fine shooting over his wide estates, but he appeared in Norfolk, renting Castle Rising and giving good sport to the Prince of Wales and Prince George. He was also often to be seen in Bertie's company in Paris, where he was known as *'le petit Ecossais roux qui a toujours la queue en l'air'*.[30] Alexandra liked him. He was straightforward, rough and outspoken, reminding her of her brother-in-law, the Emperor Alexander. He was a frequent and welcome guest at Sandringham and his was the only bachelor house at which she had ever been entertained.[31] Yet many in society wondered that the Queen showed such favour to the Earl of Fife and that Alexandra should welcome him as her son-in-law. Although the newspapers carried lengthy descriptions of his noble lineage, there were dissenting voices. The Marquis of Huntly talked of an ancestor named 'Creely' Duff so called as he was said to have started life as a packman.[32] In a book of reminiscences published anonymously after Fife's death, the following appeared:

> There was no accounting for not a few of Queen Victoria's likes and dislikes. Why, for example, did she so tenderly love Macduff? I use the 'tenderly love' advisedly, for I have been assured by one very close to the Queen that she did, indeed, tenderly love him . . . And yet very certainly his best friend would not dare assert that there was anything specially lovable in Macduff. He was essentially a coarse man, extraordinarily selfish and utterly contemptuous of the feelings of others – this is, of course, if they could be of no service to him. His language to his sisters was Billingsgate at high tide, and to his inferiors, he rivalled even Randolph Churchill in his coarseness. It was my misfortune

once to be in the room when a tailor came to try on some clothes, and the way he spoke to that unfortunate man – telling him he smelt like a polecat – 'Don't put your d–d filthy paws so near my face,' etc. – was pitiful. He could be amusing at times; was always particularly nice to me and so I rather liked him – or rather did not dislike him; but that he was not a lovable man is a fact which, I think, no one who knew him well can dispute. But the Queen certainly loved him; he could do positively anything he liked with her. Once at a servants' ball at Balmoral, while he was standing by her Majesty looking on (wearing, of course, the tartan he had no right to wear, and knew he had no right to wear, for . . . he was descended from a petty attorney and no more connected with the noble Duffs than I am connected with the Pope) Macduff coolly suggested they should dance a reel together! Her Majesty, after a moment's hesitation, consented, retired, and reappeared in a few minutes wearing . . . a short skirt. They danced together, but Macduff (doubtless invigorated by his well-loved alcohol) chose the kind of reel usually danced by sweethearts – hands locked across the bosom and danced it in rather an improper way.[33]

In Macduff's family tree was one William Duff of Dipple, a merchant of Morayshire who, after his death in 1722 was thus described:

He had of land 30,000 mks.* yearly and £80,000 Scots of money of his own acquiring. He was not above his business in all its denominations . . . He always pretended that he knew nothing but plain simplicity. He attended at Old Miln all night and day whyle his melder of corn was in the miln, slept on a rack and shared a pint of ale with his own and other Tenants. He dealt also in salmon, meale and grain and greatly in malt. In short his progress and success were miraculous. For five years preceding his death, he drank a pint of claret, or two bottles, every day.[34]

In the eighteenth century the family added the 17,400 acre estate at Balmoral to their Scottish empire. And what probably counted most with Queen Victoria was that it was sold to her beloved Albert for 30,000 guineas in 1852. Yet she thought it quite unnecessary to further gild the Fifes by making Macduff a Duke, but the Prince of Wales insisted, turning the issue into a

* The Mark (Merk) Scots was a silver coin, value 13s 4d.

personal one.[35] So it was that the line of that wily old merchant, Dipple Duff, entered the pages of the Almanach de Gotha, under the heading of 'Maison Duff'.

On Saturday, 27 July 1889, HRH Princess Louise was married to the Duke of Fife in the Private Chapel at Buckingham Palace. Glucksburg relations from Denmark and Greece were there in force and the Queen was at her brightest, smiling at all and patting many of them. Alexandra looked divine in a costume of grey and silver brocade draped with silver embroidery over a satin revers. Her headdress was a tiara of diamonds and sapphires covered with crêpe de chiffon. But it was hardly tactful of a guest to comment that she looked younger than her daughter. Marie Mallet was there:

> The Chapel really looked better than one had expected, the little pillars were wreathed and festooned with ivy and white roses, and huge palms sprouted from the alabaster pulpit which not being available for any other purpose was used as a gigantic 'cache pot' by the Prince of Wales' express desire. The congregation were all provided with seats but mine was taken from me for the Prince of Wales so during prayers I had to fall down upon both knees to the risk of my new gown and the intense amusement of my friends. However, the ceremony was not lengthy, both the Bride and Bridegroom's responses seemed inaudible and the latter lost his way in the 'Have and to hold' sentence so the Archbishop had to repeat it, there was also a good deal of fumbling with the ring but there were no tears and very little agitation. I thought the bridesmaids' dresses quite hideous . . .'

Contrary to the forecasts of many, the marriage turned out to be a happy one, the Duchess of Teck commenting that they both seemed so thoroughly happy and contented together that it did one's heart good to see them.[36] They were two of a kind, being content with their own company. Louise's circle of friends was small and much of her time was spent in Scotland and she was happiest at New Mar Lodge, Braemar. There she became a devoted, and expert, fisherwoman, only turning for interest to music when weather and season forbade her the river.[37]

In the autumn Alexandra learned that her daughter was pregnant and, at forty-six, was looking forward to becoming a grandmother, her excitement mingled with the hope that it would be a boy, in due time to inherit the new Dukedom of Fife. But, as had happened in each case with herself, the event was premature and she was not able to be present. The birth took place on 16 June. It was a boy, but he was born dead.[38] So her own loss, eighteen years earlier when Alexander John died, was repeated. The question had to be asked – would the frailness of Alexandra's children re-appear in her grandchildren? For the time being the truth was hidden from her. At 5 a.m., 17 May 1890, Louise gave birth to a daughter at Sheen Lodge, Richmond, and Alexandra was there. At 7 o'clock she wrote to her friend Admiral Stephenson: 'At last the happy event has come off and I am a *grandmother*. This time I got a telegram and no mistake! I started off at half past 3',[39] and to her son, George she wrote: 'At five o'clock, thank God, . . . I held my little naked grandchild in my arms! It squeaked like a little sucking-pig.'[40]

The castle at Fredensborg, the summer palace of the Danish royal family, where
Alexandra stayed on a summer visit to Denmark while her father was King

A family gathering at Fredensborg. Princess Alexandra is second from the right,
standing between her father, Christian IX of Denmark and her brother, King George
of Greece

The Princess of Wales at the age of forty-five in 1889

TEN

❧❧❧

Alexandra's Relations

Throughout the Victorian period the competition continued between the Houses of Glucksburg and Coburg to populate the palaces of Europe, and it was not until the end of the century that the two families were merged in marriage and the question became more one of survival than of competition.

Alexandra's younger sister Thyra made a marriage which upset the apple-cart of Europe. Her husband was Ernest Augustus, Crown Prince of Hanover, Duke of Cumberland and Teviotdale, Duke of Brunswick. He was the grandson of that hated and feared son of George III, Ernest, Duke of Cumberland, who had succeeded to the throne of Hanover in 1837, Queen Victoria being precluded by Hanoverian law. He died in 1851 and was succeeded by his blind son, George, who, in his turn, died in the year of Thyra's marriage. But in the Seven Weeks War of 1866 the Prussians had overrun Hanover, ousted the monarchy and confiscated much of its wealth.

Queen Louise, who hailed from Hesse-Cassel, was the motivating power behind the marriage, but a section of the Danish people disliked one of their Princesses marrying a German and suggested to King Christian that the Duke and Duchess of Cumberland should be refused permission to visit Denmark. The Prussians were highly suspicious of the union, as they knew that the Cumberlands – or Hanoverian royals, as they continued to call themselves – hated the Hohenzollerns. And hate them the Cumberlands certainly did. Whenever they passed through Germany by rail or carriage, they refused to dismount in order not to defile themselves by treading on German soil. The Cumberlands lived in exile at Gmunden in Austria and at the court of

E

129

Emperor Francis Joseph were granted the rank of King and Queen. Proud of his British ancestry, the Duke dressed his servants in the scarlet uniforms of the days of George III.[1] As Alexandra also hated the Hohenzollerns, her sister's marriage suited her well.

It was a strange twist of fate indeed that was to link the Cumberlands and the Hohenzollerns in marriage. Thyra had six children, her eldest son being George William, known as 'Plumpy'. When he returned to Gmunden from London after the Coronation of George V and his Queen in 1911, he told his family of a strange and clear dream which he had had.

> 'I dreamed that I was driving my car somewhere in north Germany. It crashed against a tree and I was killed. The Emperor happened to be in his summer home quite close by and he sent two of his sons to accompany my coffin as well as a detachment of his bodyguard.'[2]

In 1912 George William set out from Gmunden to drive to Denmark. In north Germany his car skidded off the road, hit a tree and he was killed. Emperor William sent two of his sons and a detachment of Hussars to the spot to escort the bier. The news of the accident was telephoned to the Cumberlands and the dream was recalled. For Thyra, the shock proved so great that her hair went white overnight.

Although the feud between the families continued undiminished, it was thought only fitting that the Kaiser's consideration and courtesy should be acknowledged and the dead man's brother, Ernest Augustus, was sent to Potsdam to convey appreciation. There he met the Kaiser's only daughter, Victoria Louise, and, although the atmosphere at tea in the garden was distinctly chilly, he fell in love with her on sight, and she with him.[3] Family differences were overcome and they were married in Berlin in the summer of 1913. This union placed Queen Alexandra in a sad and difficult position when war broke out a year later.

The most dramatic moment in the whole tangled story of Alexandra's relations came around lunch-time on Sunday, 13 March 1881, on the road by the Catherine Canal in St Petersburg. Emperor Alexander II was returning from a military review when a bomb was thrown at his carriage by a Nihilist. He escaped injury, but his escort and passers-by did not. He stepped down to inquire after the wounded and another bomb was thrown, the blast of it being heard all over the city. The Emperor was lacerated, his legs hanging on only by the ligaments. He whispered, 'Quick home, carry to Palace, there die'.[4] They took him to the Winter Palace on a one-horse sleigh and there he died. The Cesarevitch became Emperor Alexander III and Dagmar,★ his wife, the Empress Marie Feodorovna.

Alfred, Duke of Edinburgh, and his wife Marie,† daughter of Alexander II, raced to St Petersburg. The Prince of Wales wished to follow them and told the Foreign Minister so. The Queen was against the journey, knowing full well the risk entailed, that there were even conspirators in the Russian police and that no one was safe. Alfred cabled that the Emperor and Empress would appreciate the presence of Bertie and Alix. Lord Dufferin, the British Ambassador, was in favour. When the Queen learned that Alexandra was planning to go, she dug her toes in. But Alexandra by now knew her own strength and she pleaded and insisted. Reluctantly, the Queen gave her consent, telling Lord Dufferin, in so many words, that, if anything happened, it was his fault.[5]

On the way across Europe other mourners joined the Prince and Princess, among them Crown Prince Frederick of Prussia at Berlin. And so the royal party reached the Russian frontier, a rich target for a Nihilist bomb, including, as it did, the heirs to the thrones of Britain and Germany. The Imperial train awaited them, surely the most sumptuous palace on wheels ever built. Over a thousand feet long, it had nine vestibuled cars connected throughout, and individual sleeping quarters for every passenger. Once the Imperial train of Napoleon III, the Russians greatly enlarged it, fitting it to their own railway gauge. For security reasons, its route and time-table were invariably different to that published.[6]

Bertie and Alexandra joined the Emperor and Empress in the Anitchoff Palace where they were virtually prisoners. From the

★ Throughout these pages the name 'Dagmar' will continue to be used in spite of her new title.

† Prince Alfred married Grand Duchess Marie Alexandrovna in 1874.

windows they watched squads of men digging a trench round the building as a defence against bombs. The only exercise they could take was in a small, snow-covered garden, no larger than that of a terrace house in London. Alexandra found Dagmar thin, pale and suffering from shock, for she had seen her father-in-law's body soon after he was brought to the Winter Palace. There were other reasons. The only 'outing' of the day was a visit, under strong guard, to the church where the body lay. It was the custom that his relatives should kiss his exposed face; an ordeal, as the wounds had caused early decomposition to set in.

The funeral route to the Fortress Church was six miles long and on every yard of it there was the possibility that a bomb might be thrown or shots ring out. The service itself was a test of endurance, owing to the extreme length of the Orthodox liturgy and the fact that there were no seats. 'All ladies had to appear in perfectly plain black, lustreless woollen dresses, made high to the throat. On their heads they wore a sort of Mary Queen of Scots pointed cap of black crape falling to their feet.'[7] Further discomfort was caused by a rumour that the foundations of the church had been mined.

Queen Victoria had decided that the Prince of Wales should invest Alexander III with the Order of the Garter and the ceremony took place in the throne-room of the Anitchoff Palace. As usual, the insignia, the star, the ribbon, the collar and the sword were carried in separately, each on long, narrow cushions of red velvet trimmed with gold. The Emperor and the few spectators took up position in the throne-room. The Prince of Wales made stately entrance, followed by five members of his staff bearing the red cushions. At this point a clear, feminine voice was heard to say: 'Oh, my dear! Do look at them. They look exactly like a row of wet-nurses carrying babies!' Dagmar looked at Alexandra, and Alexandra's hand went to her mouth. They both went into fits of laughter. Alexander fought for self-control but, after so much strain and sadness, reaction proved too strong. His great girth began to shake and he could not contain his laughter. The incident was not reported to Queen Victoria.[8]

The Prince of Wales then began his long journey back to London but, to the amazement of many and the consternation of Queen Victoria, he travelled alone. Alexandra stayed behind because her sister needed her. Queen Victoria sent a message of protest, but Alexandra remained unrepentant and unimpressed. 'Never mind, dearest Mama,' she replied on the day before she left Russia, 'I have nearly come to the end now . . . It really was very kind of my Bertie to let me stop . . . and, after all, it would have mattered much less if anything had happened to me than to him! Besides, I think one is bound to try and help those who are near and dear to us.'[9]

King Christian made it a rule that controversial political matters were barred when his family gathered about him. It was his daughters who were the fire brands, Dagmar the most influential, Alexandra the most outspoken. In an open telegram she had referred to Germany as the 'Robber State'. When the Prince of Wales planned to stay an extra day at Cologne so that he could meet a member of the Prussian royal family, she returned to England without him. She refused to cancel her Silver Wedding celebrations because of the death of Emperor William I. She slated her son George when he attended a Holy Communion service in Germany and, after he had accepted the colonelcy of a German regiment, she castigated him: 'And so my Georgie boy has become a real, live, filthy blue-coated Pickelhaube German soldier. I never thought I would live to see the day!'[10]

Alexander III was a simple, straightforward, giant of a man, very much in love with his wife. He enjoyed his visits to Denmark for there he could relax and enjoy himself, free of the ever-present threat of assassination which hung over him in Russia. He was a great joker. From behind a curtain at Fredensborg he squirted King Christian with water from an instrument the name of which cannot be mentioned. As he watched ladies curtseying at a State reception, he squeezed a rubber contrivance hidden in his coat tails which produced a rude noise at the critical moment of genuflection. He was ever keen to show off his strength. His ability to break horse-shoes in half was tolerated but when he bent the heavy silver royal dishes the Danish sense of humour was strained. His outstanding achievement was to order the horses to be taken from the royal carriage, take their place in the traces and draw the King and Queen round the courtyard.[11] On one occasion his strength became crucially important: his train was derailed in Russia in an attempt on his life and he held up the roof of the compartment long enough for his family to escape.

But the marriage of Alexander of Russia with Dagmar of Denmark produced a strange and tragic parallel to that of the Prince of Wales with Alexandra of Denmark. The Wales children had proved to be weak and lethargic, and a deep disappointment to Queen Victoria, none of whose strength they inherited. The story was now repeated in Russia. With a father of Alexander's gigantic strength and a mother as vivacious and tireless as Dagmar, it could have been expected that their children would be physically strong and boisterous. The reverse was the case.

In Nicholas, Alexander's heir, were merged the weaknesses of the Wales' boys, Eddy and George. Nicholas had the same shyness which hounded Alexandra's children. Like Eddy, he was a mother's boy and needed her support. But he looked more like George; in fact physically they were so alike that, in adult life, they were often mistaken for one another. Intellectually he was brighter than George but lacked the latter's mental stability. Nicholas, whose eyes were liable to twitch,[12] was weak and both Queen Victoria and the Prince of Wales noted this very early in his life. There was the same tendency in all three boys to do nothing unless pressed. It was practically impossible to arouse Eddy's interest in anything but sex, while during Imperial meetings the eyes of Nicholas were fixed firmly on the clock. When the time came for George to prepare himself for kingship he did little beyond stick stamps in albums and shoot small birds. 'Though Nicholas gradually outgrew the more marked symptoms of his earlier weakness, he remained pallid, frail, and of nervous disposition. He never showed the exuberant vitality of youth, and an explanation of his extreme shyness and reserve was possibly to be found in constitutional peculiarities.'[13]

In 1893 Nicholas came to Britain for the wedding of his cousin George, and Mr T. P. O'Connor, an MP, wrote:

> 'I saw the Tsarevitch during his trip to this country. One day he paid a visit to the Peers' Gallery of the House of Commons. I was immediately struck – as everybody was – with his extraordinary resemblance to the Duke of York. It is curious how persistent some family strains are. The little royalty of Denmark has created more replicas of the original

type than any other living Royal House. And thus when you see the children of one Danish princess, you see the very picture of the children of the other princess – though the fathers be of two such different types in every respect as the Prince of Wales and Alexander III. The type appears to be more persistent, however, than vigorous. The Tsarevitch certainly did not give the impression of either mental or physical vigour. It was hard to realize that this slim, not very tall, and decidedly delicate-looking stripling was the son of the giant who could twist tin plates in the hollow of one of his brawny hands.'

ELEVEN

Social Interlude

Bishop William Connor Magee was invited to stay the weekend at Sandringham. 'All seedy and dishevelled from my day's journey,' he was invited by the Princess of Wales to come and sit beside her. He found the company pleasant but a curious mixture. 'Two Jews, Sir Anthony de Rothschild and his daughter; an ex-Jew, Disraeli; a Roman Catholic, Colonel Higgins; an Italian duchess who is an Englishwoman, and her daughter, brought up a Roman Catholic and now turning Protestant; a set of young lords and a bishop . . .'[1]

The Sandringham house-parties were an interesting and integral part of the social life of late Victorian England. They were different from the gatherings at Marlborough House, which were more impersonal, smart and fast. In Norfolk the tempo slowed and the guest list was more varied – politicians and churchmen, artists and singers, dukes and their duchesses, ambassadors and sportsmen, continental royals and Americans. Some of those invited were impressed, some bored, some critical of the Prince's role as the great panjandrum, but most enjoyed themselves and all were agreed that the Princess was the most kind and thoughtful hostess in the British Isles.

Bertie was jealous of his reputation as a host and his social weekends were a ceremonial of his own devising, utterly divorced from the rules of Windsor. Here in Norfolk he laid down his own code of behaviour, rite and procedure. From the time that his guests arrived at Wolferton's spotless and polished station and the smart carriages whisked them away up the hill and through the woods to the 'Big House', every moment was organised. All guests had to be weighed, all except Lady Rosebery, *née* Hannah de Rothschild,[2] whose pregnancies followed one another with alarming rapidity. Tea was at five and dinner at eight-thirty. No lady could retire before the Princess and no gentleman before the host, and no excuses. A man of seventy-five, desperately tired, once slipped away prematurely, only to hear a sharp knock on his door and to receive a summons to return at once.

These parties give a clear insight to the Prince's mind. They were minor affairs, very vain glories, and yet they were of importance to him. It was the repetition which he enjoyed, as if he were a stage star playing a well-known part to exactitude. Ten or fifteen years afterwards he could recite who attended on a certain date. There must be no hitches to upset the even flow of happenings. Guests must move without hesitation to their allotted places at dinner and it was the duty of an equerry to see that they were in conversation. A woman who wore a dress too tight for her, tripped on a step and fell, was not asked again. All must enjoy themselves, or at least assume a facial expression which pointed to this happy state. Throughout the years there was only one outstanding failure. This was an elderly cleric who sat in deep gloom and from whom nothing but monosyllables could be extracted. Bertie played his ace of trumps, producing from his pocket his latest photograph, resplendent in fancy dress. No one, he thought, could resist that. The old cleric regarded it for a few moments and then intoned sadly, 'Poor old Buller . . .'[3]

Alexandra always wanted her guests to be happy and comfortable; but she also did all she could to prevent them irritating her husband. As first-timers could not be expected to be *au fait* with the Sandringham rigmarole, she would single out those who she suspected might drop a brick. The men she would invite to her boudoir, while the women, as they dressed, would hear a knock on the door and in would slip the Princess of Wales. The briefing and the guidance was given so sweetly, so tactfully, with such an abundance of smiles, that there was no possible chance of offence being taken.

Alexandra's boudoir was a room which oozed cosiness and happiness. Every table, cupboard and inch of wall space was covered with her memories – photographs, statuettes, programmes, letters, lockets of hair, views, everything that reminded her of past happy moments. It was an ideal place for a shy guest to relax and feel at home in, but for one bellicose inmate. This was a white parrot, sitting on a perch among the bric-à-brac.[4] By the name of 'Cocky', he was over a hundred years old and crusty, apt to flash a peck at strangers who came within range. Alexandra could do anything with him and had taught him to say 'God save the Queen' if there was a lull in the conversation.[5] 'Cocky' would take a lump of sugar held between her lips. A visiting Pole was horrified at his hostess taking such a risk and exclaimed, *'Madame, il vous mangera!'*[6]

Alexandra had a sixth sense about young ladies who might break the Sandringham house rules through ignorance or high spirits. (One that escaped her was a mischievous miss whose exhibition dance so pleased the Prince that he offered her one wish as a reward. Her reply – 'Sire, Sir Ernest Cassel's head on a charger' – earned for her a long period of excommunication.) So there would come a tap on the bedroom door and in would glide Alexandra, ostensibly 'to see that you had everything you wanted', but in reality to drop a few hints.[7] One such hint was that conversation should be concentrated on *things* rather than *people*. The result of saying that someone's son looked just like Lady . . . or, worse still, that a groom bore an amazing likeness to the old Duke of . . . could be catastrophic, contemporary means of birth control being most unreliable.

When the West Norfolk hounds met at Sandringham during the time of a house-party, Alexandra had to keep a most watchful eye on events. The Prince expected all fit-bodied guests to ride, forgetting that some of them were tyros or had not ridden for some time. After such a day Lady Walburga Paget regarded her full nude length in the mirror; she wrote: 'Wednesday we went out hunting. It poured in torrents from ten to four in the afternoon, and yet we remained out the whole day. My agonies would be difficult to describe. I resembled a variegated rosebud with not one single white spot left on my mutilated body . . .'[8]

There was another point which the host overlooked. While his own mount was perfectly schooled and fully exercised, other horses from the Sandringham stables were short of work and apt to play up in inexperienced hands. If some unfortunate was to ride down hounds, the Prince would certainly flare with anger and the hunting fraternity have some hard words to say about that 'lot' from Sandringham. Alexandra, expert horsewoman as she was, quickly spotted those in difficulty and would tactfully suggest that they go home as soon as hounds began to draw. But in one case she was not so merciful. The loose mode of living of one of the men guests had incurred her disapproval. As he struggled with a fractious mare, she was heard to say: 'He is being punished for his wickedness.'[9]

Alexandra preferred as guests men who 'did' something – politicians, churchmen, musicians. Sir Arthur Sullivan was a favourite and so was Signor Tosti. Disraeli and Gladstone, with his wife, were always welcome, as were Charles Kingsley and Parson 'Jack' Russell. Aware of the taste of the last named for port and fish, she saw that he was amply supplied.[10] Although she was well liked – sometimes adored – by members of the aristocratic families, their interests and background were far removed from hers and conversation of equal interest to both sides was not easy to find. The talk of the British 'upper crust' was restricted to killing things – birds, animals, men – while Alexandra was concerned with life and happiness; she it was who was instrumental in bringing to an end the cruel sport of pigeon-shooting at Hurlingham. Having attempted to follow a bulletin about how Harry was sticking pigs in India, how Arthur was after elephant in Africa and how the new coverts were progressing at Cumberland Castle, she might, bored and handicapped by her deafness, lose the trend and contribute a remark on a subject far removed. She therefore gained a reputation with some for being distrait and not over intelligent – all intelligent people naturally being interested in Harry's doings in India or his slaughter of pheasants. When over-pressed, Alexandra would find an excuse to make for the piano and there recuperate in gay Hungarian dances, or even a struggle with a Schumann concerto.

As a hostess, she failed in only one direction – German royals. She was duty bound to entertain them at intervals, but she dreaded it, knowing that her loyalty to Denmark would outlast her tact. She was once overheard in a conversation with a Hessian Prince, the topic being the ownership of a certain piece of territory. 'It is German,' said the Hessian. 'It is Danish,' said Alexandra. 'It is German,' said the Hessian. 'It is Danish,' said Alexandra. This exchange was repeated four times, becoming chillier on each occasion. 'It is Danish,' said Alexandra with frigid finality. Then, pretending that she could no longer hear, she swung round and flashed a smile of triumph at her daughter.

When Emperor Frederick died in 1888, and his son William succeeded, the new Emperor invited himself to Sandringham. Alexandra had attended Frederick's funeral and had been infuriated by William's rudeness and callousness towards his mother. The clash of the two supreme egotists, the Prince of Wales and the German Emperor, ended in a battle royal in the Norfolk countryside. William departed two days before his visit was scheduled to end. As his carriage moved away from the front door of the 'Big House', where the Household was gathered, Alexandra was heard to say, 'Thank God, he is gone.'[11] She may have said it louder than she intended owing to her deafness, on the other hand she may have used this as an excuse for a general expression of her feelings, for she could be very mischievous.

She had no problems with the Gladstones, who found Sandringham a happy contrast with Windsor, or with Lord Beaconsfield. She and Benjamin Disraeli had great fun together. They were sitting beside one another when Alexandra noticed that the statesman had no Orders, while the bodice of her dress was ablaze with them. 'It is a shame that you have no decorations,' she said. 'Here, I will bestow one upon you,' and she pinned her menu to his lapel. When, in trying to cut a hard roll, the knife slipped and cut his finger, she bound it up with her handkerchief. He said: 'When I asked for bread, they gave me a stone. But I had a Princess to bind up my wounds.'[12]

Alexandra was little impressed by titles or decorations. She said to Mrs Gladstone at a time when her husband was prime minister: 'You don't want your William to be called anything but Mr Gladstone. You don't care about names and titles and orders. When I think how people trouble and struggle about these things and what dreadful persons get them, I cannot understand it at all. You are too proud of your William to want him to be anything else or to wear stars.'[13] The Gladstones blossomed in the sunshine of Alexandra's smile, although they had to put up with a good deal of ragging from their host, one reason being that the G.O.M. was too good a whist player for Bertie's liking. Although Gladstone did not smoke, he was condemned to blow smoke through his nostrils,[14] while his wife was led to the bowling alley and there subjected to unaccustomed exercise.[15] A drawing of Gladstone appeared on a screen in the billiard room. He was in company with eminent Victorians such as Matthew Arnold and Lord Salisbury, displayed in 'very dubious positions' and surrounded by a chorus of naked ladies.[16] But it was all taken in good part and, when Mrs Gladstone was ready for bed, in would come Alexandra and insist upon tucking her up.[17]

The churchmen were on part time duty, as they were called upon to preach on Sundays and then the tenants were treated to the best of Magee and Wilberforce, Dean Stanley and 'Jack' Russell. Church affairs were strictly the province of the Princess, although her husband, remembering his father's prowess at the organ, assumed for himself the unearned role of musical pundit. The organist at the Church of St Mary Magdalene was a local tradesman and but a moderate performer, and the Prince decided that he must be replaced. He thus instructed his wife and the Rector. Neither had the heart to do so and together they decided to take no action, hoping the Prince would forget. A few weeks later Gladstone came to stay and his favourite hymn, 'Rock of Ages', was on the board. The organist spotted the steely-eyed statesman in the congregation and lost his nerve, the last verse consisting of a ghastly and unrecognizable wailing of the pipes. The Prince flushed and fidgetted and, as the service ended, strode quickly from the church and took up position on the grass beyond. Alexandra and the Rector held back. 'Come here, both of you,' roared Bertie. They shuffled up, penitent, before the flock and 'caught it good and proper'.[18]

After dinner was the time for cards or perhaps a game then in fashion. One such was called 'Mental Photographs', in which those taking part were supposed to build their likenesses by stating their characteristics and tastes. Alexandra was drawn in and gave an insight of herself; *Favourite dish*: 'Yorkshire pudding' – *Favourite art*: 'Millinery' – *Favourite occupation*: 'Minding

141

my own business'.[19]

Alexandra adored dancing and the nights of the annual balls were the most important of the year. There were four of them, the County, the Farmers', the Servants' and the ball to celebrate her birthday, held in early December, when she stood beneath the great candelabra and received three hundred guests. For the social occasions there was much jockeying for invitations, for tuft-hunters were thick upon the Norfolk ground. The occasion which she and Bertie enjoyed most was the Servants' ball, an intimate occasion when everybody knew everybody and there were no pretences. A tenant left a record of one such jubilant night:

> The ball opened with a country dance, the Prince and Princess leading off with the heads of the respective departments. . . . The house-party, equerries, ladies-in-waiting, and all invited from the neighbourhood, were ordered to join in, no shirking or sitting out allowed, and when the sides had been made up, the Prince and the Princess set off with their partners, round and round, down the middle and up again, and so on to the end, the Prince the jolliest of the jolly. . . . His own Master of Ceremonies, signalling and sending messages to the band, arranging every dance, and when to begin and to leave off, noticing the smallest mistake in the figures, and putting people in their places. In the 'Triumph', which is such an exhausting dance, he looked as if he could have gone on all night and into the middle of next week. . . . It was a mercy to have a Quadrille now and then for a little rest. . . . Then a jig was started and it was so pretty to see the way the Princess danced it, while the state liveries of the footmen and the green velvet of the gamekeepers and Highland costumes, mixed up with the scarlet coats of the country gentlemen, and the lovely toilettes and the merry tune, made a sight to be seen or heard. Almost before one dance ended, the Prince started another, and suddenly the Scotch pipers would screech out and the Prince would fold his arms and fling himself into a Highland fling, and so on fast and furious until far into the small hours of the morning. . . .[20]

Alexandra did not excel at organized out-of-door games. On the tennis court she was unable to get the ball across the net[21] and could never differentiate between the rules of golf and hockey. Once finding two balls teed up on a green ready for her husband to drive off, she and Princess Victoria selected clubs and, using them as hockey sticks, engaged in a race to get their ball into the hole in the shortest time. They then departed. On his arrival Bertie found the new balls reduced to oblong shapes, divots littering the grass.[22] But Alexandra excelled in other fields of sport. Apart from being a superb horsewoman, she was an expert, and exceeding fast, tandem driver. Viscount Knutsford recalled how, as he sat trembling beside her, she took a right-angled corner and shot through a narrow archway without reducing speed and with the offside wheels of her low pony cart well clear of the ground.[23]

Skating was another of her achievements and the lake at Sandringham was an ideal rink. Torches flared round the banks, coloured lights hung from the trees and a band played on the island. The villagers and the staff gathered at one end and the house guests at the other and hot negus was served from a tent. While the inexperienced were pushed across the ice in chairs fitted with runners, each bearing a little light, Alexandra, dressed in a Siberian costume, glided effortlessly around, shaming all opposition.

One important name was missing from the list of those who periodically visited Sandringham, that of Queen Victoria. She came only once in the eight years after Alexandra's marriage – and then only because Bertie's serious illness made her presence imperative. In the remaining thirty years of her life she made only one brief stay and then it was mainly because her grand-daughter, Louise, was shortly to give birth and she wished to be informed about, if not present at, the birth. It is difficult to pinpoint the cause of the Queen's ostracism of Sandringham but it is a fact that throughout her long reign, she ignored East Anglia.

Nevertheless, at the end of April 1889 Queen Victoria arrived at Wolferton station and, under triumphal arches, was escorted to the house by sixty members of the West Norfolk hunt. Bertie and Alix spared no efforts to entertain her, the *pièce de résistance* being performances by Henry Irving and Ellen Terry, staged in the ballroom before an audience of three hundred. Victoria was intrigued:

> The piece, *The Bells*, is a melodrama, translated from the French *Le Juif Polonais* by Erckmann-Chatrian, and is very thrilling. The hero (Irving), though a mannerist of the Macready type, acted wonderfully. He is a murderer, and frequently imagines he hears the bells of the horses in the sledge, in which sat the Polish Jew, whom he murdered. The way in which Irving acted his own dream, and described the way in which he carried out the murder, is wonderful and ghastly, as well as the scene of his death. He had carried his secret about with him for thirteen years![24]

Next morning she left. Sandringham had seen the last of Queen Victoria.

However, the Queen was ever quick to call upon Alexandra's gifts as a hostess if unusual guests headed towards Buckingham Palace or Windsor. The summons came when potentates of the East – 'Oriental gentlemen' she called them – insisted upon visiting her. It was, therefore, no accident that Alexandra was on Deeside when Queen Elizabeth of Romania, alias Carmen Sylva, came to stay with the Queen at Balmoral in 1890. Queen Elizabeth was fifty-seven, wore her hair short and was an outstanding character among the royalties of Europe. She was a talented author, writing under the name of Carmen Sylva. She was equally at home with poetry, prose and plays and her particular interest lay in Romanian folk-lore. While she was well able to cope with the etiquette and procedure of a royal visit, the three young ladies in attendance upon her were feeling very far from Sinaia and facing their first evening at the court of Queen Victoria with considerable trepidation. Among them was twenty-four year old Hélène Vacaresco, a poetess who helped her mistress with her compositions.

Hélène sat in her bedroom, staring at a large divan upon which was laid out the wardrobe which she had brought with her. She simply could not make up her mind which dress to wear. She consulted her maid, who proposed the most showy, sparkling with gold and diamanté. She asked Queen Elizabeth, who was not very helpful. There came a knock at the door. There stood the Princess of Wales, come to enquire if she was comfortable and had any problems. Hélène melted under the smiles and the chatter and confided that she indeed had a problem – what to wear. So, together, the two went through the assortment laid out on the divan. 'Too heavy and gaudy for you,' said Alexandra, laying aside the choice of Queen Elizabeth. She shook her head at the maid's selection. Then, holding up a red skirt, she exclaimed: 'Oh, how nice! Why don't you wear this?' It was embroidered with yellow flowers, a gold thread ran through the fabric, and it was of the style once worn by the Tziganes beauties, the gypsies of Romania. Hélène admitted that it had been her own first choice but she had put it on one side as being 'hardly suitable'.

'But if I forbid you to appear in any other?' said the Princess.

'I will obey, Madam,' answered Hélène, smiling.

A knock came at the door. Hélène opened it and there stood a footman who announced: 'The Queen desires you to go to her immediately.' Hélène thought that he meant Queen Elizabeth and replied that she was being honoured by a visit from the Princess of Wales and would be along shortly. The footman looked somewhat perplexed and walked away. Alexandra overheard and her hands went to her face. 'Oh dear,' she said, 'You have made a terrible mistake. He means Queen Victoria. There is only one Queen to us, and she puts up with no excuses or delay, so run along quickly.'

Hélène, overawed at the summons, set off in the prim gait prescribed for ladies-in-waiting. 'Don't let him get there before you,' urged Alexandra. 'Can't you change that Court step of yours into a good run? Here, give me your hand.' Seizing it, the Princess led her at a smart trot along the corridors and overhauled the footman just before he reached the Queen's door.[25]

Queen Victoria was in a happy mood and Hélène soon relaxed, but found that all she could express was praise for the Princess of Wales. The old lady in the white cap listened and nodded and smiled. Then she paid Alexandra what must have been her greatest tribute. The Queen said:

> And you have seen only one side of her. For many years the Princess has tried to spare me the strain and fatigue of functions. She opens bazaars, attends concerts, visits hospitals in my place, and she gives me such full and vivid

accounts of people and places that I always seem to have been present. I sometimes laughingly tell her that she is a dictionary in which is inscribed every variety of adjective connected with the words 'good' and 'true'. However terrible the load which I lay upon her slender shoulders, she not only never complains, but endeavours to prove that she has enjoyed what to another would be a tiresome duty. She even declares that a Drawing Room is entertaining! . . . Princess Alexandra holds a Drawing Room beautifully, and I am gratified to feel secure that, when I am no more, a Queen of England worthy of England's Throne will give it grace.[26]

Before dinner there was a torchlight procession and reels were danced before the castle.[27] The Queen led her guests outside, the illumined hall behind them, the darkness streaked with the flare of torches, throwing strange shadows as they bowed to the wind. As each reel ended, the sound of distant bagpipes came from the hills. The scent of the heather and the trees, the tang of the river, the dancing feet and the tartan flying, the music of the pipes, now near, now soft in the distance of the night, laid their magic upon the Romanian girl. Spellbound, she confided to her diary that these were moments which would remain clear in her memory for ever. But she was in her dinner dress and the October evening was cold. She shivered.

She saw the grey-clad silhouette of the Princess of Wales standing behind the Queen's chair. She saw her leave and return with something in her arms. She watched her place a white shawl round the shoulders of the Queen. She saw that Alexandra's arms were full of shawls and she was moving among the women, handing one to each of them. Then she went back to her post behind the chair of Queen Victoria.[28]

TWELVE

❦

Loving Kindness

Alexandra was a crusader for the dignity of man, a woman with an unquenchable desire to see people and creatures happy and one who regarded the infliction of unkindness as grounds for an immediate declaration of war. George Dangerfield said of her: 'She had an instinctive kindness and an almost childlike zest for life which were quite irresistible.'[1] Happiness was written in stars across her sky and sadness was a dark cloud upon it. Seeing on Christmas Eve at Sandringham a new footman from Scotland who was depressed and clearly home-sick, she gave him a pair of gold cuff links, saying: 'This is beside your staff present. It is from *me* to *you*.' She won her smile, as she always did. No horse that ever served her was destroyed and the Duke of Windsor recalled that, if she saw a lame horse or one pulling too heavy a load, she would stop her carriage and upbraid the driver.[2] She castigated the headmaster of Eton for flogging the boys. No plea for help was unanswered while her generosity to the needy was the despair of her financial advisers.

By the close of the nineteenth century those who had been long about the Throne saw clearly the revolution that the advent of the Danish Princess had brought to the Royal Family. Lady Ripon, who had served the Queen in her early married days, paid such tribute and pointed out the 'enormous difference' that her presence and example had brought about.[3] Much of the change in Victoria, from a hard young woman and a middle-aged recluse into a benevolent old lady, spreading gifts when she travelled, carrying a purse full of coins to throw to beggars, seeking smiles and finding them, can be truly attributed to the fount of love and kindness springing from her daughter-in-law.

147

To Alexandra, the dignity of life was of life universal – animals and birds, the sick and the old, handicapped children and the mentally ill, wounded soldiers and cab horses. She lived, and she fought, in an age when the dice were loaded against her. The physically deformed were the object of laughter and teasing and ended up in booths at the fairs. 'Walk up and see the fat lady . . .' Magazines carried jokes about old and underfed horses on their way to the knacker's yard. Endless fun was poked at the under-educated who had no 'h's'. Beggars were scoundrels and a coun-tryman who poached a rabbit for his family's Sunday dinner was condemned to trudge endlessly round the prison wheel. Rat pits and cock-fighting were big attractions and in the early days of the railways there was huge demand for cheap day tickets from London to Norwich to see a man hanged in public. Then there were the evils which were ignored – little boys choking to death as they swept the soot from chimneys, 'sweated labour', the accident rate in the factories and mines, and the dereliction of the deep slums, incest-ridden, seldom penetrated by the police let alone the public. Bertie went there once, and not again. He was in disguise and with a disguised escort of police. He wandered from alley to alley in a trance of horror. In an unfurnished room he was shaken 'by the sight of a gaunt, shivering woman, lying on a heap of rags with three almost naked children who were too cold, and too much starved, to make any response whatsoever.'[4] He pulled coins from his pocket but was warned by his compan-ions to put them back, for if the word of money spread they might well be torn to pieces by the unfortunates of that alley. As he drove away, a local government official mocked him: 'What do you think of that, old Buck?' Such conditions were no shock to Alexandra. 'Her' hospital, the London, was in the East End and she wandered the wards as she wished, and in the corridors of 'the London' one could see all the realities of hell and suffering that one chose to see. In 1904 she became President. 'It is "my" hospital and I wish to be President,' she said.[5] Her statue stands in the garden there.

Alexandra's feelings for the sick and unfortunate were never better illustrated than in the strange case of 'the Elephant Man'. In the early 1880s John Merrick was treated as an advanced case

of elephantiasis at the London Hospital by Dr Frederick Treves.★ A terrifying sight, he was taken up by a showman who
displayed him in a booth at fairs around Europe. When, in 1886,
he became too ill to travel about, the showman put him on a boat
bound for London, placing in his pocket a card bearing the name
of Dr Treves. He was given a little money but was too sick and
disturbed to care for himself.

'One morning railway passengers at Liverpool Street station
who entered the general waiting-room were seen to slip out
again with horrified faces. Eventually the staff were informed
that huddled in the darkest corner was a human monster of the
most horrible description, who appeared to be ill. Some women
had fainted at what they had seen and several men had become
physically sick.'[6] After being hunted around the streets of London, 'the Elephant Man' reached London Hospital. He was so
dreadful a sight that he had to be separated from other patients
and young nurses could not face up to attending him. Dr Treves
informed the Princess of Wales of the case and she went round to
see him. She was warned by the matron, but merely replied, 'I
go'.

She went to John Merrick's bedside, shook hands with him,
smiled, looked at him straight and sat down. She found him
intelligent and under her care he regained some degree of
confidence. She took the then president of the hospital, the Duke
of Cambridge, to see him and, accustomed as the Commander-
in-Chief was to grim sights during his service in the Crimean
War, he found him 'a most painful sight'.[7] Merrick's most treasured possession was a signed photograph given to him by Alexandra and he would let no one touch it. Each year until he died
she sent him a present at Christmas, with a card bearing a
personal message.[8]

Alexandra would arrive at 'the London' without warning.
She knew all the nurses and she liked to make tea in the matron's
room. One day she walked into the receiving-room and watched
a man having his arm examined. 'It is broken,' she said. It was.
When she had gone, someone said to the patient, 'Do you know

★ Then Professor of Pathology. He was appointed successively Surgeon to
  Queen Victoria, Kind Edward VII, Queen Alexandra and King George V.
  He was created a baronet in 1902.

who that was?' 'Yes,' he answered. 'I always send for her when I
am ill.' A soldier, wounded in the leg, told her that he was afraid
that in future he would always walk with a limp. 'Don't worry,'
answered Alexandra. 'I have a stiff leg and watch what I can do.'
And she swung her leg over the bedside chair. She told a story
against herself. She was on the theatre floor in the days before it
became the rule that surgeons should wear special dress for
operations. She met two distinguished doctors wearing white
smocks and bandages round their heads. Thinking that one of
them was a patient, she patted his arm and said: 'Never mind, it
will soon be over.'[9]

Alexandra will always be remembered for her successful
efforts to introduce to England the Finsen lamp for the cure of
lupus,* a disease considered at the time incurable. Dr Niels
Finsen, a Danish physician, had written a paper in 1896 'on the
employment in medicine of concentrated light rays' and with
government and private backing set up a Light Institute in
Copenhagen. While on holiday in Denmark, Alexandra visited
the Institute and was enthralled by the cures being made. On her
return she insisted that such lamps should be used at 'the London', but came up against opposition from the medical staff. She
insisted, became most obstinate and said that she would pay for it
herself. Accordingly a doctor and two nurses departed for
Copenhagen and soon a special Finsen department was formed at
'the London'. 'Nothing like perseverance,' commented Alexandra, and those words of hers were engraved on the lamp by the
hospital authorities. 'More like obstinacy,' was the comment of
the royal donor.[10] The result was sensational. As Lord Knutsford
described the introduction:

> From all parts of England, miserable beings, who had hid-
> den themselves away from the sight of their fellows to die
> by inches, crept out into the light again and . . . hurried to
> 'the London' in an endless stream. They saw the 'lamps of
> hope' and would not be denied. It was impossible to cope
> with the hundreds of applications. In a very few days we had
> a waiting-list for two years ahead . . . For twenty-six years
> the lamps treated 100 patients a day.[11]

Although the stress has been placed on 'the London', Alex-

* A spreading tuberculous or ulcerous inflammation of the skin.

andra's interest in hospitals, homes and nursing establishments covered the British Isles, as is witnessed by 'Alexandra' wings and wards to be found everywhere. In three months, as Princess of Wales, she visited Hunstanton Convalescent Home; West End Hospital for Paralytic and Epileptic Children; Hospital for Consumption and Diseases of the Chest, Ventnor; Hertford British Hospital; Norfolk and Norwich Dispensary; Hospital for Sick Children, Great Ormond Street; Alexandra Orphanage, Hornsey Rise; West End Hospital; St Saviour's Church for Deaf and Dumb; French Hospital, Leicester Square; Royal Hospital for Incurables; Royal Normal College for the Blind, Upper Norwood; National Orphan House, Ham Common; and the Hospital for Consumption, Brompton.[12] And there were other particular favourites of the Princess, such as Barts, and the Home for Incurables at Streatham, which owed its establishment to her.

Alexandra's outstanding contribution to the advancement of nursing concerned the care of the wounded and the welfare of the fighting services in general. In this she was fired by the examples of Florence Nightingale and her sister-in-law, Princess Alice, Grand Duchess of Hesse and the Rhine. When faced with official opposition to her plans, it was the principle of Miss Nightingale which she followed: 'Keep what you know to be right before you, and never cease to try and get it. Aim high and people will follow you in the end.' Although she had clashed with her sister-in-law over the question of religious beliefs at the time of her husband's serious illness in 1871, Alexandra held Alice in great respect. She had tended the wounded in three wars and the Alice Hospital in Darmstadt was a memorial to her work. When she died from diptheria in 1878, Alexandra was deeply moved.

Her chance to help the troops came during the fighting in Egypt and the Sudan in the early 1880s, fighting which culminated in the death of General Gordon at Khartoum. Alexandra had fretted and fumed at the delay in sending out a relief force and now she took action. There already existed in England an organization known as 'The National Society for Aid to the Sick and Wounded in Time of War'. Now Alexandra formed her own branch and swiftly made her own rule book. Being tied to the Red Cross, the work of her branch was restricted to the care of the wounded, promotion of the welfare of the fighting men in general being prohibited. She ignored the restriction and sent out books, games, comforts and a recreation hut.[13]

At Sandringham Alexandra took on the combined role of district nurse and head mistress. A tenant there recalled that she came to visit a sick member of his family at ten o'clock at night and returned at eleven with special food and medicines. A bed-ridden old woman of Babingley was provided with a resident nurse.[14] If there was a death among the villagers while Alexandra was away, a telegram of sympathy always arrived. When her personal maid, Louisa Jones, fell seriously ill, the Princess stayed by her bedside for two days, Louisa dying in her arms.[15]

The village school was built by the Prince and Princess in 1867. Education was wide and far beyond the standard of the day. On a visit to Norfolk the Empress Frederick was intrigued by Alexandra's 'little technical school where the children are taught to make charming things in wood and iron-work and brass and copper'[16] and, when she returned to Germany, she started a similar school there. News spread of the forward-thinking at Sandringham and a woman correspondent of *Home Words* magazine arrived to report. Her first impression was one of pleasure that she could not find a single public house on the estate – fortunately she did not venture down the hill to Dersing-ham where the Prince's chair stood in the bar of 'The Feathers'! 'Instead of public houses,' the lady wrote, 'there are technical schools for boys; cosy reading rooms and libraries; a hospital for sick servants; a model kitchen, where cooking is taught; a spinning-school, where delicate girls receive instruction in an occupation they can follow at home; a place where girls are instructed in house-work and in scientific dressmaking; and every help and convenience a working community needs for the development of its higher life.'[17] Here was the forerunner of the village Community Councils of today.

It was the little tragedies of children and animals which opened the floodgates of Alexandra's emotions, while the great sadnesses were endured dry-eyed and with fortitude. Unhesitatingly she kissed the decomposing face of the dead Emperor of Russia. She remained as unshaken as an experienced nurse at the sights that she witnessed in the London hospital. When her husband was operated upon for appendicitis in 1902 she held him while the anaesthetic was administered and then stood quietly by to watch the operation and the doctors had to ask her, firmly, to leave. Yet when her first car arrived she made the chauffeur's life a torment with her warnings about not running over dogs. On an occasion when the Gluckburgs were gathered at Bernstorff, the King of Greece, on his first bicycle and somewhat unsteady, collided with Alexandra's Pekinese. Alexandra was carrying a tea tray to her mother who was resting in the garden. As the dog yelped, she flung the tray in the air and screamed, 'He has killed my dog, he has killed my dog.' What she then said, according to her nephew, Christopher of Greece, was enough to blow up a printing press. The injury to the Peke was found to be minor and after the crisis another nephew, Nicholas, used to give an imitation of his aunt, gesticulating, shouting, swinging her stiff leg. It was his party piece for years and Alexandra, in fits of laughter, always demanded an encore.[18]

Alexandra's heart melted when she found a child in trouble. She had been out Christmas shopping and slipped back through a side door of Marlborough House. Standing in the passage was a thin girl holding a parcel. She said that she had brought round some underwear ordered for the young Princesses. Alexandra took the girl into her room, inspected the garments and admired them. Smiling, the girl said that she had done most of the work herself. Then the sad story came out. Her mother was an invalid and she had to go out to work to make enough money to live on. She had learned to use a sewing machine and, she confided, one day she hoped to own one so that she could work at home and look after her mother. Alexandra gave her tea and ordered that a basket be packed with food for the mother. The girl departed with a full stomach and quite unaware of the identity of the lady with whom she had been talking. On Christmas Day a sewing machine arrived for her, with a note reading – 'A Christmas Gift from Alexandra.'[19]

She hated to feel that she had an advantage in life over others. On her birthday, when the Fabergé eggs arrived from Russia and the necklaces from Paris, Berlin and Vienna, she would wander round, saying: 'All this for me? Quite ridiculous, quite ridiculous.' Each morning she dealt with the appeals. A man released from prison asked for help. Charlotte Knollys read out his letter.

'£5,' said Alexandra. Miss Knollys objected, pointing out the man's failings. '£10,' answered Alexandra, 'because in that case he will need it.' When officialdom clamped down on her, she would summon a footman and send him off with an envelope, the money in it.

Sydney Holland, known as The Prince of Beggars for his work in collecting funds for hospitals, told how she did it. She summoned him to Buckingham Palace and told him that she was going to scold him, apparently under the impression that he had been unfair to Barts and had been interfering with her schools at St Katherine's. 'I won't stand it,' she said. She then questioned him about the electric cure for cancer and the new out-patients' department at the London Hospital, and presented him with another Finsen Lamp. As he rose to go, she said: 'Oh, no, you are not to go yet.' From the fold in the sofa behind her, she fished out an envelope. In it was £1,000 towards new quarters for nurses. As Holland stammered his thanks, she brought out another envelope from the same hiding place. In it was another £1,000, in notes, as a gift to London Hospital. No palace watch-dog could have suspected that she had £2,000 hidden in a sofa.[20]

THIRTEEN

The Dangerous Years

Throughout her forties Alexandra underwent a series of painful experiences. In the years when members of the Royal Family were being lampooned by publications such as *Truth*, she was the only one against whom no word was spoken. She was the peerless princess. Queen Victoria, emerging from the ill odour which had surrounded her during the long association with her ghillie, John Brown, who had died in 1883, was still being criticized for long periods of seclusion at Balmoral, for German bias and meanness. The financial transactions and escapades of Prince Alfred, Duke of Edinburgh and later of Saxe–Coburg and Gotha, were castigated. But it was Albert Edward, Prince of Wales, who was the main target and under constant fire. In the streets only two figures aroused the thrill of loyalty – George, the old Duke of Cambridge, riding to the Horse Guards, and Alexandra, Princess of Wales, smiling and waving from her carriage.

The root cause of many of the royal troubles lay in the wayward Prince Eddy. It was his weakness, his leaning towards homosexuality, which upset the balance of the family life of Queen Victoria. Alexandra, backed by the natural maternal instinct to protect her young, had the courage and the patience to cope with the problem, but lacked knowledge and experience of such affairs. But her husband had neither the courage nor the patience. Queen Victoria summed up the position exactly when she wrote in 1892: 'Poor Bertie – his is not a nature made to bear sorrow, or a life without amusement and excitement – he gets bitter and irritable.'[1]

When the Prince came to realise that his eldest son was not merely lazy and backward but also sexually unstable, he opted

155

out of the problem. Homosexuality was intolerable to him and, during the years when his judgement and example should have been at their peak, he shelved the burden and lost contact with the wishes of his wife. Night after night he gambled. He chased around Europe intent on shooting the maximum of birds and animals. He made the wrong friends. He turned to the money lenders. He upset the court of Germany, who were only too pleased to have the chance to snub the British heir. He upset the Emperor of Russia. Before the 1887 Jubilee it was rumoured that the Queen would abdicate in favour of her eldest son. Henry Labouchere, in *Truth*, gave many, and potent, reasons why this could not be:

> Those trips upon which you so frequently start, to Paris,
>   to Baden, to Nice,
> A king must attend to his country's affairs, and be ready
>   for all that befalls,
> Instead of assisting at 'Battle of Flowers', or dancing
>   at Carnival Balls.[2]

It was in 1883 that Alexandra first became aware that Eddy's backwardness was abnormal. Previously she had attributed it to his childhood weaknesses and that he had grown too fast, confident that, with manhood, he would leave his handicaps behind. But, after receiving an adverse report, she wrote to his tutor, Dalton: 'It does indeed seem strange that at his age he does not yet see the great importance of exerting himself to the utmost . . .'[3] Dalton had previously reported of his charge that he 'sits listless and vacant . . . This weakness of brain, this feebleness and lack of power to grasp almost anything put before him, is manifested . . . also in his hours of recreation . . . It is a fault of nature . . .'[4] The nail had been hit squarely on the head but it was a hard blow for the parents to absorb. Bertie had attributed his own youthful trials and handicaps to the arduous programme set for him by his father. When his turn came to be a parent, he had followed an opposite path, ensuring that no strain was applied. Yet the failure of his experiment was even more obvious.

After the separation from his brother, Eddy declined further. During the summer of 1883 a selected band of tutors descended on Sandringham and attempted to prepare him for Cambridge.

One of them, J. K Stephen, reported: 'He hardly knows the meaning of the words *to read*'.[5] On 18 October the Prince of Wales took his son to Cambridge. Determined not to repeat his own experience at the university, when he had been made to live at Madingley, he installed Eddy as a member of Trinity, with rooms in college. Whether this well intended measure was wise is to be doubted.

Word had already got around of the strange characteristics of the elder son of the Prince and Princess of Wales and on 24 November 1883 there appeared in *Punch* a page of cartoons depicting his life at Trinity. The centre piece was entitled '*The Prince after brushing his hair*.' Eddy is shown standing on a balcony. Two undergraduates are regarding him. One says: 'Isn't it beautiful!' And the other adds: 'Too lovely to look at!'

Prince Eddy received the attentions of both high society and homosexuals. He had not the will power to resist the temptations of love as offered by either sex. He had his attractions, visual though they may have been, for both. Word of his wanderings reached Sandringham and an irate father descended upon Trinity. In 1885 Eddy was taken away from Cambridge and in June was gazetted a lieutenant in the 10th Hussars. He was pursued on to the military scene by scandalous verses from the pens of his college cronies. There were no goodbyes.

But the army soon gave up any hopes of building him into a budding military commander. Regimental duties bored Eddy stiff. He considered his General to be a 'lunatic' and objected to cavalry routine such as 'the Officers' ride' when, as he wrote, 'one had to go jogging round and round the riding school in a very tight and uncomfortable garment called a stable jacket.'[6] His excuse for not taking an interest in the daily life of the army was the usual one of his kind – that he just did not see the point. He was kind-hearted, democratic, soft spoken, unambitious, and a pleasant enough companion at whist and, in the main, his fellow officers liked him, but they failed utterly to galvanise him. Under instruction he was described as being 'dawdly' and it was noticed that he fidgetted with his hands and feet, an unwelcome trait at Aldershot. When the Commander-in-Chief arrived on a visit of inspection and expressed the wish to see Prince Albert Victor carry out some elementary drill movements, the Colonel of the 10th begged him not to insist, saying that the Prince would make a complete mess of it.[7]

It might at least have been expected that Eddy would make an effort to impress the C.-in-C., the Duke of Cambridge, cousin to the Queen. When the Duke celebrated the jubilee of his military service and was honoured by banquets and messages from the crowned heads of Europe, Eddy never even noticed. Lady Geraldine Somerset, lady-in-waiting to the old Duchess of Cambridge, wrote: 'Prince Eddy . . . his own near relation, known him intimately since birth, an officer under his command, neither comes to him, nor writes to him, nor takes the slightest notice!! . . . It is no want of proper feeling, but sheer stupidity!! Alas! that fatal apathy and inertness, sleepy apathetic laziness and total want of initiative.'[8] Later, sitting next to the Duke at a dinner, Eddy admitted that he knew nothing of the Crimean war and had never heard of the battle of Alma.[9]

Distressing rumours came to the Duke's ears regarding the youth's behaviour. He himself had been a rake in his youth and knew much about the dangers lurking in London for a young officer of the royal blood. Despite his high position, George of Cambridge was not an heroic type and held both the Queen and the Prince of Wales in considerable respect, in particular Victoria. After Albert's death the Queen had turned to him for advice and help and she used him as a channel for transmitting reproofs to Sandringham. The time came when the Duke realized that something drastic must be done about Eddy. On 6 January 1887, he despatched the following letter to the Prince of Wales:

> My Dear Bertie,
>
> You were kind enough to ask my opinion the other day as regards the best course to be adopted, from a general point of view, for Eddy's future plans, and I therefore now, after full consideration, think it well to point out to you that I consider it would be for his advantage to leave the 10th Hussars, having been appointed to that Regiment since June 1885, and having thus been during the greater part of two summers, or drill seasons, at Aldershot. The Head Quarters of the Regiment will soon move to Hounslow for London duties, and I do not think that this would be a desirable station at present for so young and inexperienced a man,

who would be surrounded by temptations of every description, which it requires great firmness of character to resist . . . I would suggest his being sent for a time abroad, to a Garrison Town like Gibraltar, where his whole time and attention would reasonably be expected to be devoted to military duties. . . . I should myself prefer his being attached to one of the battalions of Infantry now stationed at the Rock. . . . Sir Arthur Hardinge, the present Governor, happens to be well known to the Queen, as also to yourself and Alix, and he could receive such personal instructions from you, regarding your intentions and wishes, as you might think desirable, and you would have perfect confidence in his carrying them out most conscientiously. . . . Great interests are involved in Eddy's future career, and certain sacrifices must be made to attain the objects in view to teach him and accustom him to habits of discipline and the knowledge of the business which he can better attain in the manner proposed than in any other way that presents itself to my mind.

I remain,
My dear Bertie,
Your most affectionate Uncle,
GEORGE.[10]

The advice given in this masterpiece of tact should have been accepted by the Prince and Princess of Wales, but, to the Duke's chagrin, it was not. After events point to the conclusion that Bertie would have been glad to have Eddy well out of the way and under tight discipline and that it was Alexandra who demurred. She had already been parted from her elder son for three years as he cruised around the world on *Bacchante* and considered that the absence might have contributed to his failings. She believed, and continued to believe, that if she was near *him* she could influence *him* for the good and restrain *him*. From Marlborough House she could keep an eye on *him* at Hounslow and was convinced that her great love would conquer. So Eddy soldiered on. Meantime there came an event which overshadowed the aberrations of a young officer in the 10th Hussars.

It was the Golden Jubilee year of 1887 and on 21 July a splendid and colourful procession wound its way from Buckingham Palace to Westminster Abbey to celebrate the fiftieth year of Queen

Victoria's reign. 'Happy and glorious' was the message carried to the cheering crowds and to Britain's vast Empire across the seas. Thirty-two princes rode in that procession, outstanding among them being Frederick, Prince Imperial of Germany, wearing the wholly white uniform of the Cuirassiers, with silver breast-plate, and on his burnished steel helmet the great silver crest of an eagle with outspread wings. But Frederick had cancer of the throat and had to wear his tunic open at the neck. The burning question was – would he survive his father, William I, who was in his ninety-first year? The person most concerned was his wife, Vicky, Princess Royal of England. Apart from the personal tragedy, there were many things which this brilliant daughter of the Prince Consort wished to do as Empress. She relied for her husband's care on a British doctor, Morell Mackenzie, a choice that was far from popular in the German medical profession and at the German court. Alexandra was also deeply concerned with the survival of Frederick, for, if he became Emperor, there was hope that North Schleswig would be handed back to Denmark, and for herself and her father there was no dearer wish. If Frederick's bombastic son, William, succeeded, there was little hope of that. On 9 March 1888 William I died and Emperor Frederick III came from the sun of San Remo to the cold snow of Berlin. He was a liberal-minded man and was in conflict with the right wing extremists. As he drove to his palace he was greeted with the words, written large on wall and placard, 'Cohen I, King of the Jews'.[11] He could scarcely breathe or speak and he reigned, as a cypher, for only one hundred days. When he died, young William II, at loggerheads with his mother and suspicious of the steps, financial and otherwise, which she had taken during her short spell as Empress, surrounded her house with armed guards. One of his first announcements was that Germany would never surrender a yard of territory gained by his glorious grandfather, and Alexandra knew that her hopes concerning Schleswig were finished. She also feared trouble between William and her brother-in-law, Alexander, Emperor of Russia.

Divided as they were in their opinions regarding Eddy, the Prince and Princess of Wales were unanimous on the subject of Emperor William II. They were both disgusted by his behaviour to his mother at the time of Frederick's death. 'That young fool,'

The Princess of Wales and her daughters trout fishing at Birk Hall, near Abergeldie

The Queen's garden party at Buckingham Palace, 1896. The Prince and Princess of Wales stand in the foreground

Queen Victoria with her son and daughter-in-law on the occasion of her golden
jubilee in 1887

commented Alexandra. 'He gets more foolish and conceited every day.'[12] But while William admired and courted her favours and kept her photograph upon his desk, the position for Bertie was much more difficult. There was a natural antipathy between uncle and nephew. The Prince of Wales, worried over finance and the dissipations of Eddy, became, as his mother said, under such circumstances, 'bitter and irritable'. To him, the German Emperor retained the status of nephew, little older than Eddy and in the same category. The uncle was the senior in the trade union of royalty and he objected to imperialistic gestures from Berlin. William, imbued since boyhood with Junker propaganda, had already earned for himself the nicknames of 'Gondola Billy', 'The Only' and 'William the Great'. Suffering from a withered arm, he felt himself unfairly handicapped and, to counteract this, became the supreme egotist. Lord Salisbury was of the opinion that he was 'a little off his head' and 'not quite all there'.[13]

As he toured around Europe in 1888, the Prince of Wales, in unguarded moments, made remarks to the detriment of William, laughingly telling of events in his childhood and referring to him as 'William the Great'. Word of this reached William's ears and he was furious. In October both he and his uncle were in Austria, the Prince timing his movements so that they might meet in Vienna. He was aghast to be informed, through official channels, that the Emperor would not visit Vienna if his uncle was there. The Prince had no alternative but to give way and he disappeared on a hunting expedition. It took the best part of a year to patch up the incident, and only patched was it to be.

Alexandra's hatred of Germany increased and the royals divided up into 'the Sandringham set' and 'the German set', in competition all along the line, from politics to yachting. She saw clearly the dangers which lay ahead. This was shown beyond doubt in 1890 when she submitted a memorandum to Lord Rosebery on the dangers of Britain exchanging the North Sea island of Heligoland for the Sultanate of Zanzibar. Gladstone studied it and described it as 'a very remarkable . . . document'.[14]

Then, in October 1889, came the Cleveland Street scandal. It was revealed that men high in Society were visiting a homosexual brothel off Tottenham Court Road. The names of Lord Euston, Lord Arthur Somerset and Prince Albert Victor were being mentioned. Lord Arthur Somerset, son of the Duke of Beaufort, was Superintendent of the Stables to the Prince of Wales. At first Bertie refused to believe the charge made against his friend, whom he called 'Podge', but later expressed satisfaction to Lord Salisbury that Arthur Somerset had been allowed to flee the country. He condemned homosexuality as a 'filthy vice' and considered any man addicted to it an 'unfortunate lunatic'. It emerged that Eddy's visit to 19 Cleveland Street had been merely out of curiosity, but the rumours continued that he attended such clubs and was there referred to as 'Victoria'.[15] It was well past the time that Alexandra's beloved son was removed from the London scene. Fortunately an opportunity now presented itself – a wedding in Greece.

As a relief to her deep mourning and to escape the persecution of her eldest son, the Empress Frederick had taken her daughter Sophie to Copenhagen for a holiday. Alexandra was there, and she and her relations showed the Germans what happy family life should be. Vicky wrote to Queen Victoria:

> Dear Alix was the flower of the flock with her two sweet girls. Dear Tino (Constantine of Greece) and Georgie (Prince of Greece) were certainly the finest of the young men, and also the most intelligent. The noise they all made and the wild romps they had were simply indescribable. Once or twice I was obliged to laugh right out when they were all carrying each other. They seemed happier and to enjoy themselves more than children of five or six. Tino and Georgie are as strong as two young Hercules! I only wonder no arms or legs were broken. The Queen of Denmark's furniture must be unusually strong – one sofa had to have the springs renewed . . .[16]

Sophie fell in love with Tino, the 'Greek Hercules', and he with her, and there was no stopping them. The wedding took place at the end of October in Athens. The Prince of Wales then took Eddy to Egypt and put him on the *Oceana*, India-bound. At Bombay the Duke of Connaught was waiting to receive him and to make sure that there were no more sexual adventures. Yet, on his way home in May 1890, Eddy escaped close guardianship and tarried a while in Egypt. There the Khedive offered the Prince the type of entertainment which the East thought fit for princes. Eddy was 'thin and yellow' when he reached home. Queen Victoria noticed the deterioration and described him as 'pale and drawn'. The parents were united on one point – Eddy must marry and quickly, or all would be lost.

First the image must be refurbished. He was created Duke of Clarence and Avondale and the Queen decreed that the practice of referring to him as Eddy should cease forthwith. Soon after the return from India, Labouchere published a cruel and pointed sketch.[17] In an imaginary visit, the representative of *Truth*, using hypnotism as a basis for her talk, interviewed members of the Royal Family. All of them, the Queen included, were castigated – with the exception of Alexandra.

> No, fair Princess, *you* do not need
> The gift we call hypnotic;
> The power you sway o'er all round
> Already is despotic.
> Your every word, your every glance
> Is able to the land entrance.
> Your will we willingly make law
> Whenever you express it;
> You have magnetic influence,
> Though little you may guess it.
> None can *your* potent charm resist –
> You are our subtlest hypnotist!

Truth turned to Prince 'Eddie',

> '. . . . who sat stiffly in his chair,
> His spotless 'spats' inspecting with a mildly vacant stare,
> Asked him what he thought of India, and what throughout his stay
> Had impressed itself upon him in the most distinctive way?

> *Prince Eddie:*
> You ask me what impressed me most
> Whilst Hindustan I travelled o'er?
> My answer is, A certain man
> I came across at Shuttadore.

> *Truth:*
> Ah! 'twas methinks some Rajah great;
> Who bid you to a gorgeous feast?

163

Or p'rhaps a famous Pundit, versed
In all the learning of the East?
You shake your head. Then 'twas, perchance,
a Fakir steeped in occulat lore?

Question and answer continue until Eddy finally comes out with
the truth:

> *Prince Eddie:*
> No, no, it was not one of these
> Who won my heart at Shuttadore!
> No, 'twas a low-caste laundry-man,
> Who, spite my aide-de-camp's rebuffs,
> Contrived an order to obtain
> To 'dress' my collars and my cuffs!
> He starched them as they'd ne'er been starched
> Since I had left my native shore,
> He 'dressed' them with consummate knack,
> Endowing them with gloss galore.
> He made them stiff and spotless, too,
> Fit for a Prince to wear once more,
> And this is what impressed me most
> Whilst Hindustan I travelled o'er –
> The skill displayed by Cundra Dass,
> The laundry-man of Shuttadore!'

The Prince of Wales left for the Continent armed with a list of
suitable brides for Albert Victor, prepared by Queen Victoria.
For the past year the Queen had been trying to bring about a
match with the youngest daughter of Princess Alice, Grand
Duchess of Hesse. But the girl, already in love with the young
Cesarevitch of Russia, was having none if it. In May 1890 the
Queen wrote to the Empress Frederick, telling her that the
marriage was definitely off:

> It is a real sorrow to us . . . but . . . she says – that if she is
> *forced* she will do it – but that she would be unhappy and he
> too. This shows great strength of character as all her family
> and all of us wish it, and she refuses the greatest position
> there is.[18]

The next on the list was Margaret, sister of Emperor William
of Germany. Margaret was rather plain and very fond of horses
and, for once, Albert Victor put his foot down and said, 'No', to

the relief of his mother, who considered that one Hohenzollern in the family was quite enough.

Meantime the Prince of Wales was having troubles of his own. They were financial. For years past he had been 'in the red' to the extent of some £20,000 a year and neither the country nor his mother felt the need to help him out. When he travelled to Paris, Bad Homburg or Cannes, his hotels were picketed by money-lenders, only too anxious to oblige the heir to the British throne. The presence of these touts was a considerable worry to the government. Suddenly it became obvious that the pressure on the Prince's pocket had been relieved and his constant appearances with Baron Maurice de Hirsch pointed to the answer. Known as 'the Baron Centpercento', Hirsch was a fabulously rich Hungarian, richer, it was said, than the Rothschilds. He had made his fortune by banking, building railways and by 'cornering' sugar and copper, and his acumen had brought him many enemies. Germany was closed to him, he was excluded from the Austrian Court and Alexander III frowned his disapproval. The Prince of Wales took a liking to the Baron, valued his advice and backed him on his social climb. Soon Hirsch was to be seen at dinner parties at Marlborough House. He rented a handsome property near Sandringham and a shoot near Newmarket. But the Queen stood firm, refusing to ask him to Buckingham Palace. Her son took offence, referring to this as a 'personal slight'.

Alexandra and Bertie were drifting further and further apart and more and more often he disappeared to the continent. So she was facing alone one of the greatest trials of her life, as new disclosures about Eddy flowed in. He had been treated for gonorrhoeal infection;[19] he suffered from gout.[20] A famous actress claimed that she had a son by him.[21] Alexandra had considerable knowledge regarding venereal diseases and, as for the shock of an illegitimate child, she had had personal experience.*[22] To add to the worries a rumour spread that her younger

---

* In 1870 her sister Thyra fell in love with a Danish army officer. In 1871 she became pregnant and was hidden at Rumpenheim. Thyra was not allowed to see the baby, who was handed over to a laundry-maid. After a series of angry interviews with King Christian, the father shot himself two months later.

son, George, had been secretly married in Malta. Life there was notoriously fast and the Fleet was a magnet for young ladies in search of romance and a husband. It was they who, on their return from visits to the island, spread the story, each professing to inside knowledge. It was gossip which refused to die. But it made the marriage of Eddy all the more vital. Suddenly Alexandra saw her chance.

Eddy announced that he was in love with Hélène Louise Henriette, the nineteen-year-old daughter of the Comte de Paris. The Comte de Paris was a grandson of King Louis Philippe, head of the French Royal House and Pretender to the French throne. So Hélène was a Catholic. Alexandra saw no great handicap on the religious side. Her sister had adapted herself to the Russian creed and her youngest brother, Waldemar, had married Marie d'Orleans, a Catholic. The families were close friends, so Alexandra saw no valid reason why Eddy, the heir presumptive, should not be united with Hélène. Being a Dane, she did not fully appreciate the British Constitution.

The Comte de Paris was a staunch and strict Catholic, while his wife was more flexible. An extraordinary, masculine woman, she smoked a pipe or fat cigar and had the habit of inspecting the 'downstairs' quarters armed with a riding crop. With this she would tap across the back domestics whom she considered were slouching, bidding them to stand up straight.

In his own limited fashion, Eddy was in love with Hélène. But his feelings were no doubt warmed by the fact that she was in love with him, and this was a completely new experience, and one he treasured. There was little real emotion in his make up – propelled only by the sexual urge he had no resistance, and fell victim to those members of either sex who encouraged him. For expediency's sake he could put on a good act and give an impression of being in love. But his only real interests lay in his hair, his clothes, his collars and his cuffs.

Queen Victoria had already issued a warning to him not to become involved with Hélène, but Alexandra thought that she could get round her mother-in-law. So she hatched a plan with her daughter Louise. In August 1890, while the Prince of Wales was safely out of the way at Bad Homburg, Alexandra travelled north with Eddy to stay with the Fifes at Mar Lodge, Braemar.

Among the guests staying there was Hélène. Eddy proposed to her and was accepted. The next step was to obtain the blessing of the Queen. Here Alexandra moved most cannily.

The Queen had just arrived at Balmoral from Osborne. She was always glad to be back on Deeside and at such times was at her most amenable. Alexandra decided to take advantage of this happy state.

Early one morning in late August a carriage drove up to the front door. Into it Alexandra bustled Eddy and Hélène, tucking a rug around them, handing them a picnic lunch, laughing and waving as they moved away. Through quiet Braemar, past the Fife Arms, and along the Crathie road the sun shone down, catching the diamonds of the sparkling Dee. The trees were showing the first rich tints of autumn. The trotting hooves and the tumbling river made sweet music. It was a morning born for lovers.

The Queen was beginning her day's work on state papers in the hut on the castle lawn, her highland servant behind her, when the carriage drew up. She was an incurable romantic and adored surprises. Eddy standing before her, professing his love, brought back to her a picture of Albert coming towards her up the stairs at Windsor on an October evening in 1839, a star of operetta come to claim her hand. Tears filled her eyes and she gave her blessing. Alexandra was thrilled but, unfortunately for her, the Queen's blessing was not enough.

The Comte de Paris would not have it. The Pope would not have it. British statesmen would not have it. Even the Prince of Wales, who was unrivalled at putting a case for a lost cause – he once convinced a bishop that he hated gambling – could make no headway. The result on Albert Victor was typical. Struggles and arguments were not for him and his ardour switched. He developed a passion for Lady Sybil St Clair Erskine. Contrary to his instructions, she kept his letters but gave her heart elsewhere.

Then once again, the attention of Society was drawn away from the marriage plans and vagaries of the heir presumptive. A romantic liaison shifted its attention towards his father, the Prince of Wales who, balding and nearing fifty, now fell madly in love with Lady Frances Brooke.

FOURTEEN

Scandal, Tragedy and a Wedding

Frances Evelyn Maynard was born on 10 December 1861. Her father, the Hon. Charles Henry, was heir to Viscount Maynard. Her mother was the daughter of Henry Fitzroy, doubly descended from King Charles II through the Dukes of Grafton and of St Albans. Charles Henry died in 1865, four months before his father, and the title became extinct. Lord Maynard left most of his estate to his granddaughter Frances, including Easton Lodge, his stately home in Essex, with its 14,000 acres and £21,000 in rents.[1] By the age of four Frances was extremely rich.

In 1866 her mother married the fourth Earl of Rosslyn and had five children by him, the eldest son being Lord Loughborough and the eldest girl, on marriage, Millicent, Duchess of Sutherland. Frances, known as Daisy, was closely woven into the peerage. As Lord Rosslyn's family home was in remote Fifeshire, Frances, her sister, and her step-brothers and step-sisters, were brought up at Easton Lodge. 'Miss Daisy' was a very important person about her estate. Her interests were centered on horses.

By the time that Daisy was at schoolroom age, Queen Victoria was faced with the problem of finding partners for her children and growing grandchildren. Since the Franco-German War, German Princes and Princesses were regarded with disfavour by the British public, and elsewhere royal suitors were thin upon the ground. So the Queen looked around for candidates among the great houses of Britain.

While the leading families held the Monarchy in respect, they

168

were not impressed by the royals. Prince Albert, for instance, had been most unpopular with the aristocracy. His cold hand-shake, his love of money and his obvious desire to reform the way of life of the landed gentry had made him many enemies, while many did not accept the Prince of Wales as one of them-selves. In addition, there was the handicap of having the Queen as a mother-in-law and enduring the servitude which she demanded. A young man invited to Balmoral fled the Castle at first light when a friendly equerry tipped him off that he was a prospective bridegroom. Another feigned madness, having a grave dug in his park and spending the afternoons staring into it.

Of course Queen Victoria did not appreciate this. She consi-dered her advances to be the ultimate in honours. Neither, apparently, did Benjamin Disraeli: when Frances Maynard was seventeen he suggested her as a bride for Prince Leopold. The Queen listened to her beloved adviser, pondered on the matter and decided that it was a good idea. But her plan for uniting haemophilic, intelligent, artistic Leopold with Daisy was unsound. The girl was autocratic, petulant, very full of her own importance and, at seventeen, obviously developing into a crea-ture of sexual dynamism. Fortunately, Leopold had already selected Princess Helen of Waldeck-Pyrmont, while Daisy's attention had been caught by the roving eye of Lord Brooke, heir to the Earl of Warwick. The Prince dutifully proposed to Daisy Maynard. To his relief, he was refused. A few hours later Lord Brooke tried his luck and was accepted. The Queen was peeved but outwardly friendly relations continued. Prince Leopold was best man at the wedding and the marriage register was signed by Albert Edward, Prince of Wales.

For five years peace reigned at Easton Lodge and Daisy bore three children. Lavish house parties were given which Bertie and Alexandra often attended. Daisy would inform her guests, with the suspicion of a wink, that the stable clock always rang at six o'clock in the morning.

Alexandra and Daisy were opposites. Alexandra was a happy and contented person; Daisy was neither of these things, and admitted so herself.[2] Alexandra had been carefully brought up, taught to look after herself and be careful with money; Daisy had been born an heiress and spoilt. Alexandra could walk into a cottage and be accepted as one of the family; Daisy was 'the squire' and of a class apart, for the British would not have it any other way. Alexandra was shy and hid her light; Daisy was only happy when she was the centre of attention. Alexandra's face was soft; Daisy's eyebrows were arched, her ears set low, her nose short and sharp and her mouth and chin were firm and hard, her dynamism, her carriage and her strength attracting her to men. Furthermore, she was imperious, unscrupulous and a sensationalist, her better qualities well hidden.

After those five years of 'nesting', Daisy became bored. Her husband spent much time shooting in Ireland and she took a lover. She chose a man as ruthless as herself, Lord Charles Beresford, a distinguished and brave sailor who was brother of the manager of the stud at Sandringham. Lady Charles objected and retrieved her husband, temporarily at least. Daisy sent a bitter and incriminating letter to Charles, which Lady Charles got hold of and would not part with. Daisy, spitting with fury, played for the Prince of Wales. He, nearing fifty and grandfather, crumpled, did as he was asked and looked towards a bed at Easton Lodge for his reward. By so doing he not only risked a punch in the nose, he put his own marriage at stake.

Charles Beresford had been on a friendly terms with the Prince of Wales for twenty years and accompanied him on the tour of India in 1875, and the friendship was shared by Alexandra, who had her own pet name for the Irish sailor. It was the Prince's influence which got Beresford the appointment of Fourth Lord of the Admiralty. Here Beresford's direct and impetuous approach to naval matters, and his demands on the treasury, met with opposition. So Bertie counselled his retirement from politics and his return to the bridge of a man-of-war. A secondary reason for the advice was that Lord Charles was having an affair with Daisy Brooke. He was a menace with the ladies. (Once, in high spirits at a house party, he opened a wrong door and leaped into the bed, which he supposed housed a willing partner, only to land between the Bishop of Chester and his wife.) After some delay Lord Charles retired from the political scene and returned to the sea and the arms of his wife, ten years his senior and already adorned with pieces of hair which were not her own. Lady Charles became pregnant. The news infuriated Daisy Brooke. She dashed off an indignant and impassioned letter, accusing her ex-lover of infidelity and inferring that he had no right to have a child by his own wife. In her husband's absence, Lady Beresford opened the letter and was also furious. Determined to put a stop to Lady Brooke's approaches, she placed the letter in the hands of George Lewis, the leading Society lawyer in London. She told Lord Salisbury what she had done.

Learning of this, Lady Brooke realized the appalling situation in which, by her temper, she had placed herself. She saw that her only salvation lay with the Prince of Wales. She arranged for an appointment with him at Marlborough House and there the deed was done. She played her part and, glancing up from her dramatic recital, she saw him looking at her 'in a way which all women understand'.[3] It was as if he were suddenly put under a spell, a spell such as that which was to enwrap his grandson, also Prince of Wales, forty years later. For her part, Daisy was not in love with Bertie. She came to like him, enjoy his company and admire his better qualities, but the men she liked were of a very different calibre, men like Charles Beresford and Joe Laycock. Above all she was concerned with saving her reputation and disengaging herself from a scandal which Society would neither forgive nor tolerate.

Bertie danced for her. He visited George Lewis after midnight and demanded to see the letter. He was allowed to read it, was thoroughly shocked and asked that it be handed back to the sender. This George Lewis refused to do. So the Prince went to see Lady Beresford and asked for the return of the letter. She too refused. He visited her a second time, now using a softer approach but intimating that he would not be meeting her on the social scene if she did not acquiesce. Not to be asked to Marlborough House was the equivalent of social ostracism, for, if the Prince of Wales was avoiding a certain lady, so would the big hostesses, only too anxious to encourage royal patronage.

Lady Beresford saw the danger and told her husband. It was early in January 1890 and he was about to rejoin the cruiser *Undaunted* in the Mediterranean. He stormed round to Marlborough House unannounced and there found the Prince and Daisy Brooke enjoying a *tête-à-tête*. The sight further enraged the

171

Irishman. He pushed HRH down on to a sofa, called him a coward and blackguard, raised his fist and stormed out uttering threats of revenge.[4] Bertie, apparently so deeply in love that he was blind to the danger, ignored the threats and proceeded to cold shoulder Lady Beresford. When shown lists of house guests for a weekend house party which he was to attend, and her name appeared, he would cross it out and substitute that of Lady Brooke, informing the hostess that he thought it best not to meet 'the angry woman'[5] until she had cooled off.

Up to this time Alexandra had remained outside the fracas. Her mind was fully occupied with marriage plans for Eddy and she had been visiting her family in Denmark. Now the Prince involved her by persuading her to invite Daisy to Marlborough House. To Lady Beresford, this was the last straw and she despatched a series of bitter letters to her husband in the cruiser *Undaunted*.

While Alexandra was at Mar Lodge in August 1890, engineering Eddy's engagement to Hélène, Bertie travelled north to Yorkshire for Doncaster races. Thereafter he was to rejoin his wife at Abergeldie Castle on Deeside. The St Leger was an annual event for Bertie and in past years it had been his custom to stay with Christopher Sykes at Brantingham Thorpe. But Christopher, like other men who entertained the Prince, found the financial strain excessive and he was now near to bankruptcy. The Prince, therefore, accepted an alternative invitation, that of Arthur Wilson, a wealthy shipowner, who lived at Tranby Croft. The change in plan did not suit the Prince and, to further his annoyance, Lord and Lady Brooke, who were to have been members of the race party, could not attend owing to the death of a relative. To take his mind off the absence of Daisy, and also from what he was going to say in a few days time to his mother about the engagement of Eddy to a Catholic, Bertie sought relief in baccarat. The Wilsons were not habitual baccarat players and a makeshift table was put up.

Among the players was Sir William Gordon-Cumming, Lieutenant-Colonel of the Scots Guards, known to the Prince as Bill. He was no friend of Alexandra's, who referred to him as 'a vile snob'.[6] Young Arthur Wilson, the son of the house, happened to be one of Sir William's subalterns. Times were changing fast. Thirty years earlier, if a subaltern had seen his colonel cheat, he would have kept his mouth shut, for the good of his hide and his future. But young Wilson saw Sir William manipulate his stake and passed the word around his family. Next evening Sir William was watched and seen to cheat. He was forced to sign a paper saying that he would never play cards again. The Prince signed as a witness and held the paper. Sir William left the house next morning.

The following day the Prince met Lord and Lady Brooke at York station and travelled north with them to Abergeldie. Somehow Daisy found out about the goings on at Tranby Croft. She was known as 'the babbling Brooke' and very soon the cat was out of the bag. Sir William learned that the secret of Tranby Croft was open knowledge and, furious, threatened legal action in the civil court. The Prince of Wales did his very best to deter his action, but was baulked. Worried and unwell, he passed into his fiftieth year.

Now that the marriage of Prince Albert Victor and Hélène appeared highly unlikely, the Prince of Wales lost patience with his son, deciding that he would never make any progress in the army and was merely wasting his time. He began to snap at, and make fun of him, telling the children of the royal family: 'Don't call him Uncle Eddy, call him "Uncle Eddy-Collars-and-Cuffs".'[7] Bertie wanted the young man out of the way and his solution was to send him off on a world tour, the sea journeys to be as long as possible. Alexandra's idea was very different. She wanted to keep him in close contact with her. He stayed with her in Scotland until the late autumn and was at Sandringham for the New Year.

Among the guests at the twenty-seventh birthday party on 8 January were the Duke and Duchess of Teck and their daughter, Princess Victoria Mary, known as 'May'. This raised some comment as the Prince of Wales was not enamoured of either the Duke or the Duchess. The Duke was poor, and a stroke suffered in 1884 had affected his reason. The Duchess, sister of the Duke of Cambridge, was known as 'Fat Mary'. She was hearty, good fun at a fête, and permanently short of money. Their daughter was well read and intelligent, but shy and poor at conversation, and suffered from an inferiority complex as a result of her par-

ents' financial straits. The Wales girls labelled her a bore and
condoned with men placed beside her at dinner. She was well
built and had the unseen advantage of a fine pair of legs.

The suspicion that something was being hatched in Norfolk
was increased by a paragraph appearing in the Press on 24
January:

> The chief social event in which Royalty has been interested
> has been Lord and Lady Warwick's house-party to meet the
> Duke and Duchess of Teck and their children, including
> Princess May.[8]

As Lord and Lady Warwick were the in-laws of Daisy Brooke,
the influence of the Prince of Wales was obvious.

Beyond the problems of finding a wife for his heir, Society
was also intrigued with the Prince's other problems – the boycott
of Lady Beresford; the relationship between Alexandra and Lady
Brooke; and the legal action being brought by Sir William
Gordon-Cumming. It was worry over the last of these which
caused Bertie to cancel his planned visit to Cannes. As he
confided in Prince George, he dared not go away.

Then, on 21 February, there appeared in the circumspect
Illustrated London News an article by Frederick Greenwood entitled, THE OFFENCES OF 'SOCIETY'. It began:

> If great scandals never failed to 'clear the air', a certain
> unfortunate lady might console herself with the thought
> that the imprudence which destroys her peace will do a
> world of good to Society. Great scandals are generally
> supposed to have that result; but, in truth, they yield a very
> mixed crop of consequences, and it is often seen that the bad
> ones exceed the good . . .

The 'unfortunate lady' was none other than Alexandra. The
writer went on to slate the 'Society craze', attributing this largely
to 'the enormously increasing number of wealthy idlers contributed by Trade', ever anxious to touch the skirts of established
Society. This was a hit at certain friends of the Prince. The article
went on to point out that suburbia followed the example of high
social circles and that the result would be that the number of
games of baccarat played in middle class homes would increase
dramatically as a result of 'recent revelations'. Near the end came

174

the telling sentence:

> But the general effect of the hubbub on those against whom
> it is addressed is sure to be good. The rapidity with which it
> has run through all classes of the community . . . shows
> how careful 'Society' should be in choosing its amusements
> nowadays. Baccarat is an illegal game. . . .

It might appear that the editor was putting his circulation at
risk by so castigating the *nouveau riche*, as his magazine was to be
found on all their hall tables. Yet, in his campaign, he had strong
backing. There had already arrived at Lambeth Palace a deputation of titled or influential ladies. They addressed Archbishop
Benson of Canterbury. In the words of his son, E. F. Benson;

> With the best and highest motives they had come to ask my
> father if he could do nothing to stop the moral rot which,
> they affirmed, was ruining London. Girls newly 'come
> out', they said, of high tone and upright intentions, were
> speedily corrupted by it, and what they had been brought
> up to regard as evil they soon regarded as natural and
> inevitable; young married women had no standard of mor-
> ality at all, and the centre of the mischief was the Marl-
> borough House set. They wanted my father to start a sort of
> moral mission for women of their class and to hold devo-
> tional meetings for them at Lambeth, thus creating a power-
> ful and influential nucleus of those who aimed at high ideals
> and would not tolerate the looseness of life which was
> becoming general.[9]

To give impetus to their meetings, they suggested that the
Princess of Wales should be invited to attend. The Archbishop
agreed to hold the devotional meetings, but opted out of inviting
the Princess. So the ladies invited her themselves.

Alexandra proved the model of diplomacy and referred the
matter to the Queen. The Queen said, 'No', and for a number of
reasons. The obvious one was that the ladies were clearly criticiz-
ing the heir to the throne. Another was that the ladies were
placing upon the shoulders of another the responsibility for the
morals of the country. Alexandra, the poor little princess from
Denmark, had been elevated to number one. That did not suit
Victoria at all. She played canny. She said: 'I can't understand
why princesses should want to go to Lambeth meetings. It's all

sacerdotal. I can't think what it's all about.'[10] If she did not know, she was soon to learn.

The baccarat case opened on 1 June and the press and their artists made the most of it:

> The sensation of the week has been the action brought by Sir William Gordon-Cumming against five defendants – Mrs Arthur Wilson, Mr A. S. Wilson, Mr and Mrs Lycett Green, and Mr Berkeley Levett – who accused him of cheating at baccarat, at the house of Mr Wilson at Tranby Croft, in September of last year. The trial took place before the Lord Chief Justice, and a chief feature of it has been the attendance of the Prince of Wales on the bench and his evidence on the second day. The court has throughout worn the air of a theatre rather than of a court of justice, the bench and both the galleries being filled with ladies, who used their opera-glasses with freedom to discover the notabilities in court . . .[11]

> 'This court is not a theatre!' said the Lord Chief Justice . . . as a burst of applause emphasised the close of Sir Edward Clarke's brilliant speech for the plaintiff. If it is not, it has certainly looked very like one – a court at which, as at the Haymarket, there is no pit, and the floor has been exclusively reserved for the stalls and boxes. All through the trial the bench has bloomed out into a very parterre of tints in the newest hats and bonnets; the galleries, especially when the sunlight caught them, have been dazzling . . .

> The summing up was, with all its fine balance, steadily in favour of the defendants. The plaintiff's last hopes must have waned as he gazed, with steel-grey eyes and level glance that never wavered, on the kind, firm, spectacled face turned now on his desk, now on the jury-box. One's eyes were involuntarily attracted to that figure, pathetic in its isolation and hopelessness. There was a solemn pause as the jury's names were read over after their brief absence from the court. 'Verdict for the defendants,' almost whispered the foreman. Even then the bronze face and statuesque form did not flinch. For a moment he sat as if a little dazed, but square and upright and handsome as before. Then he slowly left the court, and passed to his doom, a Spartan to the end. The verdict was intensely unpopular. The jury were loudly hissed, and the defendants so seriously mobbed that they had to take refuge in a neighbouring court.[12]

176

As Sir William departed to begin his life sentence of ostracism by Society, the clamour broke over the head of the Prince of Wales. It was as if it was he who had been on trial, although in reality he had been the loser at the baccarat game and had not noticed the cheating. *The Times* expressed the wish that he, as well as Sir William, had signed a paper saying that he would never play cards again. The *Review of Reviews* added up how many times in fifty years prayers blessing the Prince of Wales had been said in British churches and wondered if the effort had been worth the while. Religious publications took the opportunity to damn gambling in all its forms. A German paper published a cartoon showing the main door of Windsor Castle, over it the Prince of Wales' feathers and the motto, 'Ich Deal'. To the intense annoyance of Alexandra, who had stood staunchly behind her husband throughout, Emperor William protested against a man who held the rank of colonel in a Prussian regiment being involved in a gambling scandal. Queen Victoria was shaken and frightened and wrote to the Empress Frederick; '. . . the Monarchy almost is in danger if he is lowered and despised.'[13]

Sir William Gordon-Cumming was not the only man to cause worry to Bertie and Alexandra. Two others now added to their burden – Lord Charles Beresford and His Imperial Highness the Emperor of Germany.

On 3 June, while the baccarat case was in progress, the first state ball of the season was held at Buckingham Palace. The Prince and Princess of Wales attended, Alexandra startling the fashion world by being dressed entirely in black.[14] The social columns listed the ladies invited, and described their costumes – Lady Londonderry, Lady Brooke, Lady Dudley, Lady Caledon, etc. One name was missing, Lady Beresford's. The inclusion of Daisy Brooke, and the exclusion of herself, was the last straw for the unfortunate and persecuted Lady Charles. She put her London house up for sale, informing her friends that she had suffered enough humiliation. And she despatched a bitter and angry letter to her husband. Fortunately for the Prince of Wales that letter took a considerable time to reach *Undaunted*, cruising in the Mediterranean.

177

Meantime Prince Albert Victor had been officially informed that his proposed marriage with Hélène of Orleans was finally off. The courtier who conveyed the news had expected the Prince to show some sign of a broken heart, or at least disappointment, but no, the news was received with the usual vacuous grin. On 16 June the Wales were guests at a garden party given by the Duke and Duchess of Teck.

Emperor William's visit early in July had been of his own suggesting and was not welcomed by certain of his relations and by certain statesmen. It was his third trip to Britain since his accession and his grandmother now decided that it should be a state visit. He stayed for four days at Windsor and five days at Buckingham Palace with his wife and children. There was a packed programme, including a water party at Virginia Water, a night at the opera, a military review, a procession to the city and a garden party at Marlborough House. Despite the strain through which he had passed, Bertie managed to remain genial and avuncular. Alexandra played hostess to perfection, and assisted the Queen, but behind her fan she was poking fun at William's pomposity and joking about the number of valets and hairdressers in his train.

A point of contrast emerged from the glittering scene, the contrast between the two grandsons of Queen Victoria, William and Albert Victor. William, although only five years older, was married and with children. He looked and behaved like an emperor. Bombastic and pompous he may have been, but he was a power and a man. Poor Eddy appeared weak and innocuous beside him.

The visit passed off without incident, at its close William sailing from Leith for a Channel cruise on the Imperial yacht while his wife and children enjoyed a seaside holiday at Felixstowe in Suffolk. The damage done to the Prince of Wales did not emerge until a few months later. The staff of *Truth* spent those months working on their notorious Christmas issue. It covered the Kaiser's visit and gave the Kaiser's imagined views of the Tranby Croft baccarat scandal and the society kept by the Prince of Wales. It was one of the most damaging publications of the nineteenth century, met with an unprecedented demand and was particularly sought after in army messes. Soon copies were changing hands at £5 a time.

Another damning pamphlet was also in embryo. In reply to his wife's plea for help, Lord Charles Beresford sent her a virulent letter addressed to the Prince of Wales, instructing her to hand it to the Prime Minister, Lord Salisbury, for onward transmission. In it Lord Charles called the Prince 'a blackguard and a coward' and threatened that, unless he received a public apology, he would resort to publicity. Lady Beresford revealed what that publicity entailed. Her sister, Mrs Gerald Paget, had written a pamphlet entitled *The River*[15] which told the full story of the Prince's love affair with Daisy Brooke. Although the Prime Minister managed to persuade Lord Charles not to send his first, fiery letter to the Prince, substituting for it one which might lead to a settlement of the affair, the circulation of *The River* in society drawing-rooms exacerbated matters.

Alexandra was so deeply upset by this new development, and so worried about the future of Eddy, that she was no longer able to discuss problems with her husband. To the relief of both, they went their separate ways, Alexandra to Denmark, Bertie to Germany. He left on 14 August, she a week later. It was during this week that Sir Francis Knollys conferred with her. He put forward three alternative plans for the future of Prince Albert Victor. In brief, they were that he should be despatched on a protracted colonial tour; that a shorter colonial tour should be combined with visits to the capitals and courts of Europe; and that he should stay with his regiment and marry Princess May of Teck in the following spring.[16] The first was the selection of the Prince of Wales, who, swamped with worries of his own, simply wanted Eddy out of the way for as long as possible. The Queen was in favour of the second plan, putting forward the view that as yet Eddy knew next to nothing about the continent and its politics, a lack which would prove a grave handicap to him when he became King. Her eyes were not shut to the aberrations of her grandson – in fact she knew a great deal about them, and both Sir Francis Knollys and Sir Henry Ponsonby, her private secretary, were puzzled as to where she got the information – but she did not know of, nor could she have comprehended the shadier incidents in his life. Here the hands of the Prince of Wales were tied and he found it hard to answer his mother's point that there

179

were girls in the colonies who were just as 'fast' as they were in Europe. But the final decision rested with Alexandra and it was her wish that Eddy should stay with his regiment in Ireland for the winter and marry Princess May in the spring. Before leaving for Copenhagen she took the precaution of instructing Prince George to visit his brother in Dublin and to keep an eye on him.

When it was announced in the Press on 22 August that the Princess of Wales would not be returning to England until 30 October, there was a great deal of gossip and speculation as to whether she would ever return. Two and a half months was a long time to be away from her husband and for a part of that time both were to be on the Continent. More and more people learned of the contents of the pamphlet, *The River*, and sympathy for the Princess grew. The fear that she would not return, and that her marriage was at stake, increased with the news, at the end of September, that she had altered her plans and was leaving Denmark to stay with the Duke and Duchess of Cumberland at Gmunden.[17]

During October the Emperor and Empress of Russia paid a visit to Denmark, joining Alexandra and her parents at Fredensborg. 9 November was the Silver Jubilee of the marriage of Alexander and Dagmar and it was planned to celebrate the occasion with festivities at Livadia in the Crimea. 9 November was also Bertie's fiftieth birthday. His wife gave preference to her sister's jubilee. So now, on this most important occasion, his wife was not to be present! It was a bitter disappointment for him. And her absence had impact beyond the boundaries of Sandringham. The Corporation of London wished to celebrate the birthday in some public way, but this the Prince rejected, telling the Lord Mayor that, much as he appreciated the suggestion, he preferred to spend the day quietly with his family. Yet with his wife and two unmarried daughters away, the family gathering would obviously be limited. But the sons were available. On 22 October Prince George travelled to Dublin to visit his brother and to return with him to Sandringham for the 9th.

Thereafter drama piled upon drama. To prepare Sandringham for the arrival of the guests, the servants lit fires in the bedrooms. The brickwork in one chimney was faulty, and timber caught fire. The outbreak was discovered early on the morning of Sunday the 1st. The staff hurried from their beds to man the Sandringham fire engine and the Lynn brigade raced to the scene. On the third floor were the bedrooms of the ladies of the royal household. Built in the open-timbered style, the spaces between floor and ceiling had been filled with sawdust to deaden the sound of footsteps. These rooms blazed like a haystack, the roof fell in, and it was noon before the fire was under control.

All the contents of the rooms on the second and third floors were destroyed, and the damage was put at £15,000. The rooms on the first floor, the Queen's Room, the bedrooms of the Prince and Princess, the Bamboo Room, the Prince's Cabinet and the White Library, escaped. But for the fact that the Prince, when he rebuilt in 1870, had constructed the second floor on iron girders and concrete, there would have been no Sandringham left.

As luck would have it, the Prince of Wales was spending the week-end with Daisy Brooke, a point which would have escaped public attention but for the press reports on the fire. He hurried to Norfolk, recruited an army of a hundred carpenters and decorators and insisted that 'the Big House' be habitable by the 9th. It was. But it was several days before Alexandra learned of the disaster to her beloved home. On 31 October she arrived at Danzig on the imperial yacht *Polar Star* in company with her parents and the Emperor and Empress of Russia. They then set off in a special train on the long haul to Southern Russia.

During the emaciated birthday party at Sandringham, Prince George complained of a headache. Three days later he had a raging temperature and his father hurried with him to Marlborough House. There typhoid was diagnosed. Telegrams flashed out to Livadia. On the 17th Alexandra and her daughters began their journey home. For five days and five nights they travelled, bulletins compiled by the Prince himself awaiting them at all the major stations. He and Eddy met her at Charing Cross and she stepped out on to the platform looking as trim as a dress taken from a bandbox. She arrived in time to cope with the crisis in George's illness, but for another four weeks he was kept in bed.

Once Alexandra was assured that George was on the mend, she set about the arranging of Eddy's marriage. On her instruction, the Prince of Wales left Marlborough House to visit M. de Falbe (formerly Danish Minister) and his wife at their home, Luton Hoo, in Bedfordshire.[18] On 2 December the de Falbes gave a house party. Among the guests were Princess May of Teck, Prince Albert Victor and, as supervisor of operations, Colonel Oliver Montagu,[19] Alexandra's mentor and loved friend. Next day Eddy took May into a scented boudoir, proposed and was accepted. That night May danced round her bedroom, singing, 'Fancy it being poor little me . . .'

It took a strong reason to bring Queen Victoria to London, but now she made the journey twice in one week. The first occasion was 'for the express purpose of congratulating the Princess of Wales upon the anniversary of her birthday',[20] and a huge crowd gathered outside Marlborough House. But it was more than birthday wishes that she brought with her. There was also deep gratitude and relief that Alexandra had returned to be beside her husband and once again take her place in the royal team. It was an accolade. The second trip was to give her congratulations on Eddy's engagement. 'Marlborough House', she said, 'was all brightness and joy'.[21] And so it was – for a time.

But now the Prince of Wales, exasperated by the continued circulation of the pamphlet *The River*, took urgent steps to put an end to it. Lady Beresford telegraphed her husband, urging him to return and protect her. He arrived on 17 December and demanded an immediate apology from the Prince for his behaviour, in lieu of which he would put his case before the public. For the following week Lord Salisbury was in constant touch with the Queen, during this time the Prime Minister receiving the following memo from Sir Francis Knollys:

> I think Lord Salisbury should know that the Princess of Wales is still more angry with Beresford than even is the case with the Prince; and especially with his letter, which she describes as most disrespectful and improper.
>
> She warmly supports the Prince in everything connected with the unfortunate affair, and is anxious to do all in her power to assist him.[22]

Alexandra was in particular angry at the timing of the ultimatum. With her younger son recovering from typhoid and her elder son just engaged, that timing could not have been more harmful. The Beresfords saw the danger. To fight the Prince alone was one thing, to tackle him with the best loved lady in the land and the injured wife acting second and shouting encouragement from his corner was quite another. Still the Irish sailor held on and was on the point of summoning the press to his house when agreement was reached. Lady Brooke was to be excluded from the court for a time and a letter of apology from the Prince was accepted. But the blows of Beresford had done their damage. As settlement was not reached until 24 December, the Prince was unable to spend Christmas at Sandringham, and that increased the rancour and resentment which was to remain with him for many a year.

The arrangements for the wedding of Eddy and May were quickly announced – they had, in fact, been fixed before the proposal. The ceremony was to take place in St George's Chapel, Windsor, on 27 February 1892 and apartments were being prepared for the couple at St James's Palace. The invitations went out. The widowed Empress Frederick was invited but not her son, the Emperor, which enraged that young man. It was a pointer to Alexandra's increasing antagonism towards Germany and its ruler.

1892 opened threateningly. London was draped in freezing yellow fog and the ice was thick on the lake at Sandringham. An epidemic of influenza was sweeping the country. Prince Victor of Hohenlohe, the Queen's nephew, died and mourning put an end to royal festivities. Eddy attended the funeral and, as he stood shivering by the graveside in the freezing wind, he developed a cold. The Tecks arrived in Norfolk *en famille* on 4 January. On arrival they found that Princess Victoria and two members of the Household were down with influenza. Princess May, herself suffering from a heavy cold, was already having second thoughts about her future. Since her engagement the Prince of Wales had been continually urging her 'to keep Eddy up to the mark' and to make sure that he did this and that.[23] She began to wonder if her role was to be that of wife or nurse. She expressed her doubts to her mother. The Duchess snapped back: 'Of course you can do it, May.' She was thinking of the long years of her own struggle with her eccentric husband, and dreaming of being one day the mother of the Queen, free at last from debts to obliging gentlemen such as Mr Debenham.

On the 7th Eddy went out shooting but had to return and retire to bed. The next day, his birthday, he managed to totter down to see his presents but could not face his birthday dinner. Pneumonia developed. Only Alexandra and May were allowed to sit by his bedside. A screen was erected in his tiny bedroom and over this the others in the house party peeped, as if at a side-show. Eddy's eyes remained fixed on his mother and he did everything that she asked him to do. In the early hours of the 14th word was passed that he was dying and for six hours some fifteen persons crowded around his bed. He died at 9.35, raving, his mother holding his hand. So much was she a part of this son who had been born three months prematurely, that she said afterwards that she also felt that she was dying. Those who watched her marvelled at her courage, but inwardly she was near to breaking point; at urgent call, Oliver Montagu hurried to her side. Time and time again, her hand in his, she returned to the tiny room to see the dead body, now surrounded by flowers. It was a *chapelle ardente*, where artist William Simpson sketched the scene. That room was left just as it had been when Eddy was alive through many years to come, the water in the jug changed, the soap renewed when it mouldered. It was Albert and Victoria all over again.

Alexandra said her real farewell to her son in Sandringham church. She had wanted him buried there, beside her Alexander John. But custom decreed that he must lie at Windsor and his father agreed. As the coffin left St Mary Magdalene Alexandra realized that the story of herself and Eddy was over. She looked towards the pew where he had sat beside her since he could toddle. Soon there was to be a plate there, recording that 'this place was occupied for twenty-eight years by my darling Eddy, next to his ever sorrowing and loving Mother dear, January 14th, 1892'.

Fortunately the Queen was persuaded, on the ground of the risk of her catching influenza, not to attend the funeral. She therefore placed the Castle at the disposal of the Wales and their household. Alexandra knew little of Windsor. When her presence was required there for state occasions she travelled down for the day from London and did not venture beyond the state

184

apartments. The Sandringham household knew nothing at all of the geography or the customs. An equerry to the Prince of Wales, Sir Arthur Ellis, wrote of their stay there: 'In every – even the saddest occurrences of life there arises a comic side – a gleam of absurdity – which helps one to bear the gloom . . .'[24] And the staff from Norfolk certainly found both comedy and absurdity. They were continually losing their way in the long, dimly lit corridors. Servants sent to fetch an official became lost, and the same fate overtook others sent in search of them. There were accidental intrusions into bedrooms. There were wry smiles when it was discovered that lumps of sugar per cup of tea were strictly rationed – and that lavatories were supplied only with squares of newspaper.

Alexandra had expressed the wish that women should not attend the funeral service in St George's Chapel, she herself hiding away in the Queen's Closet away from the eyes of the congregation. But her husband's female relations were not to be robbed of witnessing such an historic event and they arrived in force. At the end of the service they discovered that they could not open the door of their pew and Princess Beatrice came to the conclusion that they had been purposely locked in. She complained to Sir Henry Ponsonby, who passed on the complaint. Sir Arthur Ellis fired back:

> The Prince of Wales desires me to say that – the harem of Princesses was *not* locked into the . . . pew closet but the door got jambed, and adds that they were none of them wanted at all. No ladies were to attend, and the Princess of Wales especially requested privacy – and to avoid meeting her Osborne relations. So they all came. If Princess Beatrice was annoyed it cannot be helped and she must get over it – as she likes.[25]

This was tantamount to a declaration of war by the 'Sandringham set' on the 'Osborne set'.

Telegrams of condolence poured in from all over the world and it was calculated that the bill for answering them came to over £2,000. Tributes to the goodness and worthiness of HRH Prince Albert Victor, Duke of Clarence and Avondale, came from the pens and mouths of royalties, at home and abroad, from statesmen and leaders of the church, from soldiers and ambassadors. Perhaps the saddest words were those of his father, in a letter to the Archbishop of Canterbury: 'Our beloved son is happier now than if he were exposed to the miseries and temptations of this world'.[26]

Alexandra moved as if in a trance. She had lost half of her heart – and was never to wear bright colours again. She said: 'I have buried my angel and with him my happiness.'[27] She was the strength of the family but it was a strength which sapped her spirit. Early in February she and Edward visited Osborne. The Queen saw at a glance that Bertie was ill, confirming her view that his nature was not one to bear strain and sorrow. Alexandra, although the picture of misery, was calm. 'Dear Alix looks lovelier than ever in her deep mourning and a long black veil with a point on her head.'[28]

They moved on to Compton Place, Eastbourne. The rain fell ceaselessly and the arrival of Princess May, to coincide with the day on which she should have been married, increased the gloom. At this point Bertie exhibited the diplomacy at which he was fast becoming adept. He took his family to the South of France, renting an apartment in the Cap Martin hotel, between Monte Carlo and Menton. The wisdom of this step was that the apartment above them was occupied by Eugenie, the last Empress of the French.

Eugenie was the best medicine that could possibly have been prescribed for the distressed family. She was an example of courage in adversity which was unique. For near twenty years she had been at the Tuileries with Napoleon III, tolerating his lurid love affairs, lending him courage as he aged and became ill. She had allowed her only son, fourteen years old, to accompany his father to the front line in the Franco–German war. As Regent, she had conducted the affairs of France and, when revolution came, she had made her escape with ice-cold courage. She had backed her husband in exile in England where he planned to return to France, and had watched him die in agony before he could make the attempt. Five years later she lost their only son, speared to death by the Zulus in Africa. Yet this indomitable woman had overcome all her griefs and trials, was interested in life and travel and devoted to the cause of the Bonapartes. She was fun. She was a tonic. She set a high standard. The Wales were in bad shape when they reached Cap Martin. George had suffered a relapse and Maud was ill with influenza. A nurse, Sister Edith, accompanied them. Yet here, in the sun, to the music of the Empress's laugh, the miracle happened. The Prince had rented the apartment for a fortnight. The stay was extended to five weeks. The nurse was sent home.

Still Alexandra was restless and craved to be on the move. After a few weeks at Marlborough House and Sandringham, she was away again, *en famille*, this time bound for Copenhagen for King Christian IX's Jubilee. Bertie soon tired of the family life at the Amalienborg Palace, the Jubilee celebrations and the endless inquests into the causes of Eddy's death. He headed for home, taking George with him and leaving his wife where she most longed to be – in the haunts of her childhood. Hard hit as Bertie was by sudden tragedy, for at heart he was sensitive, his was a mind that recovered quickly and forbade sadness to linger. He disapproved of a long mourning. (Once, on leaving for the theatre, he was told that a distant relative had died and was asked what mourning should be displayed; he decided that the evening's programme could continue but that black dress studs should be worn.) Now, on arrival back in England, he proceeded to Warwick Castle to attend the Royal Agricultural Society's show. He was photographed standing behind the chair in which sat Daisy, Lady Brooke.[29] Her exclusion from London's Court circles had worried her not a jot. Bertie still came to Easton Lodge, and where Bertie went so did Society. She built a special station for his convenience and would herself fetch him from the train, driving in triumph up the long avenue.[30] The Prince of Fun was back on the roundabout and all that autumn he sparkled at house parties and banged away at *battues*. He was making up for lost time.

There was to be no such resurrection for Prince George, now Duke of York. He had been shattered by the death of his brother and the return to strength after the attack of typhoid was delayed by several months. So inactive and aimless was he that an outspoken member of his father's household sent a memorandum to Windsor, pointing out that his way of life was no preparation for kingship. In the event, he had never contemplated undertaking that role and now he felt an interloper. In fact the picture of George, as given by contemporary and some future sources, of being a placid character and a hardened sailor was far from the truth. He no longer craved for an active life at sea. After taking part in naval exercises in 1892 and being violently sea-sick, he wrote: 'I hope I shall never be in any other manoeuvres . . . Hate the whole thing!'[31] He was following in the path of his grand-father, Prince Albert, and was a middle aged man at twenty-seven.

On the domestic and personal side, his position was most difficult. Queen Victoria laid claim to him, seeing it as her duty to prepare him for the throne and determined not to repeat any of the errors which she had made with Bertie. Of natural course, the Prince of Wales considered that he should have first say in his son's career and way of life, and his demands were heavy. It was later to be said that they were more like brothers than parent and child, but this was mostly because George, being afraid of his father – and openly admitting it – agreed on everything and refrained from argument. But the greatest struggle to hold his soul in bondage came from his mother. Alexandra wanted her only surviving son for herself. She wrote to him: 'There is a bond of love between us, that of mother and child, which nothing can ever diminish or render less binding – and nobody can, or shall ever, come between me and my darling Georgie boy.'[32] It was clear that, when 'Georgie boy' took unto himself a wife, the young lady in question was in for trouble with her mother-in-law.

The constant talk of marriage was the bane of George's life, for he simply did not wish to consider it until the ghost of his brother grew dimmer. Yet such a step was of obvious impor-tance to the country, so far the only grandchild of the Prince and Princess of Wales being the puny little daughter of Louise, Duchess of Fife. Societies put the case to members of parliament, the members prodded the cabinet and the prime minister raised it with the Queen, who needed no prompting as she was thinking of little else. The press put forward many candidates, among them being 'Alicky', Princess of Hesse[33] (Princess Alice's youngest daughter who had turned down Eddy) and Princess Helena Victoria, daughter of Prince and Princess Christian, who was known as 'the Snipe' owing to the length of her nose. Many people, including the Queen, were in favour of Princess May of Teck, but some time was to pass before George would consider her for the role. She was 'Eddy's girl' and therefore inviolate. The two were good friends, played bezique together and reminisced about Eddy, but, for him at least, to go beyond that savoured of the indecent. In fact George was under the impression that he already had an 'understanding', with Marie, daughter of his uncle Alfred, Duke of Edinburgh, known as 'Missy', which would blossom into a wedding bouquet in the near future.

While stationed at Malta from 1886 to early 1889, his ship had been under the command of Prince Alfred and he had seen much of the four Edinburgh daughters. He rode with them, took them on outings and was a frequent visitor at their San Antonio home. His favourite was the eldest, golden-haired Missy. Catching her alone in a corridor, he exclaimed, 'I say, Missy, my word but you're pretty,' and he kissed her.[34] Now George was the antithesis of his brother Eddy and the stolen kiss was the seal on a lifetime of loving. It was a serious matter, and maybe it was the kernel of the rumour that he had married in secret while in Malta. In any event he considered himself committed to this girl ten years younger than himself, and looked at no other.

While Queen Victoria and his father approved of, and encouraged, the budding romance, the two mothers were dead against it. They did not like one another. The Duchess of Edinburgh was devout, and wherever she moved a Russian priest and two chanters went with her. She was stout and dowdy, and her boots were so made that they fitted either foot. Haughty and very conscious of being the daughter of the Emperor of All the Russians, she resented having to give precedence to the Princess of Wales. Having better diamonds, she flaunted them.[35] She was also German-biased, her husband having been named successor to Prince Albert's brother, Ernest, as Duke of Saxe-Coburg and Gotha.

Queen Victoria had wished George to marry in 1891, but he had resisted saying – with Missy in mind – that, in his opinion 'the wife ought not to be too young; look at poor Crown Prince Rudolph.'[36] He confided in his mother, who replied: 'I quite agree with you, it certainly would be too soon in every way!!

particularly as the bride is not in long petticoats yet!!! *Entre nous*, talking about *her*! it is a pity those children should be entirely brought up as Germans . . .'[37] But, in view of the pressure mounting upon him as a result of his brother's death, a proposal of marriage was put before the Duke and Duchess of Edinburgh in the spring of 1892. The answer was a blunt No. Missy was not even consulted, in later days her daughter giving her opinion that she would have said Yes if she had been.[38] Alexandra was delighted, but Bertie furious. He considered that both he and his son had been slighted, and for some time he would not speak to the Edinburgh's. George was bewildered and uncomprehending. He wrote a personal note to Missy: 'I had supposed that you belonged to me and that one day we would be married'.[39] In June Missy's engagement to Ferdinand, Crown Prince of Romania, was suddenly announced. This preference of an heir to a country which the Queen described as 'very insecure' and where members of high society were 'dreadful',[40] was a blow to Prince George's ego and further depressed his spirits. Thereafter the planners concentrated upon his engagement to Princess May of Teck, though he took little part in the preparatory moves.

When the Jubilee programme in Denmark was over, Alexandra visited the Fifes at Braemar Lodge. Among the guests there was Oliver Montagu. He walked with her beside the Dee and taught her how to fish. He told her that his health was 'not too good' and that the doctors had advised that he winter abroad. He died in Cairo on 24 January 1893. Alexandra wrote his epitaph: 'The best and truest of men, one to be relied on in every relation of life, faithful, discreet and trustworthy, gentle, kind, just and brave, and noble both in his life and death.'[41] She went to his brother's house, Hinchingbrooke near Huntingdon, the day before the funeral. Her cross lay on his coffin on that last night and the next day she took it away as a *memento mori*. Thereafter, on each anniversary of his death, flowers from her were placed upon his grave. She was never to be quite the same in her gay approach to life and there came a trace of cynicism into her thoughts and words. As Sir Philip Magnus wrote, his passing 'left in her heart an aching void which was never filled.'[42]

By the autumn of 1892 it was being taken for granted by many that George would marry May, a belief furthered by the following paragraph appearing in the press in November:

> Extensive alterations and enlargements have been made to
> what has hitherto been known as the Bachelors' Cottage,
> situated a short distance from Sandringham House, so as to
> form a private residence for the Duke of York. It will in
> future be called the Duke of York's Cottage.[43]

The only people who were apparently unaware of the engagement were the couple concerned. The Tecks, who were strongly
in favour of it, were dropping hints and winking wisely. The
Prince and Princess of Wales were not so enthusiastic, considering that the engagement might reflect adversely on the memory
of Eddy. But the Queen and her advisers were determined and
by the New Year Alexandra had accepted the inevitable.

Shaken by the death of Oliver Montagu, once again the desire
overcame her to absent herself from the London scene and the
plannings and schemings of her husband's relations. She wanted
one last chance to have her 'Georgie boy' all to herself, and this
she managed. On 4 March, accompanied by Victoria and Maud,
they left for Italy, joining the RY *Osborne* at Genoa. They lazed
along the coast, making expeditions to Spezia, Pisa and Florence.
In Rome they had private audience of the Pope, exchanging
photographs. They climbed Vesuvius and saw the Isle of Capri
and the Blue Grotto. It was while they were on their way to
Corfu and Greece that they heard that the Duchess of Fife had
given birth to a second daughter – Princess Maud.

At the end of April Alexandra waved goodbye to her son as
he began his lone journey home. She could not bear to be on hand
when his engagement became fact. 3 May was a lovely, sunny
day. George was staying with his sister Louise Fife, at East Sheen
Lodge. The Duke and Duchess of Teck had, by prior plan, left
their daughter May alone at the White Lodge, their Richmond
home. May went round to the Fifes' for tea. Afterwards Louise
said to her brother: 'Now, Georgie, don't you think you ought
to take May into the garden and look at the frogs in the pond?'[44]
He duly looked, proposed – and was accepted. Alexandra was in
Malta when the telegram came. It was there that the rumour had
started that George had married morganatically. Perhaps she
thus thought to kill the rumour. But it would not die and *The
Star* newspaper repeated it. This led George, in a rare mood of

levity, to announce: 'I say, May, we can't get married after all: I hear I've got a wife and three children!'[45]

The wedding was at the Chapel Royal, St James's, on 6 July. 'It was the most heavenly day ever could be – such a summer's day as you get solely and only in England.'[46] At 11.30 twelve landaus, forming the first carriage procession, left Buckingham Palace, making their way up Constitution Hill and along Piccadilly. All the royalties of Europe were on parade, among them the King and Queen of Denmark. The crowds were dense and enthusiastic, but it was the twelfth carriage which roused a deafening crescendo of cheering. In it sat Alexandra the Beloved. She was sad and serious when she left the Palace but the tornado of the people's acclaim blew the sadness away and the sun of her smile was bright as she moved beneath the plane trees, gay green parasols decorating the way. When she reached the Chapel, an onlooker said of her: 'The Princess of Wales looked *more lovely* – than ever! – none can approach her!'[47] Among the older folk there was some comparison with the day, thirty years before, when she had starred on a similar occasion at St George's Chapel, Windsor. The bride did not escape. 'Instead of coming in the *exquisite, ideal* way the Pss. of Wales did at her wedding with her eyes *cast down* – so prettily – May looked right and left and slightly bowed to her acquaintance! a great mistake. The children bridesmaids were too delicious.'[48] They most certainly were, the star among them being young Alice of Battenberg. But the five adult bridesmaids, most serious when photographed, were not in the same class of beauty as Alexandra of Wales.

At 6.25 a special train took the couple from Liverpool Street station, reaching gaily decorated Wolferton at eight o'clock. There were Venetian masts and triumphal arches all the way to Sandringham. When they reached York Cottage the island suddenly became a fairyland as the rocks on the lake, the rustic bridge, the boathouse and the trees all around were illuminated by hundreds of hanging lamps and Japanese lanterns.

May, dusty after the drive from the station and tired out after an exhausting day, sat at the window of her separate bedroom,[49] looking out through the lights sparkling on the water, at 'the Big House' on the high ground beyond. There was Eddy's bedroom, remaining as it had been when she had watched him die little more than a year before. Sandringham was indeed a strange choice for a honeymoon, with its emphasis on the sad past. Throughout the engagement period there had been no sign of romance between the couple, no interchange of loving glançes, no movement towards one another. Their private notes to one another showed that they were aware of this lack and yet they were unable to behave otherwise.

It might well have been expected that the honeymoon would have been spent in some idyllic site – a suite with a balcony overhanging an Italian lake, a villa in the south of France with a private beach, or a Grecian isle. But no, Norfolk it was, probably by choice of Prince George, for Sandringham was the place that he loved the best. 'Abroad,' he was later to say, 'is awful. I know. I've been.' And the ghost of Eddy was not the only handicap with which May had to cope. She looked around her in amazement and chagrin at the decoration and furniture of her new home. Her husband had solved the problem in the manner which he considered the most practical, trouble free and economic. He had called in 'the man from Maple's'. Solid and practical the result may have been, but York Cottage ended up as a mixture of the lower decks of a warship, a boys' preparatory school and a better class hotel at a seaside resort. To May, with her connoisseur's taste, the shock was profound.

Alexandra had played no part in the preparation of the new home. She saw no romance in the marriage, and never did. George was merely doing 'stand in' duty for Eddy. Ten days after the wedding she arrived at the Big House, bringing with her her father, mother and brother Waldemar. She made her attitude clear immediately. She treated York Cottage as an annex of Sandringham and took to arriving as and when she wanted to, unannounced. Down the path she would come – on occasion at breakfast time – in company with Maud, Victoria and guests and surrounded by a pack of dogs, flooding George with family news and gossip and demanding that the couple come up and play some game in the evening. It was made clear to May that she was still 'the poor relation'.

A year passed and George and Mary came to love one another in their peculiar way. She became pregnant and hated the whole business. 'She does not wish it remarked or mentioned,'[50] wrote the Empress Frederick. At ten o'clock on the evening of 24 June 1894 a son was born to her. Alexandra cradled the baby in her arms and said softly: 'My first happiness since . . .'

The name of the boy was David.

FIFTEEN

✦❦✦

A Century's End

On 29 October 1894 the domestic life of the Wales family was shattered by the arrival of a telegram for Alexandra from Dagmar. The Empress said that her husband was dying and begged her to come to Livadia. The Prince and Princess set off at once. On arrival in Vienna they were told that the Emperor was dead. Four days later they reached the Crimea.

Throughout the summer Alexander had shown signs of tiredness and in the autumn his doctors called in a German specialist. He diagnosed an acute form of Bright's disease and Alexander was hurried south to the warmer climate of the Crimea. Daily he weakened. An expression of wistfulness and physical lassitude now settled on his face and he became hollow-eyed, his cheeks sunken. 'It was like seeing a magnificent building crumbling.'[1]

The new Emperor, Nicholas II, was by the bedside when his father died in the afternoon sun. He staggered from the room and broke into floods of tears. He was utterly crushed. He said to his brother-in-law: 'What am I going to do? What is going to happen to me . . .? I am not prepared to be a Tsar. I never wanted to become one. I know nothing of the business of ruling. I have no idea of even how to talk to the ministers!'

That spring Nicholas had become engaged to the twenty-two-year-old Princess Alicky, who earlier had rejected both Eddy and George. She was only six when her mother died and she had been brought up under the watchful eye of Queen Victoria. She was petulant, spoilt and self-opiniated. One of her Hessian relations referred to her as 'a stupid little English girl'.[2] She had been summoned to Livadia ten days

195

before the Emperor died. Kneeling before him she had received his blessing and become formally engaged. On the morning after his death she became a member of the Orthodox Church and titled Grand Duchess Alexandra Feodorovna. She had already showed that there was iron under her velvet glove, exhorting her fiancé: 'Show your own mind and don't let others forget who you are. Forgive me, lovy.'[3] Their's was a strange, exaggerated love, ripe with emotion, sugar-sweet with the language of lovers, swamped with mysticism and introspection. Alicky had both the liking and the desire for power, absorbing this from Queen Victoria, but she lacked the deep humanity of her grandmother. There was an immediate clash with Dagmar who still considered herself the real Empress of Russia.

The death of her husband at only forty-five shattered Dagmar and in the grim funeral programme which followed she leaned heavily upon her sister Alexandra, who slept beside her, prayed beside her and sat beside her as the long, black-draped train bearing the corpse and the mourners made its slow way from the warmth and sunshine of the Crimea to St Petersburg, white with snow. The Prince too was feeling in need of support. Here he was, sitting in a funeral train, attending endless services – one was repeated thirty-nine times – when he should have been enjoying his birthday shoot at Sandringham. A telegram arrived at York Cottage, ordering the Duke of York to hurry to St Petersburg with all speed. For the first time 'Georgie' had Sandringham, his wife and the shooting to himself, free of parental interference, and it was with a heavy heart that he did as he was bid. From Russia he wrote to May, telling her how much he missed her: 'I really believe I should get ill if I had to be away from you for a long time.'[4]

The funeral train made stops all along the way and the track was lined with kneeling peasants. Two days of procession and dirges were spent at Moscow, and then on to St Petersburg for the final act in the fortress church of St Peter and St Paul. For seven days the Emperor lay exposed in his coffin, while long queues of subjects passed by night and by day, while hidden choirs chanted and a priest intoned the scriptures. Interment took place on the 19th, in a service lasting over four hours. There was ordeal for those whose duty it was to kiss the lips and the Holy

Picture grasped in his stiff hand. Lord Carrington wrote: 'As he lay uncovered in his coffin, his face looked a dreadful colour and the smell was awful.'[5] When his widow bent over to make her last farewell, the arm of her sister Alexandra was about her.[6] The strain was clear on her face, but she showed no sign of giving way to it.

A week later Nicholas and Alicky were married. The Princess of Wales was dressed entirely in white for the occasion. To show his appreciation of the support which she had given, and to mark the occasion, the Emperor gave her a gold pot containing a crystal flower made by Fabergé, a large diamond in its centre. His male relations were less fortunate. They received, by custom, silver chamber-pots.

There was no private honeymoon, the couple remaining with their relations at the Anitchkoff Palace. Next morning at breakfast the Prince of Wales, watching the newly weds unconcernedly making their selection of dishes, remarked to Lord Carrington that they looked 'as if nothing had happened'.[7] Nevertheless Alicky sent her husband this note: 'Never did I believe there could be such utter happiness in this world, such a feeling of unity between two mortal beings. I love you – those three words have my life in them.'[8]

Fortunately, after so much unhappiness, 1895 was to prove a lucky year for the Prince and Princess of Wales. The immediate problem was to find suitable husbands for their daughters Victoria and Maud. Particular care had to be taken owing to the possibility that they were carriers of haemophilia. Their frequent illnesses might be indication that they were sufferers from the appalling disease – or at least carriers. In the 1890s little was known about it. Queen Victoria was completely confused by it, often repeating that it was 'not in our family',[9] by which she meant the House of Hanover. It therefore must have come through the Coburgs, who in any case were subject to most of the diseases in the medical dictionary. The Queen's youngest son, Leopold, had died of it in 1884. Of her daughters Alice and Beatrice were transmitters. Victoria (although at one time believed to be) and Helena were not, while Louise had no children, so remained an unknown quantity. Princess Alice lost a three-year-old son who bled to death after a fall. Evidence that she had passed on the disease to the female side came with its appearance in the son of her daughter Irene, married to Prince Henry of Prussia.

In September 1895 the Wales family went on holiday to Denmark and there Maud fell in love with her cousin, Prince Charles. The two had known one another since childhood, meeting at the annual gatherings of the Glucksburg clan, but Maud, being three years older, had regarded herself as being in almost another age group. Now she met a very changed character, a full-blown sailor, on leave after a six-month tour of the coasts of Iceland. Charles was hearty, high spirited, full of fun and just the man for Maud. They were engaged before the Wales returned home at the end of the month but it was not until the end of October that the public announcement was made. Both the Queen and Alexandra were delighted.

Owing to Prince Charles' naval duties, the wedding was postponed until July 1896. Britain and the Empire were already preparing for the Diamond Jubilee of Queen Victoria's reign and what better appetizer could there be. The choice of a Dane was popular with the public and a great fuss was made about it, special wedding Numbers pouring from the presses.

Charles and Maud were married in the private chapel at Buckingham Palace on the 22 July and the honeymoon was spent in Norfolk, at Appleton House on the Sandringham estate. On her engagement the Prince of Wales had given Appleton to his daughter. He wished her to have a foothold in England and he stipulated that she visit it at least once a year. He supervised the improvements himself, added a castellated wing and made many interior alterations, including the installation of central heating. On her arrival there on her wedding night there was to be no such shock as had come to Princess May when she reached York Cottage at the start of her honeymoon and saw the sombre background created by the joint efforts of Prince George and 'the man from Maples', for Alexandra had made a special journey from London to supervise the decor and make the final touches in the newly improved home. Maud had known Appleton since she was a child and needed no urging to visit the house annually. In fact she made three or four stays each year until she died in 1938.

The gardener who was there when she arrived on honeymoon was still there when she died. He said: 'This was her real home. She loved this place.'[10]

So Princess Victoria was left, waiting for a Prince to lift her off the shelf. He did not materialize. She was delicate, musical and passionately fond of animals, birds in particular. She hated ceremony. As she approached thirty, her health deteriorated and she became a hypochondriac. She tried many cures, including the waters at Harrogate, which she thought revolting.[11] Quick of mind, she became waspish and critical, but remained full of fun with those whom she knew well, such as Sydney Holland and Frederick Ponsonby. In her autograph book was the signature of her doctor, Sir Frederick Treves. In pointing this out, she would say: 'I owe that man my life twice.'[12] Sir Frederick was succeeded by Lord Dawson of Penn. After her death in 1935 the famous royal physician expressed the intention of writing a paper on the health of the Princess whom he had tended for twenty-five years,[13] but he died before achieving this.

Although there were no wedding bells for the Wales in 1897, it was a happy year for them and the bells were ringing all summer through for the celebrations of Queen Victoria's Diamond Jubilee. For Alexandra, a domestic problem was eased by the end of the love affair between her husband and Daisy, now Countess of Warwick. Daisy had been shaken by the discovery of the startling truth that the gap between rich and poor was much too wide, the prophets who appraised her of this being Robert Blatchford and W. T. Stead. The Prince was also aware of this, but was not prepared to let it interfere with the occupations of his pleasure hours. Daisy was also in need of a more exciting and ruthless lover, and she found one in the hunting fields of Nottinghamshire. She and Bertie remained the closest of friends and he continued to write her frequent letters, with compromising beginnings and endings, but only social tittle-tattle in between. Now that the fire was out, he did his best to bring back Daisy into Alexandra's social orbit, but she, playing canny, was not accepting this.

It was in April 1897 that the Princess of Wales suggested to the Lord Mayor that, to celebrate the Jubilee, dinners should be provided for the poor of London's slums.[14] The idea was accepted with enthusiasm and a fund started, Alexandra weighing in with a substantial donation. She was no financier and had little idea of the immense sum needed to feed 300,000 hungry and jubilant cockneys. But, if she was weak in addition, she was strong in charm, and knew full well how to wheedle largesse out of the rich. On this occasion it was Thomas Lipton, the tea king, who topped up the coffers, pouring into them £25,000. In the next Honours List he became Sir Thomas Lipton. And Australia made certain that the meals would be substantial by sending 20,000 carcases of mutton.[15] The feasts were held at fifty-six centres and were followed by entertainment. The Prince and Princess visited a number, outstanding among them being the People's Palace, Mile End Road, where a thousand crippled children of East London were given a day which they were never to forget.

On 22 June Queen Victoria, a little old lady with weak eyes and slow legs, drove to St Paul's Cathedral for the Thanksgiving Service. She was wearing her second best shawl and sheltering from the bright light under a white parasol. Before her sat Alexandra, 'Looking very pretty in lilac'.[16] As, at each bend and turn on the route, their carriage came into the view of a new section of the tens of thousands who waited for it, the tumult of their cheering was as if a great wave smashed against a high sea wall.

The Queen later wrote in her diary: 'No one ever, I believe, has met with such an ovation as was given to me, passing through those six miles of streets . . . The cheering was quite deafening, and every face seemed to be filled with real joy. I was much moved . . .'[17] The emotion was near to overcoming her. Her lips were pressed tight together and tears welled from her eyes.[18] Alexandra leaned forward, pressed her hand and, under cover of the parasol, wiped away a tear.

Yet still the old lady remained firmly enthroned. Now aged nearly eighty, she was perhaps waiting to die with her century and her age, yet the courage was still there, and the zest for holidays in Scotland and the South of France. There were family sadnesses still to face. Two of her children were dying of cancer.*

* Prince Alfred, Duke of Edinburgh and of Saxe-Coburg and Gotha; and Empress Frederick of Germany.

She lost two grandchildren, one from fast living and the other from disease caught on the field of battle.* Three of her grandchildren were heading for divorce.† Her favourite son-in-law, Henry of Battenberg, died of fever contracted in the Ashanti campaign. There was also the lingering fear and doubt as to how her heir would perform when she had gone. She had no fears about Alexandra, his wife.

Yet Alexandra looked forward with many misgivings to the prospect of being Queen. She hated wars and she feared violence. She had told her mother-in-law, after an attempt on the latter's life outside Buckingham Palace – 'It is no pleasure being a Queen'.[19] Marie Mallet said of the Princess at the beginning of 1899: 'Her restlessness is alarming and her one idea is to be constantly travelling. She looks ill . . . and I hear she dreads the possibility of reigning.'[20] And she was lonely in her separate bedroom. Although she played the public role of partner to her husband to perfection – and the role had become part of her life and she would have been lost without it – the partnership lasted only while they were on the royal stage together. There was little rapport or understanding of each other's inner needs. Their interests were too wide apart, their tastes and beliefs so very different. He felt the lack as much as she did, but he was able to make up the deficiency, and she was not. Bertie, now unpopular on the Continent, suffering permanent pin-pricks from his nephew William, and out of tune with Daisy, sought relief from the strain and the lack of a female confidante. Dark clouds of depression engulfed him as life's curtain began to fall on his sister Vicky and his brother Alfred. The light of relief came to him on a winter's day in 1898 at the Military meeting at Sandown race-course. There was a lady on his arm and the eyes of those in the privileged areas were fixed upon her. He had only met her once before and yet there was an aura of familiarity and one-ness about them that discouraged intruders.[21] Youngest daughter of Admiral Sir William Edmonstone, naval ADC to the Queen, her name was Alice Frederica. She was the wife of the Hon. George Keppel, twenty-nine years old – about half Bertie's age – with a four-year-old daughter. She was short, voluptuous, with tiny

* Prince Alfred of Coburg; and Prince Christian Victor.
† Grand Duke and Duchess of Hesse; Princess Marie Louise of Anhalt.

hands and feet, and a voice which sank to a whisper or rose to a shout as the emotion took her. She was dark and beautiful, ambitious yet tactful. Her husband was tall, handsome, fond of the ladies and short of money. He appeared unconcerned at his wife's aberration. In time, as his photograph appeared again and again in company with royals, foreigners became intrigued as to the reason for his presence with them and came to the conclusion that he must be the last lover of Queen Victoria.[22]

Alice took over Bertie and stayed with him to the end. She could handle him, interest him and calm him. She was invited where he was invited, with the exceptions of Welbeck, Arundel and Hatfield, fitting exceptions which held the balance of her extraordinary position. To Alexandra, she was both a blessing and a nuisance. It was a relief to know that there was someone who could rescue Bertie from the dark pond of his depression, who could influence him when he became obstinate, who kept him away from the sirens of London and Paris, of Cannes and Baden-Baden. But it was upsetting to see his spaniel eyes upon her on social occasions such as Cowes. When the Duke of York was there, and his wife was not, he wrote to May: 'Alas, Mrs K. arrives tomorrow . . . I am afraid that peace and quiet will not remain.' To which May replied: 'How annoyed Mama will be!'[23]

Personally, Alexandra never took her husband's love affairs seriously. Latterly she found in them a source of amusement. Looking from a window at Sandringham she saw her husband and Alice sitting close to one another in an open carriage, her ample bosom topping his massive paunch. She burst into fits of laughter and called a lady-in-waiting to come and enjoy the spectacle.[24] The reception of behind-the-curtain sex indulged in by members of the Royal Family has ever been a gamble. Some of those who have dared have been castigated, others enthroned. Alice Keppel was one of the lucky ones.

Equipped with Alexandra as the perfect hostess and impeccable partner in State affairs, with Alice as mistress, confidante and playmate, the Prince seemed well enough provided for in the feminine sphere. Yet he raised his establishment to a trinity. The third member, and in some respects the most powerful in influence, was a most unlikely addition. She was a nurse and a spinster of forty-six when the Prince first met her in 1898. Her name was Agnes Keyser and she was the daughter of a stock-broker. She was handsome and formidable. Determined to follow in the footsteps of Florence Nightingale, she had early turned against the social fripperies of the day and, with the help of her younger sister, Fanny,[25] set up a nursing home for army officers at 17 Grosvenor Crescent, (it later became the King Edward VII Hospital) close by the gardens of Buckingham Palace, to which she was soon to possess an entrance key.

To Bertie, as Prince of Wales and later as King, Sister Agnes played a triple role, that of 'nanny', real friend and an insurance policy against the fear of death. She did not give to him what all the other women in his life had deemed essential. In starched white cotton, she provided him, by the touch of her hand, with a strength, sanity and peace which no other love had reached. He would slip over to Grosvenor Crescent to sup with her on Irish stew and rice pudding, and the starched nurses would change the plates and hold their peace.

Bertie had been a rebel all his life. He had fought his tutors, resisted his father, outwitted his mother. He had rebelled against sitting at home of an evening with only the Danish simplicity of his wife for amusement. Now, for the first time, he did what he was told, although only when he was within 17 Grosvenor Crescent. Once outside, he was back again at his late night supper, his gambling and his fat cigars. For Alexandra, Agnes Keyser raised few problems, except for the disappointment that comes to any wife who discovers that she is insufficient as an adviser and helpmate.

Alexandra was herself beset by worries and sorely missed the comforting strength of Oliver Montagu. Throughout 1897 it was the future safety of her favourite brother, King George of Greece, which troubled her dreams. A secret society of young officers planned the resurrection of the military glories of Greece. Trouble started in Crete, largely Greek in population but for long a part of the Turkish Empire. Public opinion in Athens demanded the annexation of the island and as a result Turkey declared war. The brief campaign which followed was disastrous for the Greeks. The Turkish troops proved vastly superior and King George pleaded with his sister to do all in her power to help. Alexandra did a great deal, bombarding Queen Victoria with telegrams and even arriving at Windsor 'in an awful stew',[26] as a lady-in-waiting said. But by the end of the year Greece was defeated and the dynasty threatened. The state of the country was deplorable, the northern towns being crowded with destitute refugees and violence rife in the streets of Athens. But in February 1898 an attempt was made to kill King George and there was a public reaction in his favour. Alexandra breathed again.

Another cause for worry was the health of her eighty-one year old mother. On 2 August 1898, while she was at Osborne, a telegram arrived for her saying that Queen Louise was fading. The Princess left for Denmark that night. Queen Louise lasted for two more months, her life flickering on as a candle burns to its last drop of wax. Alexandra was constantly by her bedside. The Prince of Wales, recovering from an injury to his knee, was unable to attend the funeral in the historic cathedral at Roskilde and sent the Duke of York in his place. Although the Queen's life had exceeded four-score years, the family ties were still strong and her husband and children were shattered. King Christian was in doubt whether he could continue his task alone and his daughters banded together to ensure that one of them was always with him in the months ahead.[27] Alexandra took the first stint. This did not suit her husband or son, and letters were arriving constantly from Marlborough House, urging their return. George would dearly have loved to have gone home, as he was missing the shooting in Norfolk, but Alexandra was determined. The Prince of Wales began to fear that once again she would be absent from his birthday party at Sandringham on 9 November. She arrived home, with a very relieved son, just in time.

At about this time a pervasive loneliness closed over Alexandra, which to a degree, altered her character and her outlook. Lying in bed, sleepless in the small hours, she was haunted by the sadnesses of the past. What would her son, Alexander John, have been like now if he had lived? Had she done the right thing by Eddy? Should she have allowed him to go away for so long on the *Bacchante* cruises? Should she have taken other steps to control his weaknesses? Could she have done more for Oliver Montagu – given him more?

On an occasion when loneliness swept uncontrollably over her, she called her maid and insisted that the girl slept in her bed while she herself dozed on the sofa.[28] It was a strange situation which the maid did not comprehend. Although the Princess had a small appetite, every night a tray of sandwiches was placed outside her door after she had retired.[29] In the morning the tray was always empty. Her small dogs slept with her and it was realised that it must be they who were enjoying the snacks. Alexandra was handing out their rations and finding company in chatting with 'the little people'.

But if Alexandra was denied the simple comfort of another human presence in the long night watches, she had company enough in the daylight hours: there was her unmarried daughter, Victoria; at nearby York Cottage were Georgie and May, with regular additions coming to their family – 'Bertie' in 1895, Mary in 1897 and Henry in 1900* and there was an army of male admirers. Outstanding among them were Sir Dighton Probyn, vc, who referred to the Princess as 'The Beloved Lady'; George, Duke of Cambridge; Prince Louis of Battenberg; and the Marquis Luis de Soveral, Portugese Minister, known as the 'Blue Monkey', who became 'the great confidant of the future Queen of England'.[30] The men who worshipped her as a divine being, proof against the smuts of life, were legion and none would tolerate a word being said against her.

However, the outbreak of the Boer War on 11 October 1899 brought a change to Alexandra, galvanising her into dynamic action. Once again she became totally absorbed with the care of the wounded and, as her husband also gave high rating to the question, the two came closer to one another. On the 10th the entry in the Prince's diary was, 'P. and Pcss. dine alone,'[31] and that was a rare occurrence indeed.

Alexandra's prime consideration was to provide a modern and well equipped hospital ship to bring home the wounded. In previous campaigns she had been appalled at the callous manner in which casualties had been shipped back in the holds of cargo vessels. The Red Cross Society, of which she was honorary

---

* George VI, Countess of Harewood and the Duke of Gloucester respectively.

president, chartered the steam yacht, *Midnight Sun*, and the Princess undertook to provide the money necessary for conversion. Her branch of the National Aid Society had collected a considerable sum during the Egyptian campaign of 1885 and the balance accruing was now used for providing the necessary medical equipment and ward facilities.[32] When the fund ran out, she once again turned her appealing eyes and fascinating smile upon Sir Thomas Lipton. By the first week in December the refitting was complete and the vessel was re-christened *The Princess of Wales*. It was a family effort, the wards being named Alexandra, Louise, Victoria and Maud.

The Princess went to the docks to inspect both ship and company, and was in Napoleonic mood. Intensely modern in her thinking, she was apt to clash with die-hards who put more value on the transportation of mess silver than on bandages and her ideas on the degree of comfort were considerably more lavish than those held by the War Office. She inspected every detail, even that the medicine bottles were well enough secured to withstand heavy seas. She found no fault with the mattresses, as she had selected them herself but was upset because there was no chaplain on board and only grudgingly accepted the assurance that the captain read prayers adequately. But the engines proved beyond her and, to her chagrin, the boiler collapsed.[33] Matters were soon put to rights and, when in February 1900 s.s. *The Princess of Wales* arrived back with a full complement of wounded, Alexandra was at Southampton to meet her. On the 27th Queen Victoria, paying tribute to the work of her daughter-in-law, visited the men at Netley hospital.

In the early days of the fighting Alexandra's war work was impeded by the arrival of a most unwelcome guest. Emperor William of Germany had chosen this inopportune moment to visit his grandmother and uncle. William had, in recent years, been behaving in a most unpredictable and annoying way. In fact Lord Salisbury's earlier comment that he was mad appeared to be nearing the truth, such was his inconsistency. One month he was overflowing with kind words and pacific promises to his British relations, the next he was thundering threats to descend, in the garb of Attila the Hun, upon the white cliffs of Dover. He arrived with his wife and two sons on 20 November and, owing to his unpopularity with the British public as a result of his famous telegram to President Kruger, the press gave him only minor coverage. At Windsor he was polite, kind and thoughtful to his 'unparalleled Grandmama' and on the 25th moved on to Sandringham. There his good behaviour continued. Alexandra contained herself, although she was still bitter that, in the obituaries in the German newspapers, Queen Louise of Denmark had been referred to as a 'she-Machiavelli'.[34] But she did let herself go once. When she heard that William had brought with him an assistant to his hairdresser, responsible only for curling his moustache, she spat out, 'Ach, the fool![35] Count von Bülow, Secretary of State for Foreign Affairs, was in the party. Through Charlotte Knollys, Alexandra sent him the following spoken message:

> In his telegram to Kruger my nephew Willy has shown us that he is inwardly our enemy, even if he surpasses himself every time he meets us, in flatteries, compliments, and assurances of his love and affection. His heartless treatment of his dying father and his behaviour to his mother show that he has as little heart as he has political common sense.[36]

Bülow had known Alexandra in childhood days at Rumpenheim, respected her judgement and listened carefully to her words. Russian records, not revealed until long afterwards, proved how right was her assessment. While condoling with Queen Victoria and the Prince of Wales on the point of British defeats in South Africa, he was simultaneously 'suggesting to the Russians that the time now be ripe for a joint action to "paralyse the power of England and deal it a mortal blow." '[37]

With William out of the way, the Princess returned to action. She was perturbed at rumours about the bad housing conditions for the families of dockers sent out to the Cape to unload supply ships, and became involved in a scheme to send out portable buildings. She was told that the cheapest of these were made in Germany. 'Nothing will induce me to get them from there,' she replied.[38]

In December she decided to send out to Africa twelve of the best nurses from the London Hospital, insisting that they wore the same uniform as the nurses already there. Certain jealousies arose and Alexandra heard gossip that her ladies were not as well turned out as they might have been. Into the tent of General Kitchener, Chief of Staff in South Africa, came an angry telegram from the Princess who was generally considered to be so meek and mild.[39] Lord Roberts received a similar irate message when the nurses were prevented from entering the fighting area.[40] The gossip was stopped, the nurses were given a free hand and the Princess sent out another twenty, paying for them herself. But she was annoyed and angry that she was not allowed to make the selection herself.

Then Alexandra conceived a plan of her own with which no one could interfere, except her husband. She decided to start a small convalescent home at Sandringham for wounded officers who had no home to go to after leaving hospital. She converted and modernized an old farm house and there installed a cook and a parlourmaid. She wanted to have a full time nurse, but on this point she came up against the Prince, who proved most obstinate. He gave the somewhat odd reason that the nurse 'would get into mischief'.[41] In truth he was so jealous of the privacy of his estate that he did not want strangers wandering around it.

Meantime public feeling on the continent had become decidedly pro-Boer, anti-British, and tourists crossing the Channel were frequently greeted with uncomplimentary remarks in hotels and on the railways. The foreign press carried many hostile articles and Bertie was the target of the cartoonists. For a third of a century he had been besporting himself from Cannes to Homburg, so ammunition was in plentiful supply and some of the finished works were coarse and outspoken. The winds of change have ever proved variable in France, the weathercock swift to swing, as both Napoleons had come to realize. Now, with the bitter memory of Fashoda fresh in their minds, the French poured out their venom. It was, therefore, considered politic that Queen Victoria should not spend her customary spring holiday by the Mediterranean and instead she went to Ireland. This was indeed a *volte-face* as, when she had arrived at Nice in previous years, her reception had been so tumultuous that it had taken four regiments of infantry and a battery of artillery to control the crowds along the route from the station to her hotel.[42]

In 1897 the Prince of Wales had agreed to become president of

Queen Alexandra 1901

To be painted — with full Court-dress — order of the Garter — Pathetic expression even when smiling

From a collection of studies for royal miniatures by Gertrude Massey.
Note the artist's comments alongside

King Edward VII and
Queen Alexandra at the
opening of their first parliament,
February 14, 1901

Queen Alexandra and her grandchildren. From left to right: Princess Mary, Prince Henry, Prince George (*later* George VI) and Prince Edward of Wales (*later* Edward VIII)

the British section of the International Exhibition to be staged in Paris in April 1900. Now he refused to attend, saying that he would be wearing uniform for the occasion and, if this was insulted, the result might be war. So for the first time for many a year he missed the heady air of Paris in the spring. But, as he dearly loved his continental journeys, he decided to spend Easter with his wife's relations in Denmark, poor substitute though Bernstorff might be for his *entresol* in the Hotel Bristol.

At 4.50 on the afternoon of 4 April 1900 the Prince and Princess arrived at the Gare du Nord, Brussels. They were due to continue their journey to Copenhagen at 5.30. The small party, which included Charlotte Knollys and Admiral Sir Henry Stephenson, was travelling in one of the *berlines* which the Prince was in the habit of using for his continental journeys. Behind it was a car of the *Compagnie Internationale des Wagons-Lits et des Grands Express Europeens*. The royal party took the chance to stretch their legs, Alexandra leading her little dog. They chatted with the stationmaster and the officials there to greet them.

As the time for departure approached, they took their places in the *berline*, the Prince and Princess sitting back to the engine. The *wagon-lit* attendant was at the door of his coach and was the first to see what happened next.

As the train began to move, a youth ran from the station buildings and jumped on to the footboard of the *berline*. Alexandra saw a hat at the window and thought that someone was offering her flowers or some such token, not an unusual occurrence.[43] The youth, holding on to the carriage with his left hand, pulled a revolver from his pocket with his right and fired. He pressed the trigger four times before the Belgian officials pulled him to the platform and held him down. Two rounds misfired, one bullet broke the compartment window and the fourth passed between Bertie and Alexandra, hit the compartment wall just above their heads and richochetted back, burying itself in the cushions on the other side. The train stopped and the Prince jumped out. Seeing that his attacker was little more than a boy, he requested those who held him down not to treat him too roughly. 'Poor fool,' he said.[44]

It all happened so quickly that the seriousness of the incident was partly lost. The press was not present in force and there were

209

few spectators. As the boy was led away the Prince indicated that he did not wish his journey to be delayed and the train steamed out of the Gare du Nord.

Alexandra had always dreaded an assassination attempt. She had seen the gun, heard the whine of the bullet and the thud as it hit the wood but a few inches above her head. But, to her amazement and relief, she found that she was not frightened, remaining as cool as her husband. Luckily she had something to occupy her immediate attention, for her dog was near hysteria, barking and shaking with fear. Calming it was her antidote to alarm. But each split second remained clear in her memory, for six years later she recited to Sir Maurice de Bunsen, Ambassador at Madrid, every detail of the attack. It was the same with the Prince and much later he explained to a French detective: 'The bullet entered just here, on the right, smashing the window pane, and, before burying itself in the wood, passed across the compartment and nearly grazed my hat. I was in serious danger that day.'[45] Admiral Stephenson reported back to England:

> It was indeed a providential escape HRH had at the Brussels Station last Wednesday; and I hope and believe that both Their Royal Highnesses are now no worse for the wicked act of a madman. They were at the time quite calm and collected, and no nervousness or excitement in either of them. As soon as the train started we all had a search for the bullet, without success; it has since been found.★ It struck the wood work about a foot above the Prince's head and rebounded on to the cushion opposite . . .[46]

The young assassin was named Sipido, of Italian origin, resident in Belgium. He was a member of an anarchist club and stated that he regarded the Prince as 'an accomplice of Chamberlain in killing the Boers'.[47] He had three adult accomplices, all of whom were arrested. The Belgian authorities were lax in their security measures and Sipido escaped to Paris.

Queen Victoria was horrified and, when shortly afterwards King Humbert of Italy was assassinated, became convinced that she was next on the list. She was particularly worried about Alexandra travelling around Europe, but the Princess, purged of her fears, did not worry at all. In contrast to the attitude of the

★ The bullet is preserved at Windsor.

man in the street, the British authorities took little regard of the affair and the Prince indignantly demanded why Parliament had not recorded its thankfulness at his escape. Apparently the underlying reason was that Sipido was only fifteen and the false premise applied then, as it does today, that death is less final when handed out by the young.

Alexandra travelled on alone to Paris to see the International Exhibition, despite the fact that Sipido was in hiding there and that the Prince had considered it unwise to attend owing to the bad feeling against Britain. Staying with Charlotte Knollys at the Meyerbeer Hotel on the Rond-Point des Champs Elysées, she fondly imagined that, as she was travelling *incognita*, no one knew that she was there. The French, having no quarrel with the lovely Princess of Denmark, respected her privacy. She was joined by her brother, King George of Greece and his family, and thereafter enjoyed some very happy days. They roamed around Versailles and saw everything at the Exhibition from the Pavilion of the Nations to the smallest side-show. Alexandra was intrigued by the *Trottoir Roulant*, a rolling pavement which, to her delight, caused consternation and upsets to nervous ladies persuaded to sample it. King George took her to a restaurant for dinner, a rare treat indeed for her. The young officer accompanying the party, feeling greater privacy was required, asked the head waiter for '*un cabinet*' (a lavatory). The head waiter looked perplexed. '*Oui*', stammered out the officer, '*un cabinet pour quatre.*' Alexandra collapsed with laughter. At the end of the evening she demanded to see the bill and soundly admonished her brother for being so extravagant.[48] There is one charming glimpse of her on record: she was seen standing on a bench by the Champs Elysées, waving at, and loudly cheering, a passing carriage. Her daughter Maud, with her husband, Prince Charles, was taking part in a state drive of important visitors to the Exhibition.

The green summer days of 1900 were gay indeed. On 17 May Mafeking was relieved and Britain went mad with joy and excitement, the sounds of the cheers and the laughter of 'Mafeking Night' ringing loud and clear throughout the country. The Prince of Wales won the Derby with *Diamond Jubilee*. On the Queen's birthday, it seemed as if all London turned out for the

211

opening by the Princess of the mammoth bazaar in aid of war funds at the Royal Palace Hotel, Kensington. Many of the vast crowd had paid the guinea entrance fee just to see Alexandra, and there were continuous outbursts of enthusiasm and affection as she toured the eighty stalls.[49]

On 11 July Queen Victoria gave her last garden party. Five thousand people languished on the lawns of Buckingham Palace. It was blazing hot under a perfect blue sky while the air in the crowded tents was stifling (to provide air for a swooning lady, a well-meaning soldier cut a slit in the canvas wall: unfortunately his sword grazed the backside of a maid standing on the outside). The Queen, Alexandra beside her, drove in an open carriage drawn by two small white horses, the other royals following on foot. Many of the visitors guessed that this was the last time they would see their Sovereign, that at the next Garden Party the lovely woman of fifty-six beside her would be the star. It was the climax of the reign. Lady Monkswell said: 'This party made such an impression on me I seemed to come back from it another creature.'[50]

Quickly the Queen's health deteriorated. The strain of the war, sorrow over the death of 'Affie' and the sufferings which cancer had brought to 'Vicky' contributed. In addition she paid little attention to diet. (When told to go steady on raspberries and ice-cream, she cut out the raspberries and doubled up on the ice-cream.) At Balmoral for the autumn, early in November she drove round the cottages to say goodbye to her tenants, bidding them to keep well until she came back. But she did not return.

Alexandra was troubled as to what to give her mother-in-law for Christmas, what gift for an old and ill woman who could see little and had everything. But she knew the Queen loved a surprise and decided that, in deep secrecy, she would have a miniature painted of the Queen's two Pomeranians, Marco and Turi, whom she adored. Mrs Gertrude Massey was commissioned to do the painting and in considerable trepidation she reported to Windsor. There the help of the household had been enlisted and the artist was provided with a room containing a large screen behind which she could hide if the Queen appeared unexpectedly. The snag was that the dogs were never away from their mistress except when she was engaged on official business or out for drives. Some days the artist waited all afternoon and no dogs appeared. On others, a footman would hurriedly appear with Marco and Turi and tell Mrs Massey how long she had to work. On one occasion a party of foreign royalties, on a tour of inspection of the Castle, came into the room and stopped to chat. Hiding behind her screen, Mrs Massey was overcome by the desire to sneeze.[51] But, on Christmas Day at Osborne, Queen Victoria received the present which so delighted her. The almost illegible letter of thanks was the last that Alexandra received from her.

On 3 January 1901 Alexandra carried out her final engagement as Princess of Wales. She was hostess at a luncheon at Buckingham Palace to Lord Roberts on his triumphant return from South Africa. She retired to Sandringham, while her husband headed north for Chatsworth. This was to be the last fling of Albert Edward, Prince of Wales. The Press reported:

> The evening of Friday, Jan. 11, the last of the Prince of Wales's visit to the Duke and Duchess of Devonshire, was devoted to amateur theatricals . . . At half past nine the Prince, accompanied by the Duchess of Devonshire and the guests who had been present at the dinner-party, took their places in the ball-room. The entertainment opened with a French comedietta 'Le Bibelot' . . . Miss Muriel Wilson and Mrs Willie James danced . . . After supper the house-party danced 'Sir Roger de Coverley' in the Picture Gallery.[52]

Alice Keppel was there but her name did not appear among the printed list of guests.

Worrying messages came from Osborne about the Queen's health. Deeply upset, the Prince dined alone with Agnes Keyser on the 18th; she was the one person that he wished to talk to.[53] On the evening of the 19th an urgent call from the Isle of Wight brought the Queen's relations to her side. The German Emperor came from Berlin in a special train, driving the engine himself. The Princess of Wales and Princess Victoria travelled from Norfolk.

Queen Victoria faded slowly away, as a great ship sinks into a calm sea. On the morning of the 22nd she talked to her Battenberg grandchildren about their lessons and their pets.[54] Soon

213

after the last of the light had done she quietly slipped away as Alexandra, holding her hand, prayed by her bedside.

The yacht *Alberta* carried the dead Queen to the mainland, Windsor-bound:

> We took Her silent form to glide
> Where reached from shore to shore
> Her glorious Fleet. Each warship's side
> Rang, mile on mile, above the tide,
> The Queen's salute once more![55]

On the afternoon of Monday, 4 February, all Windsor shops and offices were closed between two and four and every window was shrouded as the local people gathered for the last act. Queen Victoria's coffin was borne on a gun-carriage, down the descent towards the forest, to the Mausoleum at Frogmore where lay the remains of Prince Albert. Behind the coffin walked King Edward VII, Emperor William of Germany and Queen Alexandra, holding the hand of Prince Edward of York, clad in a sailor suit. The royal pipers played the 'Lament' of the Black Watch.[56]

In the deep tomb Albert's coffin could be seen, his sword lying upon it. Now his widow's was lowered by her Life Guards and once again the two of them were side by side. Still holding the hand of her grandson (known as David), Alexandra came out into the darkening afternoon. The cold was piercing.[57] Albert had asked to be buried among flowers and his widow had built his last home in a garden. Today flowers were everywhere, a thick border of them lining the Mausoleum steps.[58]

Alexandra, a tear glistening under the crêpe, looked up the hill towards the grey walls of Windsor. 'I, Alexandra, Queen of Great Britain and Ireland, Empress of India, Princess of Denmark . . .' In the flower-beds the snowdrops were pushing up their heads. It was all beginning again.

SIXTEEN

'Vivat Regina'

As Queen, Alexandra was an immediate success, somewhat to her own surprise, as before her mother-in-law's death she had openly admitted that she dreaded the role and was doubtful of her capability to fill it. Yet, before many weeks had passed, she was very much the leading lady and obviously enjoying herself. She objected to the suggestion that she should be called Queen *Consort*, saying that she intended to be *Queen*.[1] She declared that, as Princess of Wales, she had never been allowed to do what she chose to do. 'Now I shall do as I like,'[2] she announced, and the raising of her annual income to £60,000 strengthened her arm.[3] She showed her new spirit when advice came from those planning the coronation as to what she should wear. She replied: 'I know better than all the milliners and antiquaries. I shall wear exactly what I like, and so shall my ladies – *Basta!*'[4]

Her success was due largely to the care and backing of her husband. Edward VII took to kingship from the first day of his reign, adapting himself as easily as the Regency rake had done eighty years before. He had been trained from birth to regard himself as a person apart and Prince Albert had drummed into him the monarchial creed. His mother had prepared the way for him. But Alexandra had been brought up in a simple, democratic way and, during her thirty-eight years as Princess of Wales, she had been friendly with all manner of folk and Edward now feared that advantage might be taken of this familiarity. He watched her carefully, checking that all treated her with the respect due to a Queen.

Within a month of his accession he created her a Lady of the Order of the Garter. This was a most unusual and unexpected honour for a woman and Garter King gave the view that the rules prohibited him placing the Queen's banner in St George's Chapel. The King pointed out that there had been a number of ladies so honoured in the fourteenth and fifteenth centuries, the last two being Margaret and Elizabeth, daughters of Henry VII, in 1495. The banner went up.[5] At the same time Edward agreed to his wife taking the headship of the projected Queen Alexandra's Imperial Military Nursing Service, a plan which matured the following year.[6]

On 14 February 1901 Alexandra underwent her baptism of queenly duties at the opening of parliament, the King having arranged that she wore the Garter Ribbon for the occasion. The House of Lords was packed and there was not room left for a mouse. The Archbishop of Canterbury, old and wide, came in late and sat down partly upon the small Archbishop of York, blotting him out. Lady Monkswell was there:

> At last the East door was opened, and the procession marched slowly in – in perfect silence. They looked a perfect blaze of colour, and the light was turned on at the same moment so that we could see it all. The King was in uniform, and carried a hat with white plumes; the Queen in black and covered with diamonds; they both had magnificents robes of state, red velvet lined with miniver, the train carried by pages, and large white ermine capes. Queen Alexandra had a little diamond crown on the top of her head and looked a perfect picture sitting in her chair of state. It was all so perfect and beautiful and unlike common life that, if it had not been for the strong sense of reality that never left one, we must have thought we were at the play.[7]

Thus began the glittering run which enriched the first decade of the twentieth century. On the royal stage the two stars were unchallenged until the curtain came down on 6 May 1910, only hours after the last applause for him had welled out as his horse, Witch of the Air, was led into the winner's enclosure at Kempton Park.

The relationship between the leading man and leading lady was strange: Alexandra was the master, stronger in character and more able to control her feelings. When some hitch occurred in ceremonial and the King became peeved and obstinate, it was to her that the courtiers turned to quieten him down. But even she was incapable of withstanding the sudden fits of uncontrollable anger which seized her husband. When his angry bellow was heard, ladies-in-waiting would hurry to the safety of their rooms and the menservants prepared themselves for an onslaught of abuse. A footman spilled a spot of spinach on to the King's waistcoat at dinner. Seizing the dish, Edward emptied the entire contents over himself and strode from the room, muttering that he might as well make a proper job of it.[8] But at other times the Queen exercised her discipline. On being told that she was late for an appointment and that the King was waiting, she replied: 'Keep him waiting. It will do him good.'[9]

However, this strength in Alexandra, together with her obvious popularity, brought out a pettiness in Edward. He began to undertake more and more minor duties on his own and refused to allow her to accept certain honorary positions offered her by societies and institutions. On his Birthday Parade he refused to allow her to drive round the review with him – the parade was for him, he said. She said that she would watch from a Palace window. But immediately he had left she ran downstairs, jumped into a carriage and drove round in the procession.[10] There was a touch of mischief and ragging in her management. When, at a Windsor evening, the King sent an order to the bandmaster to play Offenbach, wishing to revive memories of happy days spent with Hortense Schneider in Paris, she sent a counter-demand for Wagner. The embarrassed bandmaster opted out of the dilemma by playing Gilbert and Sullivan, which amused Alexandra immensely. But there was no fun or lightness in the letter which she sent to Daisy, Countess of Warwick, saying clearly that she must see the King no more.

The first months of the reign were clouded by a family tragedy which drew husband and wife together. Vicky was dying from cancer. 'Every feature and limb distorted and that charming countenance quite unrecognizable, her mouth drawn up, her teeth project, her nostrils are dilated by her terrible struggle for breath which makes her nose bleed constantly and the whole face yellow.'[11] Alexandra went to Germany to comfort her sister-in-law and be with her as long as she could. The Empress died in August 1901, three months after Alexandra's return home.

It was fortunate therefore that the sound of childish laughter echoed around Sandringham. The Duke and Duchess of York had a long standing engagement to travel to Melbourne for the inauguration of the first Parliament of the Commonwealth of Australia. The thought of being parted from her 'Georgie' so soon after Queen Victoria's death upset Alexandra deeply and her husband decided that the tour should be cancelled. Fortunately, wiser counsel prevailed. The absence proved a tonic both for Alexandra and Edward and for the grandchildren who were left in their care for eight months.

David, aged seven, Bertie, six, Mary, four and baby Henry* moved into the Big House and a world far different to any they had so far experienced. As parents, the future King George V and Queen Mary lacked humanity and understanding, reverting to the stern and restricted upbringing practised by Victoria and Albert. The father bullied his children, ruling them by the threat of an evening summons to his study where he lectured and quoted adages. The mother was simply incapable of opening the gates of maternal feeling. Once with their grandparents, life was in strong contrast. The children were allowed to romp about the dining room, talk to grown ups and play around Alexandra as she dressed; they were taken to a variety of entertainments, to the despair of their teachers who were unable to keep to the rigid curriculum which they had been instructed to enforce. David never forgot that interlude of fun and sunshine and sought to recreate it in his later years.

But it was noted that the York children were small and backward in their absorption of learning. Young Bertie had bow legs, a weak chest and stammered. It was clear they were not strong and when the last born, John, proved to be an epileptic and mentally unstable, breeding ceased at York Cottage. The transference of weakness also appeared in the two daughters of Louise, Duchess of Fife, who showed signs of physical and mental upset. The shy Duchess kept them close to her, refusing to allow them to sample the fun and free-for-all offered by their grandparents. At the time this family weakness was attributed by some to syphilis. Later it was realized that the same weakness

* Edward VIII, George VI, the Countess of Harewood and the Duke of Gloucester. George, Duke of Kent was born in 1902 and John in 1905.

218

appeared in the offspring of Alexandra's sister Dagmar – whose husband had been a tower of physical strength. But this did not apply to the youngest sister, Thyra, whose illegitimate daughter was, in the event, to live to the age of ninety-four. Both Alexandra and Dagmar were sexually cold, while Thyra was not. A recent theory for the inherent weakness of the children and grandchildren concerned centres around the Rhesus factor.* If, in truth, Alexandra and Dagmar were in the category of Rhesus negatives, then many of the problems which faced the Royal Families of Britain and Russia can be more easily understood. While Queen Mary was strong on the maternal (Cambridge) side, there was weakness on the paternal (Teck). But the introduction of the Bowes-Lyon line seems to have given the strength necessary to overcome the weakness† while that of the ebullient Mountbattens appears to have wiped the frailty away entirely.

When George and May returned home at the end of 1901, they were created Prince and Princess of Wales. Planning for the Coronation now dominated the thoughts of all, from Westminister and Windsor to the village hall, from Balmoral to Melbourne, Montreal and Delhi, for there had not been such an occasion for sixty-four years. On the evening of 28 June 1838 Queen Victoria wrote in her diary: 'At 10 I got into the State Coach with the Duchess of Sutherland and Lord Albemarle, and we began our Progress. It was a fine day, and the crowds of people exceeded what I have ever seen . . . Their good humour and excessive loyalty was beyond everything, and I really cannot say *how* proud I feel to be Queen of *such* a *Nation*.'[12] Now the railways prepared to bring a far greater multitude from all cor-

---

* The great majority of people have in their blood an antigen in common with that of the Rhesus monkey. Only rarely is it missing. It is now a factor taken into consideration when blood is grouped for transfusion. If a man whose blood carries the dominant Rhesus factor – Rh positive – marries a woman who is Rh negative, the child is likely to be born Rh positive. The osmosis between the mother's blood supply and the child through the placenta can cause trouble if the blood of mother and child is incompatible. As the mother manufacturers antibodies to fight the alien blood, children are likely to be affected, each one more so than the last.

† Queen Elizabeth the Queen Mother's father, the Earl of Strathmore, reached his ninetieth year.

ners of the country and the big liners from all parts of the Empire, and the world. The date fixed for the ceremony was 26 June 1902. On 14 June King Edward became ill.

The doctors who were called in found him fractious, rude and impatient and determined to carry on with his crowning, the most important day in his life. He had become so swollen and overweight that the measurements around his chest and his stomach were identical – forty-eight inches.[13] They suspected appendicitis, but the press was told that it was lumbago. The doctors' fears were kept from Alexandra and she deputized for her husband at a military review and at Ascot. On 23 June the King and Queen travelled from Windsor to London to make ready for the great occasion. He was wearing an overcoat, although the day was warm. C. W. Stamper, the royal chauffeur, watched them drive from Paddington station: 'The Queen kept touching his arm to rouse him, and each time that she did so he lifted his chin a little, his hand struggled up to his head, and he raised his hat. He hardly opened his eyes at all.'[14]

That afternoon the climax came. It was Sir Francis Laking's unenviable task to tell the King and to persuade him to undergo an operation. He began:

'As I said at Windsor, your Majesty, it *is* perityphlitis.'

'I don't care what you call it,' the King answered, 'as long as you get me on my feet for the Coronation.'

Sir Francis stalled. 'Inflammation of the appendix – an organ useless to man, a cul-de-sac of the large intestine where noxious matters chance to pass into its interior, where such material is retained and thus furnishes an appropriate breeding ground for bacteria and abscess formation.'

'Get to the point,' said the King.

'An abscess must find an outlet and if it opens into the general cavity of the abdomen it will cause peritonitis . . .'

'To the point,' snapped the King.

'Peritonitis is an inflammation of so intense a nature that it is generally fatal. That is why we must operate immediately.'

'*Operate* – immediately?'

'Yes, your Majesty.'

The men stared at one another for a few seconds. Then, clenching his fist, the King roared: 'Impossible!' Sir Francis was left with no alternative but to tell the sick man that it was beyond doubt that the strain and fatigue of the ceremony in the Abbey would kill him.

The King lay back, his hand over his eyes. Almost in a whisper he said that, if such was the case, he had no choice but to agree.[15] The news was kept from Alexandra, for that evening she had to preside over a dinner party for two hundred people at Buckingham Palace. She learned early next morning, shortly before the public announcement. Tens of thousands of visitors from all over the country and the world turned sadly towards their homes.

The operation was to be performed by Alexandra's old friend, Sir Frederick Treves. Soon after noon, she walked beside her husband, her hand in his, into the palace room which had been hastily converted into an operating theatre. She apologized to the doctors that he was wearing an old and favourite dressing-gown.[16] She was beside him as the anaesthetic was applied, holding him down, trying to comfort him as he struggled wildly and his face went black.[17] When he lay still and unconscious, she stood back meekly, hands clasped, waiting. To his horror, Sir Frederick realized that it was her intention to stay throughout the operation. Politely, but very firmly, she was asked to leave. Without demur she joined her son and her daughters in the room next door. The next forty minutes were the worst in her life, more poignant even than the death of Eddy. At last the door was opened and she was told that the operation had proved completely successful.

She took him away to convalesce on the royal yacht lying in the Solent. By 15 July he was out of danger and regaining his strength. The Coronation was fixed for 9 August. Alexandra said to the Archbishop of York: 'It is quite different from the *last* time. Then we were thinking too much of the pageant and not enough about the religious part of the ceremony.'[18] Different it certainly was to be, less bedecked by pomp and the leaders of the world and shortened to save the King's strength, yet it was more charged with emotion, an emotion similar to that aroused when, as Prince of Wales, Bertie was snatched from the jaws of death on 14 December 1871.

Lady Jane Lindsay was early in the Abbey:

> When the Queen appeared it was like a vision coming
> through the dark archway of the screen. I never saw any-
> thing more beautiful. Her left hand was supported by the
> Bishop of Oxford in a wonderful gold and white cape, the
> Bishop on her right in dusky red damask. During the slow
> progress the opening anthem 'I was glad' was sung by the
> choir, broken by the ringing cry of the Westminster boys,
> 'Vivat Regina'. Then came the King, his cap of maintenance
> on his head – a procession apart from hers. On reaching the
> Altar he removed his cap, bowed low to the Altar and sat
> down on a state chair on the south side. His voice taking the
> oath . . . rang through the building . . . After the oath, the
> King moved to the Coronation Chair for the anointing . . .
> Then the King was crowned, and at the moment a shout
> burst forth and a blaze of electric light was turned on, all the
> Peers crowning themselves. . . . The Peers' allegiance was
> immediately followed by a crowd of people closing round
> the Queen, who now slowly advanced to her Coronation
> chair where the Archbishop of York officiated. The gent-
> lemen with the canopy reappeared and held it till the four
> Duchesses moved up over the great space, and they held the
> poles during the anointing. Words fail to say how marvell-
> ous she looked moving down with her crown glittering
> with diamonds, a sceptre in each hand . . .[19]

Yet for Alexandra there had been one incident of crisis. Among
the Duchesses holding up the canopy was the Duchess of Marlborough. The four were dressed in red velvet trimmed with
miniver and in their pockets were bars of chocolate to sustain
them during the five hour attendance. The Duchess recounted:

> When the Queen left her throne to kneel before the aged
> Archbishop to be anointed, we rose to hold the canopy over
> her. From my place on her right I looked down on her
> bowed head, her hands meekly folded in prayer, and
> watched the shaking hand of the Archbishop as, from the
> spoon which held the sacred oil, he anointed her forehead. I
> held my breath as a trickle escaped and ran down her nose.
> With a truly royal composure she kept her hands clasped in
> prayer; only a look of anguish betrayed concern as her eyes
> met mine and seemed to ask, 'Is the damage great?'[20]

SEVENTEEN

❦❧

On the Move

There was considerable speculation and gossip over the frequent partings of Alexandra and Edward. Time and again the King travelled to the Continent *en garçon*. Alexandra, becoming piqued at this treatment, either shut herself up at Sandringham, disappeared to Denmark, or went on cruises in the Mediterranean, calling upon her Greek relations. She kept her movements to herself and on one occasion Edward complained to his son that he had no idea what 'Mama's' plans were for the coming weeks.[1] This was strange indeed, for the multitude of duties of a sovereign and his consort demand a near daily schedule for months ahead. She was not even allowed to accompany the King on the famous trip to Paris of 1903 when the *entente cordiale* was born. It was not until 1907 that she was invited by him to visit France and then 'her joy was that of a girl – she cried it from the house-tops'.[2]

There were two main reasons for Edward leaving his wife behind. The first, and the lesser, concerned his own private convenience. When on holiday at Biarritz, he was in the company of Alice Keppel and clearly Alexandra would be superfluous. In Paris he liked to be free to visit the families, and the ladies, whom he had known well twenty, thirty years before. At Marienbad his way of life was fast and social and he preferred to play it unencumbered by a wife. He attempted to give a semblance of balance to his travel programme by accompanying Alexandra to Denmark, but the old King bored him and there was little amusement.

The second reason was that Alexandra was a very outspoken woman and, now that she was Queen, a tactless remark might cause international repercussions. She was a simple woman and she saw matters straight. She hated Germany on account of the Schleswig-Holstein war of 1864 and she continued to hate Germany for that reason. 'The Duchies belong to Papa', she had said at that time, and for her there was no deviating and no forgiving. She recalled vividly both the Seven Weeks War of 1866, when the southern states of Germany and Austria were humbled by Prussia, and the Franco–German War four years later. She saw clearly that Britain was next on the list, and that Denmark would suffer in the process. In secrecy she received a newspaper published in Jutland by the Schleswig 'underground movement'. This paper related how the Danes were being maltreated – 'forced selling of their homes to Germans; burning of bibles written in Danish; schoolchildren torn from their mothers' arms and forced to learn German'.[3] If it had come to the ears of Berlin that the Queen of Great Britain was receiving such intelligence, it would have upset even more the difficult relationship which existed between the two countries.

Then there were Alexandra's links with Russia to be considered. The people of Britain, in the main, were strongly critical of the autocratic regime of Nicholas II, and the treatment of Jews was little better than it had been under his father, Alexander III. Dagmar was always horrified and astonished by her brother-in-law's philo-semitism. As a result it was not considered politic for her to visit Alexandra and it was not until 1907 that she visited England, after an interval of thirty-four years. In addition, Alexandra was a firm supporter of Greece. The Glucksburgs stuck together and if King George was in trouble (as he often was) he could rely on the full support of sister Alix.

Under the circumstances it was understandable that the King did not allow his wife to see the contents of the official boxes. But – and here came the rub – he allowed the Princess of Wales to do so, having high opinion of her intelligence and tact. He said to his heir: 'You can show them to May.'

George showed surprise and answered: 'But Mama doesn't see them!'

'No, but that's a very different thing,' was the King's comment.[4]

Hence there existed a high degree of jealousy on the Queen's

The master figure of the Edwardian era with Queen Alexandra

The little Caesarevitch with
his sailor friend. A picture
taken by Alexandra, who was
a keen and expert photographer,
during the meeting with the
Russian royal family at Reval
in 1908

The Kaiser and King Edward
at Friedrichshof, Germany
in August 1908

part towards May. She looked upon her daughter-in-law in the light of a poor relation, boring and German inclined. Then May made a slip. In a letter, the contents of which became known, she referred to the home of the Glucksburgs as 'that vile D . . . . k'.[5] This made life difficult for her husband, George, who was 'a middle of the road man', content to shoot birds, lick stamps, lecture his children and carry out official engagements with the minimum of fuss.

The reason for the King's embargo is open to a number of interpretations. One, commonly accepted in certain quarters, is that Alexandra was feather-brained and unable to comprehend matters political. This does not stand up to examination. It is only necessary to read her memorandum of June 1890 on the subject of Britain having a protectorate over Zanzibar in exchange for the North Sea island of Heligoland to appreciate her ability.* Lord Roseberry congratulated her upon it and passed it

* Heligoland is an Island in the South-east of the North Sea, and belonged from time immemorial to Denmark, until the British Government demanded the cession of the island at the Peace of Kiel in 1814, at the same time that Norway was severed from Denmark.

The island is more or less a barren rock, and one may well ask why the Government of Great Britain should have insisted on taking possession of it when Denmark still held the whole East Coast of the North Sea as far as the Elbe with no Naval Ports. Nor had Germany any Navy at all, and Holland was reduced to insignificance. That the British Government insisted on having Heligoland clearly shows the great foresight of the Minister then at the head of Foreign Affairs, and time now shows how right he was. Germany is at present in possession of the Coasts of Schleswig and Holstein, as well as of the ancient territory bordering the North Sea, and has acquired both sides of the mouth of the Elbe. She has built an important Naval Port in the Bay of Jahde, and has begun the construction of the great canal from Kiel to the Elbe which will enable her to bring her Fleet, stationed at Kiel, into the Elbe and the North Sea in a few hours' time. But Heligoland dominates the whole of the German Coast and the mouths of the great rivers flowing into the'North Sea, with the Bay of Jahde, and a British Fleet stationed at Heligoland, can, in time of war, blockade all the outlets from Germany to the North Sea, and reduce her Fleet and Commerce to inactivity. This eventuality may be remote, but if this possibility was foreseen in 1814, surely it ought not to be lost sight of by a British Minister in 1890. Moreover there can be no doubt that Germany has in view the annexation of Holland. In the treaty of alliance between Prince Bismarck and Count Andrassy in 1879 the former indeed demanded and obtained from Austria a free hand which allowed him to do what he liked with Holland. There may be statesmen in this country who would look **upon such** an event with a certain amount of indifference, but

on to Mr Gladstone who announced it to be 'a remarkable and very confidential document'.[6]

As to her tact and balance and foresight, here is an extract from an interview which she granted to the important French newspaper, *Le Gaulois*, in 1905, at a time when royal interviews were rare indeed. She declined to discuss politics but spoke of the political excitement of the day:

> In the troublous times through which we are passing we cannot but be affected by the excitement, sometimes natural, that seizes the masses of the people. – Believe me, if the social question is to be solved one day, it will be so by the exercise of virtues which women practise – the virtues of mutual love, of respect for justice and charity. You men talk of war, we women speak for peace – peace within every nation and between all nations. Brought up under the teaching of a King with a deep sense of justice, I have, like him, always sought to inculcate love and charity. I always have a dread of these warlike preparations on which the nations are incessantly occupied, of your soldiers, of your cannons – of

---

when they consider that the mouths of the Schelde, with Flushing, belong to Holland (not Belgium) it is difficult to believe that such indifference, with what might be the consequence in regard to Antwerp and Belgium, should really exist. Germany, in possession of Holland, can construct a Naval Arsenal (and will certainly do it) at Flushing within a few hours' sail from the Thames. But England, in holding Heligoland, prevents a German fleet from operating against Holland and from reducing the country in a short time both by land and by sea.

In a defensive point of view it may be said that Heligoland in the hands of England covers the East Coast of these islands against any attack, while in the hands of Germany it would be made the basis of operations against England, and our Government in a short time, or at all events in a few years hence, would have to apply to Parliament and to the pockets of the taxpayer for the millions of money which would have to be expended in Fortifications that it would be necessary to erect along the coast in order to defend it against Foreign invasion.

If England cedes Heligoland to Germany, a precedent would at once be created for Spain to claim Gibraltar (another *barren* rock and a very expensive one) and Italy Malta, and there would indeed be but little reason for our retention of Cyprus which Germany might ask for as a convenient Station for her communications with her East African Colonies. At all events the opinions of the naval and military authorities as to the strategical value of Heligoland to England (and to Germany) should be submitted to the Crown before Diplomatic negotiations are completed.   June 1890.

all the inflammable material which they are accumulating and which may break forth into a conflagration such as may plunge humanity into Mourning and afflict the common Father of us all.[7]

An explanation nearer to the truth is that Queen Alexandra was on most friendly terms with many of the leading statesmen and service chiefs and the King feared that she might turn her almost irresistible charm upon them should she learn of secret negotiations and wish to further her own beliefs as to the course which should be taken. In addition it must be allowed that such knowledge might strengthen her anti-German bias. Thus the boxes remained closed to her and the King continued to travel the continent alone.

But there was one journey across the sea upon which Edward insisted that his wife accompany him, and that was when he went to Ireland. Apart from the fact that there were no problems there regarding Germans, Russians or mistresses, Alexandra was the member of the royal family who came nearest to being loved by the Irish. Their first visit was in July 1903 and Princess Victoria accompanied them. After an enthusiastic welcome in Dublin, it was decided that the royal party should see the wilds of Connemara. With difficulty a sufficient number of motor cars were assembled and a start was made at Leenane. There the oldest inhabitant was detailed to greet them and, being unrehearsed, called for 'Three cheers for King Henry VI and his Quaine'.

The question of security on the unfrequented roads worried the head of the Royal Irish Constabulary. He decided that there must be no obvious display of force but at the same time was determined that no risks be taken. He accordingly summoned men from all over the country. He dressed them all the same – straw hat, Norfolk jacket, watchchain, knickerbockers – issued them with bicycles, stationed them a hundred yards apart and ordered them to lie in a casual pose on the verge as if tired tourists. As the royal car passed, each man sprang to attention, thereafter resuming the lounging position.

Connemara decided that a special reception should be staged and a cavalry escort was decided upon. Every man and boy who could produce a quadruped was to take part. Sir Henry Robinson was in the car with the King and the Queen:

'The motor swung round the Lough Ina road, turning into the straight for the Recess, when we suddenly found ourselves in the midst of an amazing mob of horsemen: farmhorses, cart-horses, ponies, donkeys, of all sizes and descriptions, mounted by men and boys in rags and tatters, black coats, flannels or home-made stuffs. Some had saddles, others none, some had reins, some straw ropes. There they were all waiting on the high ground up the mountainside to see the arrival of the cars, and the moment the cars came into sight they were off down the mountainside like an avalanche, yelling, cheering, laughing, knocking each other over and leaping over the ditch on to the road with a speed that sent most of them on to the bog at the other side.'[8]

A visit was made to the quarries and to honour the occasion the owner had had a marble ink stand made for the King and a harp for the Queen. He learned too late that Princess Victoria was also in the party. He bewailed:

Begorra, there'll be a bloody row in the palace over this, and it's all my fault so it is. Sure I never heard tell about the Princess coming. What's to be done at all? Oh, my God, this is fearful! Well, the only thing for me is to give the ink stand to the King and to put the little harp between the two Royal ladies, and then clear out and let them fight it out among themselves as to who is to keep it.[9]

He later recounted the moment in the royal visit which impressed him most:

The Princess Victoria, in stepping out of the carriage, brushed her skirt against the wheel and splashed it with yellow sand. And the Queen, the Queen of England, mind ye, stooped down as humble as the poorest woman in the land and brushed the Princess's skirt with her own hand! There she was with the First Lord of the Admiralty beside her, who she could have ordered to do it, and other great lords and generals, but no! humble she was, and humbly she brushed the skirt with her own hand before everyone, and an example to everyone. Oh, dear God, the humbleness of it![10]

The King and Queen made another successful trip to Ireland in 1904 but that of 1907, during Lord Aberdeen's Viceroyalty, was marred by an incident which sent Edward into a fury. The

Crown Jewels, including the star and insignia of the Order of St Patrick, were stolen from the safe at Dublin Castle. Efforts to quieten him failed. 'I don't want your theories,' he roared. 'I want my jewels.' An explanation was proffered by a Dublin jarvey as he drove an official to the railway station:

> The jules, is it? Well! Well! And d'ye say ye never heard tell what way they were took? My! Oh my! Whisht now and I'll give ye the word in private, and there's not many in Dublin has it besides meself, but I have it for a fact from a chap in the D Division that's a cousin of me a'nt. Whisper now! Sure it was the King himself took them! He was afther having great card-playing with the Duke of Devonshire, and he dhropped a power o' money, so he sent round Lord Aberdeen wan night to take them out of the safe and bring them to him and say nothin' at all about it. Sure they were his own, and hadn't he as good a right to take them as he would have to sell his own gould watch and chain? Well, now, what I'm tellin' ye is a fact, and believe me ye'll never hear tell of them jules again.[11]

The jarvey was correct in his forecast.

1903 was a happy year for Alexandra, for, in addition to the success of her Irish tour, she rejoiced at a birth and at a wedding. After eight years of marriage, Maud – Princess Charles of Denmark – had a baby boy. It was named Olav,* the only live son born to Alexandra's daughters. The wedding was of her nephew Andrew, son of King George of Greece, and Alice, eighteen-year-old daughter of Prince and Princess Louis of Battenberg.† Alexandra had been a strong supporter of Andrew in his choice and she made one of her rare appearances in Germany for the wedding. The venue was Darmstadt. It was the last royal fiesta to sparkle in Europe and differences were forgotten. Hohenzollerns came from Berlin, Romanoffs from St Petersburg, and the Greeks in a crowd from Athens. Alexandra – without her husband – was the leader of the family fun which the Glucksburgs always enjoyed when together. At the reception tall

---

* Afterwards King Olav of Norway.

† Afterwards Marquess and Marchioness of Milford Haven. He married, in 1884, Queen Victoria's granddaughter, Princess Victoria of Hesse and the Rhine.

hats were sat upon, spectacles stolen, hair-dos ruffled and rice bags flew in a fusillade. Emperor Nicholas chased the car as the bride and groom drove away and Alice hit him over the head with a slipper. Eighteen years later the last child of the marriage, a baby named Philip, was rescued from the Greek revolutionaries by HMS *Calypso*. The crew of the cruiser made much of him, and fashioned an orange-box into a cot for him.

In 1905 Queen Alexandra's influence in the international field was widened when her daughter, Maud, became Queen of Norway. United to Sweden for ninety-one years, the Norwegians now decided to go it alone. The question was – should the country be a monarchy or a republic? Prince Charles of Denmark was put forward as a candidate for King, but Alexandra, who was in Denmark at the time, counselled care, for she feared that the choice might lead to war in Scandinavia. Then it was learned that the Emperor of Germany coveted the throne for one of his sons, causing her and her husband to back the Danish Prince. King Christian IX gave his permission and the daughter and son-in-law of King Edward and Queen Alexandra became Queen Maud and King Haakon VII of Norway. The crowning was to be the last important event in the life of eighty-eight year old King Christian. He died on the afternoon of 29 January 1906, only an hour after he had danced with his daughter Dagmar to show how fit he felt.[12] The news, therefore, came as a complete shock to Alexandra and, as was her habit when upset, she locked herself away in Sandringham.

Longing to be reunited with her family, in the spring she accompanied her husband on a trip to Greece. They had been invited by King George to watch the revival of the Olympic Games in Athens. One result in the Games further exacerbated Anglo-German relations, at this time at a critical stage. The British fencing team outclassed the German and the sight of the fat German captain 'being whacked all over his body in sabre play'[13] sent the crowds into roars of laughter. Unfortunately the thousands in the stands appeared to consider that King Edward and Queen Alexandra were personally responsible for the victory and directed their cheering at the pair, a point which was not missed in Berlin.

In 1905 Alexandra made her debut as star on the foreign stage; she undertook a solo official visit to Portugal. A special interest was attached to this as the German Emperor was to follow a few days later on a similar visit. In the outcome Alexandra out-pointed William and her success established her as a leading personality of Europe. At Lisbon the King of Portugal met her on the royal yacht and escorted her to the shore in his great state barge manned by eighty rowers wearing red uniforms, and the crowds roared their approval of the lovely Queen. There was a State banquet and luncheon with Queen Maria Pia at the old Moorish palace at Cintran, followed by a drive up the steep road to the Pena Palace in carriage drawn by four mules. After the two visits were over the British Ambassador, Sir Maurice de Bunsen, wrote:

> The Queen sent for me before she left, and I had a quarter of an hour with her alone in her sitting-room at the Neces-sidades Palace. She was charming, full of impressions of the visit, which was enthusiastically received by the people, usually so quiet and undemonstrative – and especially the night of the Opera, when they simply went mad with delight at seeing her. She gave £100 for the poor.
>
> Yesterday we saw the procession of the German Emperor in the wonderful old State carriages – really well done by this little country. The crowds were not stirred to enthusiasm, as they were by the Queen, whose personal charm carried everything before her.[14]

Having noted the success of the visit to his neighbour, King Alfonso of Spain was eager to join the band-waggon, and in 1907 he asked the British King and Queen to visit Madrid. He was indebted to them both as it had been while on a visit to them that he had fallen violently in love with Princess Ena of Battenberg, granddaughter of Queen Victoria, and it had been through their help and cooperation that he had been able to marry her. The manner in which Edward and Alexandra had pushed aside the hurdle of a British Princess marrying a Catholic was the root cause of the rumour that both the King and Queen were Catholic minded and that Edward was received into the Catholic Church on his deathbed.[15] During the wedding procession through Madrid in May 1906 a bomb had been thrown, with resultant

231

carnage among people and horses. It was clear that Edward and Alexandra could not be exposed to the risk of another such outrage and Sir Charles Hardinge wrote to Lord Knollys: 'Our government must be quite firm for some years to come on the subject of a visit by the King to Madrid, as the Spanish police is hopeless, and there appears to be no prospect of improvement.'[16]

In peaceful Norfolk the King and Queen had a new interest and source of amusement in the shape of their new grandson, Olav. Olav was an only child, individual, perky, unrestricted, leading a very different life to his cousins of Wales, regimented and bullied at York Cottage. He came with his parents on frequent visits to Appleton House and the up-rated farmhouse was the scene of family teas. Olav told fierce stories of the cold of Norway in winter and informed his mother that he spoke the language better than she did because he was a native. Getting butter and jam over his fingers while revelling in buttered toast, the sarcastic parental suggestion was made that he should put both of his hands into the jam pot. He did.[17] He was a child after Alexandra's heart and ever a favourite.

EIGHTEEN

❦❦❦

Queen and Nurse

In a world preparing for the bonfire of war, Alexandra was the lady who could have been the most likely to strike the match. And war was coming, a course seemingly determined upon by Berlin. Emperor William II returned home after the funeral of Queen Victoria, softened and anglicized. Those who had war in mind soon altered that, for William was easy to influence and easily upset. For twelve years, as Emperor, he had had the whip-hand over his uncle. Now Edward VII ruled an Empire upon which the sun never set and William's title of 'All Highest' had a false ring about it. The British King, quite understandably, made the point clear, for he had been forced to swallow many slights and insults when he was only heir.

In 1902 Germany began her preparations. Spies were planted about Britain, positioned in high spots along the banks of the river Trent and at vantage points in the Midlands, sketching, making friends with the military, preparing to flash the guiding lights for the Zeppelins.

Alexandra's hatred for William increased after the death of her mother, who had been castigated in obituaries in the German Press. When in 1903 he made sudden plans to visit Copenhagen at the time of a reunion of the royal family, Alexandra was furious. Thyra, who was already there, left with her husband and daughters on the day before he was due to arrive.[1] The feud became more bitter still when Alexandra learned that, on his return to Germany, the Emperor had boasted of how he had cajoled the Danish King. At a Berlin function he had repeated Count von Moltke's observation: 'Poor King of Denmark. The founder of a new dynasty, he began his reign by losing one half of

233

the realm. Sweeping reductions were inevitable in the Court and administration. Indeed, it is doubtful if this state can continue to exist as an independent kingdom.'[2]

When the Emperor visited Sandringham in 1902, and the atmosphere was icy, a lady-in-waiting noticed that Alexandra could scarce bear to shake hands with him. There may have been a hidden cause for this. William was not only mentally unstable, but sexually also, and many in Germany expected the mental illnesses which had overtaken Frederick William IV and King Ludwig of Bavaria to claim him with the passing years. Adoring beautiful women as he did, it was upon their hands and arms that his fetish was concentrated. This perhaps stemmed from his own handicap of a withered arm. He would summon selected ladies to *tête-a-tête* meetings and then slowly peel of their long gloves, after which he would cover the length from their finger nails to their elbows with passionate kisses. Jewels were the reward for such indulgence, but some of the ladies, puzzled and amused, talked.[3] His weakness was common knowledge at the Court. Although Alexandra played her queenly role with all the control that she could muster, on occasion she let slip and made a sly dig. Noting that the Emperor was toying with his food at dinner, she taunted him: 'You ride, you work, you take a lot of trouble. Why don't you eat? Eating is good for the brain.'[4]

'He adores noise,' she told the French Ambassador. 'He meddles with everything, he will play the part of Charlemagne and domineer over all the Sovereigns. He will undertake everything at once and, though he always assumes an air of assurance and superior knowledge, he is often mistaken . . .'[5] Comments began to appear in the press about her obvious dislike of all things German. Her name was coupled with that of the more outspoken critic of Germany, Dagmar, the Dowager Empress of Russia. When the two sisters met in Denmark, as they often did, there were suspicions that they were hatching trouble. After King Edward's death the *Frankfurter Zeitung* declared that the two had long been in league to prepare for a world war and that they were 'the centre of the international anti-German conspiracy'.[6]

Although mistrusting German intentions, George and Mary, Prince and Princess of Wales, had always liked William II and there is no doubt that to a certain extent they were fooled by him.

After all, he was a close relation and he still had his supporters in the British Royal Family. Prince and Princess Christian, never popular with Alexandra, had strong German links and their daughter, Marie Louise, had married a German, and the fact that the marriage had ended in disaster did not affect their friendship with the Emperor. The son of the late Prince Leopold, Duke of Saxe-Coburg and Gotha, was under the Emperor's thumb, while, in the words of Sir George Arthur, the Prince of Wales regarded his German relations with 'a languid interest',[7] and resisted William's urgent demands that he visit more frequently the German regiment of which, reluctantly, he had been made Colonel.[8] He did not face up to the probability that shortly he and his cousin would be the heads of great nations locked in the catastrophe of war.

Emperor William had been given cause to suspect the animosity of Alexandra. In his preparations for war, which continued unceasingly, he had seen the importance of the neutrality of Denmark, but a Denmark strong enough to ensure neutrality – while allowing Germany to use the Baltic ports. He had accordingly visited Copenhagen and, as he thought, made good progress in this direction with King Christian, who had a horror of his country being over-run and wished for neutrality, but neutrality in its true sense. Thereafter, Christian was invited to Potsdam and again the Emperor thought that his plan would succeed. Bülow was entrusted to take the visiting monarch home to Denmark and to fix the details. But suddenly Christian went cold on the idea and 'talked with animation about every subject under heaven, but sedulously avoided the neutrality issue'. The Emperor searched for a reason for the sudden change of heart and, to his satisfaction, found it. It was none other than Queen Alexandra.[9]

He was soon given further grounds for his suspicions. In 1904 Admiral Sir John Fisher had been appointed Britain's First Sea Lord. He was a man who 'adored the ladies and detested the Germans'. Among the ladies he adored was Alexandra and he admitted that he would have liked to marry her. She wrote to him as 'Dear Admiral Jack' and progressed to 'My beloved Admiral . . .' They were two of a kind, bound together by belief and taste, a similarity in social outlook and a common foe. They both liked dancing and for him, and him alone, she allowed the carpet at Windsor to be rolled back after dinner. It was as if Oliver Montagu had come back to lighten her autumn days. They had the same sense of fun and her letters to him were always lighthearted.

Fisher and the Queen were at one in their interpretation of recent European history. He believed that the turn in events would have been altered if the British fleet had been sent to the Baltic at the time of the Schleswig-Holstein war of 1864 – as we have seen, a course urged by Bertie and his wife. He was also in agreement with Alexandra that Heligoland should not have been exchanged for Zanzibar. He wanted the strength of the fleet to be in the North Sea, *'where the fight will be!* perhaps off the Heligoland (which was won by the sword and given up by the pen!)'.[10] The King had complete faith in Fisher and showed it by appointing him to be his principal naval ADC, thus having direct contact with him. Lord Esher, a close friend of Edward's, assured Fisher in 1904: 'The King will always back you.'[11]

Fisher came into office at a time when Germany's naval might was looming up as a peril. It would have been a simple solution for him to match ship for ship, however disastrous the end result might prove. But with the scientific and industrial progress which came with the new century a wind of change was blowing through the electorate, bringing with it demands for more measures for social equity, such as pensions and better education. Many felt that public expenditure should be so directed rather than be lavished on expensive ships of war.

Fisher found his answer in increased efficiency, and was absolutely ruthless in obtaining it. The die-hards still adhered to the nineteenth-century gunboat policy, with ships, mostly outdated and often over-crewed, scattered around the globe, ready to fire a round or two as an antidote to a native rising or foreign insults to the flag. He introduced a new and highly efficient class of warship named the Dreadnought, of some 18,000 tons and highly armed. He cut out much dead wood, commenting: 'Reduced navy estimates are no sign of reduced naval efficiency. On the contrary, swollen estimates engender parasites both in men and ships which hamper the fighting qualities of the fleet. The pruning knife ain't pleasant for fossils and ineffectives, but it has to be used . . .'[12] The die-hards who clung to the old naval ideas formed up against the First Sea Lord and the navy was split right down the middle. At the head of the opposition stood Admiral Lord Charles Beresford. Neither the King nor the Queen had ever forgiven 'Charlie' Beresford for the part which he had played in the Lady Warwick affair, so 'Jackie' Fisher received unswerving royal support, but for which, as he said, his enemies would have eaten him! Fisher put forward the sensational suggestion that the German fleet should be scuppered at its moorings. So robbed of her sea might Germany would be unable to fight for many years. 'My God, Fisher, you must be mad!' was the King's comment. Other ears heard of the proposal and soon it became the main talking point in every ship of the British Navy. Emperor William learned of it and, in his fury, said that there was not a man in Germany who did not pray for the death of Sir John Fisher. Some there took the threat seriously. 'An invasion scare which convulsed Germany in November 1906 was followed in January 1907 by a fantastic rumour that Fisher was coming, which caused panic in Kiel for two days.'[13] The following year Fisher again put forward the plan, but the King refused to consider the idea, and the First Sea Lord lamented that Britain 'possessed neither a Pitt nor a Bismarck'.[14]

Fisher had another plan for quashing the German threat which this time indicated Alexandra's influence. The plan was to land a British force in Schleswig-Holstein without the announcement of a declaration of war. To Alexandra, such a declaration was unnecessary, as she was in touch with the 'underground' in Schleswig and still considered that the Duchies belonged to Denmark. 'When Fisher spoke of Britain's "betrayal of Denmark" and claimed he could capture the Kiel canal and recover Schleswig and Holstein, she prayed that the government would let him do so.'[15] The Emperor, well informed as usual, wrote: 'Fisher can no doubt land 100,000 men in Schleswig-Holstein, and the British Navy has reconnoitred the coast of Denmark with this object in view.'[16] Alexandra's prayer remained unanswered, the government giving an emphatic No. In fact the Liberal government was back-stepping. In the summer of 1906 it wished to cut the number of new Dreadnoughts to be built from four to three. Fisher, due to confer with the King, asked the Queen if he might have a seat on the royal train. She replied: 'Yes, with pleasure I will give you a seat in my train if you will give us a fourth Dreadnought.'[17] He promised her that it would be on the stocks by the time her birthday came round in December. He got his seat.

In Queen Alexandra, Fisher had a staunch friend who was not afraid to go into the fight. His drastic measures called down upon him vicious attacks from the Press, at home as well as abroad. After one such the Queen telegraphed him: 'It is alright. As I knew, pure invention and G . . . lies. Alexandra.'[18] She did not use a cypher, but sent the message straight, knowing full well that by doing so her words would become public knowledge.

In 1907 King Edward made a determined effort to better Anglo–German relations, and in particular the relations between himself and his nephew. He still believed that it was possible to avert war between the two nations, but insults and acrimony were now pouring from the German Emperor about the British King. At a dinner in March 1907, before three-hundred guests, William began to talk freely about the English policy and grew more and more excited. 'He complained bitterly of the intrigues that his uncle, the King of England, was carrying on against him. He said he knew all about them from private letters from France, and King Edward was equally hard at work in every other country. The whole press of the world, including that of America, had already been mobilised against him by English money, and it was extraordinary how much personal animosity his uncle's attitude revealed. He ended with the words: "He is a Satan; you can hardly believe what a Satan he is." '[19]

Obviously something had to be done. The King invited William and his wife to make a State visit to Windsor in November. The reply was couched in a most affable style: 'We are most thankful to you and Aunt Alix for the kind invitation. It is a most suitable thought of you to invite us to Windsor, and it would give us real pleasure to come over. I can well imagine that we might have good sport in the dear old park I know so well. Best love to Aunt Alix and believe me, ever your most affectionate nephew . . .'[20]

King Edward personally supervised every detail of the coming visit, the entertainments, the honours, the sport. Among the guests invited to the Castle to meet the Emperor were twenty-four royalties, including three queens. There were few visible hitches during that November stay and it was believed that the understanding between King and Emperor were better than they had been at any time since the notorious Kruger telegram. But Alexandra had told Bülow in 1900: 'My nephew has shown us that he is inwardly our enemy, even if he surprises himself. . . in flatteries, compliments, and assurances of his love and affection.' She was to be proved right once again.

One evening Emperor William dined with his suite. When the meal was over, the footmen withdrew, leaving the Germans alone. The gallery above was in darkness. An inquisitive boy who worked in the Castle wine cellar slipped silently through the gallery door and listened. The Emperor rose, his glass in his hand. He gave a toast, and that toast was repeated along the length of the hall. The toast was – *DER TAG* (the day). The boy left the gallery as silently as he had entered and retired to bed. He held his silence for the sound reason that he feared for his job. His 'crime' was that he had dared to eavesdrop on his 'betters' and it was doubtful that anything which he had to say or reveal would alter the position.

In 1907 a story appeared in the British Press that the Emperor Nicholas of Russia was about to abdicate. It was said that a secret villa had been purchased near Copenhagen for his retirement and that a well known London interior decorator had been engaged to carry out the alterations. Five bathrooms and electric central heating were being installed.[21] In fact the new owners were Queen Alexandra and her sister, Dagmar the Dowager Empress of Russia. The two had decided, at the funeral of King Christian, that they wanted a hideaway, somewhere where they could do exactly what they liked and have a rest from the royal roundabout. Alexandra had never been on such close terms of intimacy with her eldest brother, the new King Frederick VIII, as she had been with Willie, the King of Greece, nor had she seen eye to eye with her sister-in-law, Louise of Sweden. Ever since her marriage Alexandra had treated her parents' homes as her homes. But now she and her sister were dependent upon invitation, not the same thing at all. So they bought a house called

Hvidore, which, being translated, means 'White Hours'.

Hvidore lies to the north of Copenhagen on the road to Elsinore. A milk-white Italianate villa, its entrance was off a quiet village road. From its windows could be seen the ships passing along the Sund, the white coast of Sweden on the horizon. Comparatively small, no pretence was made of converting it into a miniature palace. To make the point clear, the sisters had engraved over the chimney-piece in their living-room, 'East, West, Home is best', and had both signed their names below it.[22] Allocation of rooms was settled by the simple process of tossing-up and a small kitchen allowed them to make tea and snacks for themselves when they felt like it.[23] Dagmar said: 'What is the use of my four hundred rooms at Gatchina? I never use more than two.'[24] The gardens were their delight, both kitchen and flower. A tunnel was built under the road, giving access to the beach of the Sund, a small stretch of which was fenced off to provide privacy. Here the sisters competed in finding pieces of amber.[25]

Visitors either fell in love with Hvidore, or hated it. There was criticism that passers-by could look straight in through the windows – and see the plethora of knick-knacks from the sisters' past as well as a giant carved Bornholm timepiece which played a hymn tune every hour. King Edward only visited Hvidore once. He considered the central heating entirely inadequate and kept his overcoat on. Crouched before a ghastly electric fire of imitation blazing logs, he declined to inspect the view from the roof. He suddenly recalled that he had urgent business to attend to in Copenhagen and ordered his car.[26] Alexandra had need of the relaxation that Hvidore offered for she had deep worries on her mind, her anxieties centering round the health of the King.

A serious decline in Edward's physical state began in February 1905. Prior to that he had suffered from minor attacks of bronchial catarrh, due to excessive smoking, and weight problems, due to excessive eating. Alexandra could do little about either. Cigars were a part of his day and a part of his image and he refused to curtail them. His appetite was gargantuan. Starting the day with a glass of milk in bed, he would breakfast on plates of haddock, chicken, eggs and bacon. Turtle soup taken later in the morning did not lessen his appetite for lunch at half past two, and he was prompt in the hall for a tea of buttered scones, sugar cakes and shortbread. At dinner he would often take all twelve courses. Alexandra told his doctors that the amount of food which he consumed was 'just terrible'[27] and that they ought to do something about it. But he would listen to no one. Then in February 1905 came the first serious attack of bronchial catarrh. Thereafter the second month of the year was regarded as the danger period. In 1906 the attack was even more serious and the King was advised never to face the fogs of London in February, but, because of the opening of Parliament, he refused to agree. In 1907 his physicians were summoned urgently to Buckingham Palace. The strength ebbed from him and he could not sleep at night. Moods of deep depression engulfed him and he talked of abdication. He lost the will to enjoy himself. 'My son will reign, my grandson never,'[28] he would mutter. And then: 'Willie is only waiting until I die to declare war.'

It was difficult for Alexandra to play the nurse-role which was necessary to the prolongation of his life. Firstly came the obstacle of the other two women who held his interest, Mrs Keppel and Agnes Keyser. Secondly, he was constantly away on his own, often at shooting parties. When she complained of being left alone at Balmoral, George commented: 'Mother dear . . . doesn't understand of course about the shooting . . .'[29] Thirdly there was the contemporary ruling that one must not be ill or tired, that etiquette was predominant. And Alexandra, despite the great sympathy which she extended to the wounded, to chronically ill children and hospital cases, adhered to the discipline, attending dinner when she felt unwell, standing for long periods when protocol demanded that she did so. She had learned the hard way.

Lord Ormathwaite recalled an evening when he was 'in waiting' at Windsor. It had been a long and busy day and he was weary. In the seemingly endless pause before dinner, the company remained standing. Relying on the noise of the band music and the deafness of the Queen, he remarked to his neighbour: 'Are we never going to sit down tonight?' Alexandra heard him – some people believed that she could hear more than she made out. She strode across the room to where a line of large gilt and scarlet brocade chairs stood against the wall. Seizing one, she pushed it, unaided, across the floor to where Ormathwaite was standing and commanded him, 'Sit down'. He demurred, and she repeated the order, loud and clear. He did so. Then, with the sweetest of smiles, she turned towards the astonished company and said: 'Poor thing, he is so tired.'[30]

By 1907 Alexandra had really become Queen in the hearts and minds of the public. Now sixty-two – she looked much younger – she had left behind the image of the beautiful Princess of Wales which she had held for nearly forty years. From now on she was to be more often by her ailing husband's side.

The following year, she accompanied the King to meet the Emperor and Empress of Russia in Estonia, a visit which both the prime minister and foreign secretary considered would be 'productive and of great good.' The left of the Labour Party, on the other hand, roared its disapproval of this meeting, Ramsay MacDonald describing it as 'hobnobbing with a blood-stained creature'.[31] There was a debate in parliament and the King showed his anger towards those who voted against the visit by withholding, from three of them, invitations to a royal garden party. Other difficulties were that Lord Rothschild wished him to remonstrate against the cruel treatment of Jews in Russia and Sir Ernest Cassel wanted him to put in a word about a proposed loan.

The journey presaged to be unfortunate when, shortly after *Victoria and Albert* left the Thames on 5 June, a fierce gale blew up and soon few were standing upright on the royal yacht, noted, even in calm weather, for its uncomfortable motion. On approaching Kiel the royal party received a shock. The German North Sea fleet lay at anchor, forming an impressive and threatening sight, while the evolutions of the torpedo flotilla excited the admiration of all the naval officers on board the royal yacht.[32] It was dark when the entrance to the canal was reached and the King landed to greet the Emperor's brother, Prince Henry of Prussia. As the royal party made its way along the quay, it was observed, in the pale shadows of the summer night, that the entire waterfront area was massed with troops, line upon line of them, grey, still as statues, numberless. The display of German military might was again on show on the following day as the yacht passed through the canal, cavalry trotting beside her all the way. Alexandra pulled down the blinds in her cabin, and kept them down, until the open waters of the Baltic were reached.[33]

There was one sad member among the royals – Empress Alicky, the sole German present. She was for ever watching for slights from her mother-in-law, who held seniority of place over her, and when a dinner-party was given on *Victoria and Albert* Edward and Alexandra suspected that she might refuse to take her place if Dagmar went in before her. There were whispers between host and hostess. Immediately dinner was announced Edward quickly took an Empress on each arm and, bidding them to keep step, led them in together.

But 'Alicky' would not be comforted. One evening Sir Charles Hardinge, a member of the British party, found the festivities on *Standart* somewhat wearying and took a turn on deck. He heard the sounding of sobbing. Hidden in the shadows, deep in an armchair, he came across the Russian Empress, weeping uncontrollably. He asked if he could be of assistance, but she answered that there was nothing anyone could do and asked to be left alone.[34]

The outstanding feature of the Reval meeting was the happy relationship engendered between the British King and Queen and Emperor Nicholas, which switched an atmosphere of Russian suspicion into one of cordial trust. The King made his nephew an Admiral of the British navy, to the latter's great delight. But the news was received with some misgivings in Whitehall, which caused Fisher to comment: 'It's a jolly good thing we have a King who knows how to act, as cabinet ministers seem to me always like frightened rabbits!'[35]

The success of the visit, and the obvious diplomatic superiority of his uncle over himself, infuriated Emperor William. When Count Metternich, the German Ambassador in London reported at the end of the month that the British people desired peace and that was the King's policy, he wrote in the margin: 'Untrue. He aims at war. I am to begin it, so that he does not get the odium.'[36]

An incident illustrates how efforts were made to better the King's relations with Emperor William. Sir Edward Grey, the Foreign Secretary, thought that the only man who could do it was the King himself. Accordingly it was arranged that the two should meet at Friedrichshof in August 1908, Edward being on his way for his annual cure at Marienbad while Alexandra went on holiday to Denmark.

The King's first state visit to Berlin in 1909 was unfortunate in many ways. Politically it did little good. As Frederick Ponsonby, Assistant Private Secretary to the King, a member of the British party, wrote: 'To my mind the effect of this visit was nil. One felt that a few charming men really liked us, but with the majority I derived the impression that they hated us.'[37] In addition, there was resentment that the British King had postponed his visit to the German capital until the ninth year of his reign and had given preference to Paris, Lisbon, Rome, Vienna and the Scandinavian capitals. From the personal angle, it was ill-planned, and in the event near catastrophic, for the journey took place in February and by this time it was well established that the King's health was at its lowest ebb in this month. He was exposing himself to the risks of a climate even more severe than that of London. If, as many people thought then, and some still think now, the postponement of war in Europe depended on the life span of the King, it would appear that, at sixty-eight, he would have been better occupied resting in the Mediterranean sun rather than undertaking a long journey and a packed, three-day programme under continual strain. It was an ordeal for Alexandra too, for in January she had an attack of influenza, so serious that not even her son was allowed into her room. There were thoughts of the fate which had overtaken Prince Eddy, suffering from the same illness in the same place in the same month. But Alexandra's reserve of physical strength and her courage won through and she was her usual gay self by the time the party left London on 8 February.

Edward was wheezing, coughing and cantankerous as he left Dover for the Channel crossing. Looking back as the royal yacht *Alexandra* left harbour, he saw the Royal Standard flying above the castle. A message was flashed to the War Office that this flag must only be flown when the Sovereign was in residence and that the mistake must not occur again.

The Emperor had planned an exact routine for the arrival at Berlin, every move measured to an inch. He marshalled his family and relations in considerable number by the red carpet where the door of the King's coach was to halt. But Edward had made his way along the corridor to see his wife, whose saloon was some hundred yards away. And it was out of this saloon that he stepped on to the platform. There followed an unseemly run by the Imperial family, swords clanking, hats askew, skirts ruffled. To complete the processional calamity the horses drawing the carriage of Queen Alexandra and the German Empress resolutely refused to move. They had to change into another vehicle and the whole parade was disorganized. This infuriated the Emperor, knowing full well as he did how good a horsewoman his English aunt was. During the family luncheon at the Royal Castle King Edward dozed off.

By the second day Edward was suffering from bronchial catarrah and Alexandra's moment of triumph came. In the interval at the opera he was due to move among the audience and say a few words to everyone. He simply could not face it. Alexandra rose and took on the task single-handed. She staged a superb performance, although she could hear little and understand less. Beauty and charm such as hers had seldom, if ever, been seen in Berlin. Frederick Ponsonby's comment was, 'I have never seen anything better done',[38] high praise indeed from a man who had travelled all the courts of Europe.

For this gala performance the Emperor had organised the spectacular play *Sardanapulas*, which could hardly be classed as opera as it was a series of splendid pictures interspersed with songs. The King fell asleep during the last scene. On stage was a funeral pyre. Little tongues of flame licked its foot and then burst into a vivid blaze. Edward awoke with a start and, with all the speed his girth and health would allow, made for the door.

After luncheon at the British Embassy there was a near tragedy. The King was chatting to an old friend, the beautiful Princess Daisy of Pless. He began to cough and choke and collapsed on the floor in a faint. As the guests panicked, Alexandra ran to him, undid his collar and brought him round. The room was cleared and his doctor, Sir James Reid, called. A quarter of an hour later Edward was sitting up in a chair, puffing at a newly-lighted cigar. He assured the returning guests that he was quite all right. But Sir Charles Hardinge was of the opinion that he was not and that there had been collusion between doctor and King.

245

On the 13th, in severe weather conditions, the royal party set off for home and, although the farewells appeared cordial enough, there was bitterness in many hearts. The King had been selective in handing out decorations to commemorate the visit, in fact much more sparing than sovereigns who had visited Berlin on previous occasions, and those who had dreamed of being handed out the garter were empty chested and did not like it. For the Emperor's part, he was not fully satisfied with the attitude of the Queen. When he referred to her as 'dear aunt', she retaliated with 'dear nephew', when he considered that she should have used 'Willie'. In addition she had lectured him about his diet and been critical of his refusal to allow young members of his family to dance the modern two-step, restricting them to minuets and the like.

Two days later the King opened Parliament and then made off for Biarritz, Alice Keppel in attendance. But Alexandra was deeply worried about her husband's health; she did not doubt Alice Keppel's ability to care for him, but appearances demanded at least equal shares of her husband. In any case she did not like the French resort – that 'horrid Biarritz', she called it – but nothing would deter Edward from making his annual visit. There he set up his 'court' and became the only one who mattered, happy in the reminders of the Second Empire, in the place Napoleon III had called 'his little Osborne'. There, surrounded by British cronies, he was comparatively free of inquisitive tourists and royals on holiday. It was also an advantage that France, a republic, was free of regal trappings and he liked the air of romance, secrecy and deference with which the French railway officials greeted Mrs Keppel. He was back in the gay days of long ago and, even if he had lost his physical bounce, at least there was no Mama to censor him.

Alexandra allowed him a month of this Ruritanian interlude and then ordered him to rendez-vous at Marseilles with herself, Dagmar and Princess Victoria. Edward became the elderly King of Great Britain again and lost his gaiety. He liked to be the master of his personal life, and that he could not be when Alexandra was about, particularly when she was accompanied by Dagmar. However, the King, aboard the royal yacht sailed on to Naples.

After visiting Vesuvius the Queen and Empress continued on their way to Greece, the King returning to England.

Thus began the green summer days of the last of the King's years, a summer boiling with political crisis over the relative strength of the British and German navies. But, despite the tension, Edward and Alexandra touched the peak of popularity of the reign. The date, 26 May 1909 – the place, Epsom Downs. The King's horse, Minoru, was second favourite for the Derby at 4 – 1, an American-bred colt, Sir Martin, receiving slight preference. Minoru, royal jockey Herbert Jones up, was drawn on the inside but got smartly away and was well placed behind the pace-makers before the mile post, Sir Martin tracking him. Then the American horse crossed his legs and fell, blocking those behind him.

At Tattenham Corner the purple, scarlet and gold colours of the King were spotted on the rails and slightly in the lead. Then Louviers challenged and the two were neck and neck at the post. The suspense and the silence were nerve shattering. All eyes moved from the number board to the royal box, where stood the King and Queen, and back again. Alexandra was crying. When Minoru's number was first in the frame the crowd went mad, stampeding towards the unsaddling enclosure to see the King lead in his winner. Alexandra put away her handkerchief, kissed those around her and leaned forward to watch her husband greet Minoru and jockey Jones. The air was full of hats – even policemen's helmets – and someone started to sing 'God save the King' and the words echoed over the Downs. The King went into the crowd and was submerged by it. 'Good old Teddy! Teddy boy! Hurrah! Hurrah!',[39] people shouted and slapped him on the back. Somehow Richard Marsh, his trainer, got him to Minoru and there followed the triumph in the winner's enclosure. In the reign of Edward and Alexandra there had been no popular moments to match these.

The summer slipped quietly by, enriched by a brilliant Cowes week and the return visit of the Emperor and Empress of Russia. Then Edward went to Marienbad and Alexandra to Hvidore. In November the cauldron which had been heating up since the presentation of 'The People's Budget', thus named as it was aimed to satisfy the demands for social reform, in April boiled over when the House of Lord threw it out. A general election followed in January 1910 and the Liberals were returned by a narrow margin. It was their plan to create enough Liberal peers to force through any such bill and that needed the consent of the King and that, most understandably, he was loath to do. No political crisis ever worried him more and he fought to find a compromise. As a result of the strain and worry, his health deteriorated and he was urged to leave England in the New Year. He refused and on 21 February opened parliament with the Queen. Having been assured by Asquith that no serious crisis impended, he left for Biarritz on 6 March, Alice Keppel making her separate way there. In Paris his catarrah worsened and by the time he reached Biarritz he was seriously ill, Alice Keppel being at his bedside. Alexandra was in a difficult position, but kept in constant touch, arranging that Sir Francis Laking, the King's physician, should leave with her immediately if the illness took a turn for the worse. But the King recovered slowly and was taking drives and short walks by the end of the month. Then the snow fell, a rare occurrence for Biarritz.

Alexandra made her final bid to prevent the danger which she saw ahead. She begged him to join her at Genoa on the new royal yacht on 14 April and cruise to Corfu, meanwhile setting out for Italy herself. The King turned down her plea outright: '. . . quite out of the question, as it might be necessary at any moment for me to return (and I can do so under 24 hours at any time) should the Govt. resign, dissolve, or commit any act which entails my presence at home.'[40] The King said that, if he were to cruise on the yacht, it might take him up to six days to reach London. In fact, if the yacht had called in at Mediterranean ports to pick up the latest news, he could have been home in forty-eight hours, for that was the time which it took Queen Alexandra to return home when the summons came to her at Corfu. Twenty-four hours longer – could not the political situation have survived that one vital day? The truth was two fold, firstly that the King did not wish to leave Biarritz, and secondly, that the politicians were engrossed in social warfare. Yet the continuation of the reign of Edward and Alexandra was vital for the peace of the world. For while Edward was well-known internationally and was thoroughly versed in the secrets of the European courts, his son was hardly known in Europe, and possessed none of the panache of his father. George was bad at languages and had little in common with Americans or international financiers, He followed his father about like a somewhat retiring ADC. No Prince of Wales has made less public impact – indeed it is hard to associate George V with that title at all.

But equally important for peace was the continuation of Alexandra as Queen. Her wide-ranging connections with Europe's royalty carried a great deal of influence, quite apart from the spell cast by her magnetism and charm. Americans adored her, and if the King and the government had had the foresight to send her on a world tour, the love she would have undoubtedly engendered would probably have proved a deterrent to war. Her unfulfilled dream often expressed was to see India and the East and she would have gone had she been given the chance.

Edward came back from Biarritz on 27 April and went to the opera. He travelled to cold Sandringham and walked in the grounds with Frank Beck, his agent, discussing the lay out of a new plantation. He caught a chill. But he would take no care of himself, cancel no appointments, turn no visitors away. On 3 May a message reached Corfu that he was ill. It was not an urgent summons, but Alexandra ordered the yacht to return through the Adriatic at speed.[41] It had been suggested by her entourage that she should rest a while in Venice. 'No', she told Charlotte Knollys. 'I'm worried about the King. I think he needs me. We'll leave at once.[42] On the evening of the 5th she reached Victoria Station. Her husband was not there to meet her, as was his invariable custom, but he had arranged for her to have a box at Covent Garden that evening; the moment that she saw him she cancelled it.

> He was sitting propped up in a chair and showed the features of cardiac restlessness . . . In addition to the injections of strychnine, hypodermic injections of tyramine were employed with benefit. It was also agreed that under certain circumstances leeches should be applied to relieve the congestion.[43]

He spent the night in his chair, Alexandra in constant attendance upon him. When awake his mind was clear but his strength was waning. The leeches were not employed.*

On the morning of the 6th he insisted on dressing in a frock coat to receive Lord Knollys and Sir Ernest Cassel. He smoked a cigar. After a light lunch he collapsed.

> During the evening the King roused from time to time, and on one occasion, about 7 p.m., he rose and tried to walk. The effect of this was to bring on acute heart failure, in which the pulse disappeared, with marked pallor and sweating. After this hour the King was for the most part sleeping upright in his chair, propped up with pillows. *Her Majesty administered the oxygen, which still gave relief* . . .[44]

Now, as she gave the oxygen, as she fought to save his life, Alexandra was playing the part which she had for so long wished to do, if he had but let her. She was too late. King Edward VII died at 11.45 that night.

She could not bear to part with him and kept him as long as protocol and conditions would allow. When Sydney Holland called on 10 May to pay his last respects, he found her kneeling and praying at the bed's end in the darkened room. She had pressed a rose[45] into his stiffened hand and, with it thus clasped, at last she let him go.

---

* This mode of blood-letting marked its zenith in Europe in the early nineteenth century. By 1910 it had largely fallen out of use.

NINETEEN

❧❧❧

Before the Storm

Alexandra was utterly lost without 'her Bertie'. She said to Frederick Ponsonby: 'I feel as if I had been turned into stone, unable to cry, unable to grasp the meaning of it all. . . .'[1] Since that September day in 1862 when she had met him before the altar in Speyer cathedral, he had filled her life completely. It was not a saga of love which was over, but rather as if a mantle had been taken from her shoulders, a mantle which she had worn for forty-seven years. Without that mantle she was cold, exposed to the world – lost, as Edward would have been if she had died instead of him. They were essential parts of one another's lives. Without her he might not have reigned, so many and deep were the scandals in which he was involved as Prince of Wales. 'It is she who keeps the Throne for him,'[2] Bernal Osborne had said. And Edward had repaid his debt by guarding her, unsophisticated as she was, and allowing no word to be said against her.

Princess Daisy of Pless went to see her. 'The darling – because she *is* a darling – said, "My life is finished, there is nothing left for me." Poor little Queen, she loved being on the Throne, and I understand her loneliness. . . .'[3]

She hated change and was reluctant to leave Buckingham Palace. It was, she said, the lovely garden there which she would miss, and it was not until December 1910 that she returned to Marlborough House, which had been her London home when she was Princess of Wales.

At Sandringham she could retain the aura of the past. Her husband's bedroom was closed, everything in it left exactly as it was when he was alive. No one ever slept there again.[4] She did not give way to her grief, as Queen Victoria had done when

251

Prince Albert died, shunning all social contact, but invited close friends for week-ends in Norfolk and they found her as lovely as ever in her dress of black and silver and her small widow's cap. In the evenings she played bridge after dinner, insisting that the table be placed in the exact position where Edward had liked to have it. But one thing was missing from the old routine. There was no music, the tunes of yesterday bringing back with them emotion and sadness that she found too poignant to bear.[5]

She found relief in her grandchildren and was able to laugh and lark when they were around her. In January 1911 Sydney Holland was a guest at 'the Big House' and kept the fun going by teaching David and Olav conjuring tricks. He was demonstrating how to palm his watch. He found that he had been out-pointed and that his watch had really disappeared. He suspected one of the boys but they professed innocence. Holland teased Queen Alexandra, saying that, as he was a guest in her house, she would have to replace it. She laughed. It was later found in Lady Ripon's shawl where she had hidden it.[6]

Sandringham was the cause of family disruption in the first years of the new reign. In his will Edward had left the house to his widow for her lifetime and it was clearly his intention that she should continue to live there. He could not have considered otherwise. For nearly half a century it had been their home and their joint love and interest. Over the porch had been inscribed the words, 'This house was built by Albert Edward and Alexandra his wife in the year of our Lord 1870'. Some considered that she should hand over 'the Big House' to the new King and Queen, taking into account their large family and necessarily numerous retinue. Alexandra had no intention of doing any such thing. Continuity and memories meant as much to her as life itself and she regarded as sacred the bedrooms of her husband and her eldest son. Every corner of the house was crammed with souvenirs and reminders of the past. Without Sandringham she could not have carried on in the important role which she still played.

King George knew this. He said: 'It is my mother's home. My father built it for her.' But the other members of his family were not so understanding and there was a disagreement between husband and wife. Many years later the Duke of Windsor wrote: 'His attitude caused my mother to point out that, as a practical matter, it was rather ridiculous for one old lady to reside in grandeur in that vast mansion, while the King and Queen lacked room in their congested Cottage for a single guest.'[7] It was typical of Queen Mary to give priority to the practical over the emotional.

The household certainly suffered inconvenience in the cramped quarters of York Cottage and an equerry became so incensed that he went so far as to tell Princess Victoria, who shared Sandringham with her mother, that the position was ridiculous. Princess Victoria flared with anger and complained to her brother. In nautical language the King laced down the equerry, telling him that he could not see 'what the devil it had to do with him'.[8]

Alexandra's closest link with her dead husband, and an ever-present reminder of his ways, was his white fox terrier, Caesar. Caesar had slept in an armchair beside his master's bed and travelled with him to Paris and Biarritz, Malta and Marienbad. On his collar was engraved, 'I am Caesar, the King's dog'. He was a one-man dog and the King's frequent question to him, 'Do you like your old master?', was superfluous.[9] Caesar was a rascal, amiable enough with those he knew but apt to take exception to strangers, growling at their trouser legs. He was a snob, but not above scrounging a bone from below stairs. The royal chef, Gabriel Tschumi, recalled: 'So long as the King was not there Caesar would fraternize with the kitchen staff and knew each of us very well, but the moment its master appeared it ignored all its former friends, and not even by the quiver of an ear did it betray recognition on any inspection visits by the King.'[10] It was Caesar's delight to hunt hedgehogs and he would come back from these forays with his mouth and paws full of pricks, whining until a friendly footman removed them.

Caesar could not understand why the King was not available for fun and walks during his last illness and grew somewhat impatient. Then, on 20 May, he went for a particular walk. By Queen Alexandra's instruction a highland servant led him behind the King's coffin in the funeral procession from Westminster to Paddington station. There were eight Kings and an Emperor in the procession, but the spotlight of public attention was on the white fox terrier, looking up at the highlander as if to ask what the walk was all about. It was primarily the sight of Caesar which brought tears to the eyes of the spectators. He became a hero that day and a legend and a memoir of the King published shortly after his death was entitled, 'Where's Master?'

But the wave of mass emotion left Alexandra untouched, as she considered that Caesar had neglected his duty by not comforting the King in his last hours. 'Horrid little dog,' she said to Margot Asquith.[11] Then Caesar realized that his master had gone, wandering from room to room in search of him. He sat for hours, just waiting for him to come back. He would not go near to Queen Alexandra. She, who knew more about dogs than she did about human beings, would make no advances. It was a plain case of conflict over pride of possession. Soon loneliness overcame pride and Caesar became the shadow of Queen Alexandra, sharing his love for her with a like feeling for Princess Mary, only daughter of the new King. For four years Caesar gave Alexandra comfort and company and when he died she told Lady Rothschild that 'the last living link with the beloved King' had gone.[12]

Queen Alexandra was not present at the coronation, which was held on Thursday, 22 June 1911. Many reasons were put forward for this. Some said that she was following tradition, as Queen Adelaide, widow of William IV, had not attended the coronation of Queen Victoria. Some said that the strain would be too much for her. Others, more realistically minded, were of the opinion that, if she did, she would steal the show, and she did not want to do that. In reality her reason was personal and guided by the past. Although she sent a loving letter, and a mother's blessing, to her son on the eve of his crowning, she could not fully accept him as king.

Into her seclusion at Sandringham there had come the ghost of Eddy, who had died there twenty years before. He lived again. She saw his tall and graceful figure garbed for Westminster. She saw that understanding smile which he had reserved for her alone. His Royal Highness Prince Albert Victor should now be taking the oath. She wandered about the house and gardens, repeating and repeating, '*Eddy* should be King, not *Georgie*,'[13] and the sympathy of her faithful entourage went out to her.

In truth Queen Alexandra never truly accepted her second son as sovereign. She could never bring herself to address her letters to him as 'The King', but always wrote to 'King George',[14] although she knew full well that this was incorrect, sounding, as it did, as if he was merely one of a number. Edward VII was referred to as 'My King';[15] Eddy not being available, her husband reigned on. This attitude in no way affected the bond of love and understanding which linked mother and son and, in contrast to his father's practice, George told her everything that was going on in the political sphere.

The position was difficult indeed for Queen Mary, from many angles. In fact she did not enjoy her new position. In August 1910 she wrote to her aunt, Augusta, Grand Duchess of Mecklenburg-Strelitz: 'I wish the old life were coming back, I don't like this, anyhow as it is at present. . . .'[16] While 'mother-in-law trouble' was her main burden, there were other worries to face. Rumours about her husband and herself were rife. It was said that the King drank too much and that she was frightened of him. Then the old gossip was resurrected that George had married the daughter of a British Admiral at Malta in 1890 and the journalist Edward Mylius, who wrote the story for a French magazine, was taken to court and sentenced to twelve months' imprisonment. It was recalled that Mary's cousin Marie, Duchess of Stelitz, had had an illegitimate child, the father being a footman whose duty it was to light the lamps in the bedrooms. Mary was sensitive and these rumours hurt her deeply. But her ever present problem was Queen Alexandra and the hold that 'Motherdear' had over 'Georgie'. After a few months she came to the sad conclusion that she and her husband were drifting apart. Alexandra, in her grief, was largely unaware of the unhappiness which she was causing. In fact she had deep affection and respect for Mary, but still regarded her as a poor relation and a good part-time secretary to her late husband. She could not bring herself suddenly to change her approach and feelings and bend the knee. Perhaps because she was Danish, she had not the deep, inborn respect for the monarchial system which was a part of Queen Mary's life, as she was to show so clearly in after years.

Alexandra early made clear her attitude to the new reign. At Edward's funeral she insisted upon taking precedence over the new queen, a precedence which was not hers by right. She refused to give a date when she would vacate Buckingham Palace. Upon being given some advice by Emperor William as to how to behave as mother of the king, she replied: 'Willie dear . . . I am afraid that I have not heard a single word you were saying.'[17] She issued a directive as to what her grand-daughters, Alexandra and Maud, should wear at the Coronation. She retained certain of her husband's jewels which, many considered, should have been handed to the new queen. Mary commented: 'The odd part is that the person causing the delay and trouble remains supremely unconscious as to the inconvenience it is causing . . . and everyone seems afraid to speak.'[18] And that was the true position – everyone was afraid of speaking to the widow of King Edward VII. The relationship between Queens Alexandra and Mary was exacerbated by the inteference of two women, women who heartily disliked one another and had differing loyalties, and who now ranged themselves on opposing sides.

Alexandra's mentor, and constant companion, was her sister. Dagmar was not as beautiful as Alexandra, but she was more worldly wise and politically sophisticated. As the wife of Alexander III, she had become accustomed to power, and in Russia she still held that power, having seniority over Empress 'Alicky'. It was Dagmar who had insisted that Alexandra took precedence over Mary at Edward's funeral and her hand could be traced in many of the difficulties which now arose.

Backing Mary was her aunt, Augusta, Dowager Grand Duchess of Mecklenburg-Strelitz, now in her ninetieth year. She was a strong character, a redoubtable adversary, and with a Germanic slant to her thinking. Queen Mary confided all troubles to the Grand Duchess, complaining of the difficulties which Dagmar was instigating. Her aunt replied: 'I understand every word, expressed and *not*, and have *feared*, what you so gently allude to! May that pernicious influence soon depart!'[19] But the Russian Empress stayed on at Sandringham throughout 1910 and was back again for the coronation. Mary wrote: '. . . if only things can be managed without having rows, but it is difficult to get a certain person to see things in their right light.'[20] To which her aunt replied: 'Oh! were *I* there instead of Dagmar!, more I

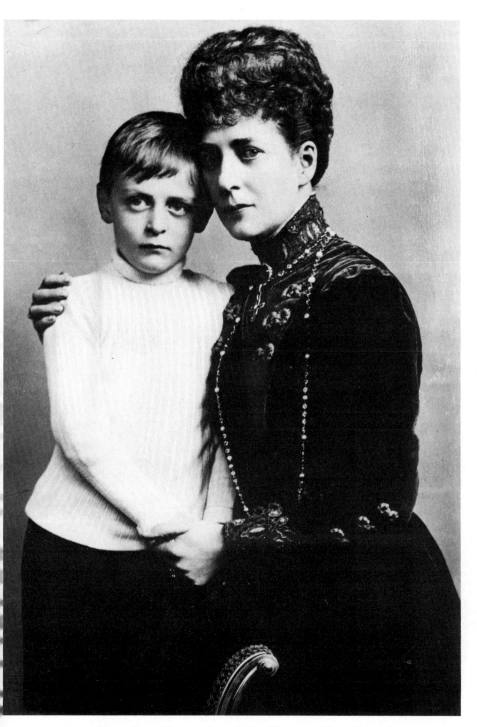

Queen Alexandra and her grandson, Prince Olav, now King of Norway

Queen Alexandra at the Royal Horticultural Society's spring show at the Royal Hospital, Chelsea, May 1914

dare not say.'[21]

An unsettling background to the differences was that Queen Mary was receiving advice from Germany, with its, by now, inevitable anti-British bias, while Queen Alexandra was being guided by the Russian and Danish views.

By nature Alexandra was independent and informal and apt to drop in upon her friends without prior notice, on one occasion being refused entrance by Lady Battersea's footman. Whenever she was in the Farnborough area she would call in, unannounced, upon the Empress Eugenie, a habit which perturbed the old Empress as she was endeavouring to preserve the dignity of the French Second Empire and liked to receive visiting royalties with some semblance of the style once accorded them at Compiègne and the Tuileries.

Alexandra now made a complete *volte-face*, abandoning all informality at Sandringham when Queen Mary was in residence at York Cottage. A new lady-in-waiting, Lady Cynthia Colville, was informed that tea was to be taken with Queen Alexandra. She imagined that this would be a casual and family affair, and dressed accordingly, plus hat. She was expecting to walk the few hundred yards between York Cottage and 'the Big House'. When Queen Mary appeared, she was dressed as for a party. She looked in horror at Lady Colville and exclaimed: 'But you can't go in a hat!' This was removed, the owner being conscious of a ruffled hair-do. Then a carriage appeared and the short drive along the driveway was made in pomp and circumstance. Queen Alexandra, in a magnificent tea gown, was waiting to receive them, behind her a maid-of-honour and her faithful retinue.[22] There was no doubt left as to who was number one.

In the public side of her life, Alexandra worked harder than she had ever done before. She was haunted by the words of her husband, spoken shortly before his death: 'I will not give in. I shall go on. I will work to the end.' Now in her comparative seclusion and with more time on her hands, health, education and charitable causes received her unstinted support. President of the London Hospital, patron of Dr Barnardo's Home, a leading figure in the field of army nursing, 'whenever any opportunity arose when her name and influence could be of use to some deserving charity she would throw the full force of her energies into the work, thus ensuring the success of the enterprise.'[23]

On 11 November 1911 King George V and Queen Mary left for India to attend the Delhi Durbar. Alexandra considered that it was most unwise for the Sovereign to be away for three months at a time when trouble was brewing in the Balkans and the threat from Germany was increasing. 'Hardly conceivable',[24] were the words that she used to describe the tour. She went to Portsmouth to see her son and daughter-in-law leave in the new P. & O. liner, *Medina*. A gale was blowing and the bunting on *Medina* and the escorting cruisers was torn to shreds. The King sat down to write to his mother, his words showing clearly his deep feelings for her: 'I shall never forget that moment when I saw you moving from the window of the railway carriage as we slowly steamed away from you into the wind and rain.'[25]

A few weeks later the Duke and Duchess of Fife and their two daughters set off in ss *Delhi* for a holiday in Egypt. Off Cape Spartel, on the African coast of the Strait of Gibraltar, the *Delhi* was wrecked when it went on the rocks. The cutter sent from a cruiser to rescue the royal travellers was swamped in heavy surf and the shore was reached with difficulty. As a result of the exposure the sixty-two year old Duke developed a severe chill. He carried on with the journey but died at Assouan on 29 January 1912.[*] By special remainder the dukedom descended to his elder daughter, Alexandra.[26]

The death of the Duke of Fife was the first of a series of family tragedies to sadden Alexandra during the following year. In May her brother, Frederick VIII of Denmark, died at Hamburg on his way home to Copenhagen.[†] Her nephew, Prince George William of Hanover, eldest son of her sister Thyra, Duchess of Cumberland, set out by road for Denmark to attend the funeral. As related earlier his car skidded off the road near Nackel and he was killed instantly. Emperor William's help and compassion in the tragedy caused the Duke to send his youngest son, Ernest Augustus, Duke of Brunswick-Luneburg, to Potsdam to thank

---

[*] The Duke's body was brought home in HMS *Powerful*. The funeral took place at Windsor, the body being removed in the autumn of 1912 to the vault in the private Chapel at Mar Lodge.

[†] He was succeeded by his eldest son, Christian X (1870—1947).

the man with whom he had been at loggerheads for many years. Ernest fell in love with the Emperor's only daughter, Victoria Louise, and they became engaged to be married. By this strange twist of fate Alexandra again became linked to the hated Hohenzollerns.

Now Alexandra turned her attention to the welfare and security of her favourite brother, King George of Greece. She had visited him the spring of 1911 and learned from him of Emperor William's plans in the Near East and of the threat of war in the Balkans. She came to the conclusion that Britain was once again shutting her eyes to dangers ahead, and said so, and once again she was to be proved right. She urged her son to give Greece greater support, saying: 'Remember England put my brother there and are bound to keep him there.'[27] But in October 1912 the Balkan wars began.

In the first Balkan war Greece, Serbia, Bulgaria and Montenegro were ranged against Turkey. On 9 November Salonika was captured by the allies, Adrianople surrendering on 26 March 1913. Peace was signed in London in May. Shortly after Crown Prince Constantine made his victorious entry into Salonika at the head of his troops on 9 November, his father arrived. Throughout his long reign King George had dreamed of this moment and he decided to stay in the Macedonian capital for a time. Despite the pleas of his family, he insisted upon walking about the town without an armed escort. He took such an airing on 18 March 1913. A man was sitting on a low wall, apparently enjoying the spring sunshine. His name was Schinas. As King George turned to go home, Schinas shot him in the back. The bullet went through his heart.[28]

Alexandra had received many tragic messages in her time, and was hardened to them, but this news proved such a shock to her that she all but fainted. To add to the sadness, King George had been within a few days of his Golden Jubilee as King of the Hellenes.[29] The assassination upset the balance of power in Europe. While King George's wife Olga,* was a Russian, the new King, Constantine, was married to Sophie, sister of the German Emperor. And that was to create many problems in the troubled years which lay ahead.

* Niece of Emperor Alexander II.

1913 was the Golden Jubilee of Alexandra's marriage and it was an occasion which her army of admirers insisted should be celebrated in a special way. She had been seen little in London's streets since her husband's death and a processional drive seemed an obvious choice. But Alexandra wanted a secondary, and deeper, reason for the drive, one that would help the sick and needy. The idea that came to her was founded on a custom of her father. King Christian IX instituted a 'Children's Help Day'. On that day he would walk through the decorated streets of Copenhagen, encouraging those who were collecting donations and urging the public to put their hands deep in their pockets.[30] Alexandra developed the idea into one which would benefit the funds of London hospitals. Women volunteers, dressed in white, would sell artificial wild roses which were to be made by the disabled.[31] The day was to be called Alexandra, or Rose, Day.

The first drive which Alexandra made – from Marlborough House to the Mansion House and back again – took place on 26 June 1912. As she had been married in 1863, this was a year premature, but the idea seemed so good, the plans were ready, and it was pointed out that she had in fact first visited England in 1862, when she stayed with Queen Victoria at Osborne.* The

---

* On 7 March 1913 Queen Alexandra received the following letter:
To her Most Gracious Majesty Queen Alexandra.
MAY IT PLEASE YOUR MAJESTY,
  We, the Lord Mayor, Aldermen and Commons of the City of London in Common Council assembled, respectfully approach your Majesty with the sincerest sentiments of loyalty and attachment to offer to your Majesty, on our behalf and that of the citizens of London, our heartfelt congratulations on the 50th anniversary of your Majesty's landing in this country as the affianced bride of our deeply lamented and much loved Sovereign King Edward the Seventh, of blessed memory, then Prince of Wales.
  We desire further to unite in the fervent prayer that your Majesty may long be spared to illustrate by your bright example the shining virtues which adorn and dignify your exalted character, and to continue to carry on the beneficent work for the happiness and benefit of the people of this country which has so endeared your Majesty to the whole nation.
  In conclusion, we pray that the blessing of the Almighty may rest upon your Majesty and upon all the members of your Royal Family.
Signed by order of the Court,
JAMES BELL, *Town Clerk.*
Guildhall, London.
March 7, 1913.

drive swept Londoners off their feet. It was a welcome return of
the gay days of 'Good King Teddy', a resurrection of distant
green summers. Alexandra received an ovation, the memory of
which, she said, 'I will cherish to the last day of my life'.[32] That
evening the London *Evening News* commented:

> 'Alexandra Day' has come and all male London is captive at
> the feet of the ten or eleven thousand pretty women in
> white, who are selling millions of roses for charity's sweet
> sake. It was a beautiful idea, this scheme of celebrating the
> fiftieth anniversary of the landing in England of Queen
> Alexandra, 'the blissful bride of a blissful heir'. That all
> London should wear her favourite flower, and by so doing
> help her favourite charities, was an inspiration.

The funds raised were a godsend to hospitals which relied
heavily on charity and the drive became an institution, one of the
chief attractions of London's summer, Alexandra the star. As the
years passed the excitement and the acclamation proved somewhat of a strain upon a woman in her seventies, but never for a
second did she allow that strain to show, ever smiling, constantly
stopping to speak to collectors and to receive flowers from
children. By 1920 the hospitals had benefitted to the tune of
three-quarters of a million pounds.[33]

On 24 May 1913, Alexandra's nephew, Ernest, married
Emperor William's daughter, Victoria Louise. Alexandra did
not accept the invitation to attend, having doubts not only about
the wisdom of the marriage, but also of visiting the German
capital at such a time of rising crisis. She contented herself by
sending the bride a present of an emerald brooch. But King
George V and Queen Mary, who liked their cousin 'Willie' and
got on well with him, decided that they would attend. The
international situation making a state visit out of the question,
they decided to go as mere relations and to take no ministers with
them.

But there was nothing unofficial or private about the great
military display which the Emperor staged for the entry of the
King and Queen to Berlin. The scene at the Brandenburg Gate
was awe inspiring and all morning the Zeppelin *Hansa* circled
over the city. After the wedding there was a magnificent dinner
at which 1200 guests sat down at the same time. The Emperor

kept jumping up to make speeches, give toasts and assurances of his peaceful intentions. These assurances were later reduced to their proper value when he told Sir Frederick Ponsonby: 'I am a man of peace, but now I have to arm my Country, so that whoever falls on me I can crush. And crush them I will!'[34]

Generally speaking, a good time was had by all. At the close Queen Mary wrote: 'William and Victoria* accompanied us to the station – Took leave of them all with regret after charming visit . . . I cannot tell you how much we enjoyed our visit to Berlin or how touched we were at the kindness shown by William and Victoria and indeed by everybody. It was a most interesting time and so beautifully arranged in every way, nothing could have gone off better.'[35]

The goodbyes exchanged at Berlin station were very final goodbyes, for of those who waved their handkerchiefs as the train pulled out King George and Mary were to see very few again. Half a century was to pass before a British Sovereign next set foot in Berlin.

A romance much more to the liking of Queen Alexandra was that which developed between her grandaughter Alexandra (Alix), Duchess of Fife since the death of her father, and Prince Arthur of Connaught. Prince Arthur was the only son of the Duke of Connaught, King Edward's younger brother. Like his father, Prince Arthur was a soldier and handsome. The couple fell in love in the summer of 1913 and were married at the Chapel Royal, St James's, on 15 October. Ten months later Queen Alexandra became a great-grandmother.† She was now sixty-nine, though this was hard to believe. An old friend, Sir Maurice de Bunsen, formerly Ambassador to Portugal and Spain, described her as looking 'like a young girl'.[36]

4 August, 1914. Queen Alexandra stood at a window of Buckingham Palace, looking down at the immense crowd in the Mall, beside her her nephew, Prince Christopher of Greece.

> Waiting in a silence that could almost be felt while the last moments of the ultimatum to Germany expired, and when

---

* The German Empress.

† A son, Alistair, Earl of MacDuff, the only child of the marriage, was born on 9 August 1914. As his father, Prince Arthur, died in 1938, he succeeded his grandfather as second Duke of Connaught. He died in Canada in 1943.

at length the clock boomed out the hour, one deep breath was drawn by all those thousands, like a mighty sigh. Then the tension relaxed and a second later everyone was laughing, singing patriotic songs and shouting for the King and Queen. King George went out on the balcony. His face was white and drawn, he had grown years older in the last week.[37]

Queen Alexandra wrote to her Danish friend, Colonel Rordam: 'God help us and our dear countries! May our dearly beloved native country stay outside the struggle and keep her neutrality until the last in this unjust war which we in Denmark knew since 1864 would come one day.'[38]

She told her son, the King: 'I always told you Willie was a bad man. Now perhaps you will believe me!'[39]

She had been uttering her warnings for exactly fifty years.

TWENTY

༯ ❀ ❀ ༯

1914–1918

Queen Alexandra entered the years of war bearing on her shoulders a personal burden of which only few were aware. It was the threat of a scandal breaking loose, a scandal which would not only do irrevocable harm to the memory of Edward VII, but also undermine the good name and standing of the royal family at a time when full loyalty and trust were essential.

It all began on 24 June 1914. On that morning Alexandra made her Rose Day drive while 20,000 rose-sellers collected for charity. The crowds were dense, the cheering deafening, as she drove down the Mall to lunch with the King and Queen at Buckingham Palace. Meantime, at her desk at Easton Lodge, Essex, Daisy – Countess of Warwick – was writing a letter. It was addressed to Arthur du Cros – to whom she owed £16,000 – and told of her intention to publish her memoirs, which were to include the letters to her from Bertie, when he was Prince of Wales. She had called in to help her the notorious author and journalist, Frank Harris, author of *My Life and Loves*, and he had advised her that the venture should net her £100,000.

Arthur du Cros was a millionaire. He and his father had developed the invention of John Boyd Dunlop, a veterinary surgeon of Belfast, of a pneumatic tyre for bicycles, thus laying the foundations of the Dunlop Rubber Company. Deciding that King George should be made aware of the situation as soon as possible du Cros contacted the Palace.

The King was already over-worked and deeply worried about the situation both at home and abroad. Sir George Franckenstein thus described the position in the spring of 1914:

264

The brilliance of social life in London contrasted strongly
with the dark and confused situation in home politics. The
rejection of the Woman's Franchise Bill resulted in repeated
demonstrations by the suffragettes, who conducted their
campaign of Votes for Women by arson, and other violent
methods. Many London museums and picture galleries had
to be closed as a precaution against these Amazons. Far
graver still was the Parliamentary situation, when the Irish
Home Rule Bill, after passing the Commons, was thrown
out by the House of Lords. Under the strong leadership of
Sir Edward Carson, the Ulsterman had won strong support
. . . The Orangemen were passionately rejecting Home
Rule for all Ireland, both as patriotic Unionists and because
they did not wish to be reduced to a minority and feared lest
Home Rule meant Rome rule coupled with crushing taxa-
tion.

The King had just completed a series of tours of the industrial
North and a visit to France. When, in May, the Home Rule bill
passed the Commons, nationalist Ireland enrolled volunteers by
the thousand and began to import arms. The King spoke with
Mr Asquith, stressing 'the increasing gravity of the situation
and the dreadful predicament which would face the Crown if
civil war broke out'.[1] Already the radical press, urged on by
threat of civil war in Ireland, was writing with contempt of the
crown and the sovereign and it was clear that a royal scandal
would cause deep harm. On the personal side King George
viewed with horror any gossip which would blacken the memory of his father, whom he had viewed with reverence, or cause
suffering and sadness to his beloved mother. At the same time
silencing such a threat by paying out a large sum of money was
out of the question. Ever careful with money, both George and
Mary were implacable in their determination that this should not
occur.

The palace was deeply concerned when the news came from
Arthur du Cros of Lady Warwick's plan. But the older men of
the Household were well trained in dealing with scandals, their
experience dating back to Bertie's wilder days. The duties of
these royal advisers had passed from father to son and been
confined to inter-related families. Men like Lord Stamfordham,
who had joined the royal service in 1880, were well geared to

265

cope with such a situation. The danger lay in the timing. Alexandra was kept in close touch with Lady Warwick's moves by three men close to her, Sir Dighton Probyn, comptroller of her household, and Viscount Knollys and Sir Arthur Davidson, lords-in-waiting.* Deeply worried over the affair, on 20 July she announced a forthcoming visit to Denmark. It had been her habit since her marriage to retire to her homeland when under personal strain and she longed to relax on the beach, and in the gardens of Hvidore. But that holiday was not to be.

On 28 July Austria – Hungary declared war on Serbia.† On the same day an Imperial Council in Potsdam voted for war against Russia and, as a natural consequence, against France, Austria being dragged into the conflict by her determined ally, Germany. On the 31st Emperor Nicholas ordered the mobilization of the Russian forces. On 1 August a state of war existed between Germany and Russia and German troops penetrated French territory. By the 3rd France and Germany were at war and the next day German troops crossed into Belgium, the sanctity of which country was guaranteed by Britain. Britain stood by her pledge and went to war.

In a private conversation with Alexandra's nephew Nicholas the Russian Emperor said:

> But I can tell you one thing: now that we have been led into this abominable business against our will, I am determined to stick to my French Ally to the bitter end. We cannot afford to lose this war, as the triumph of Prussian militarism would mean the end of all liberty and civilization. England is bound to come in and I have already telegraphed to George giving him my views.[2]

Alexandra was of the same opinion and, ungagged for the first time, she 'hurled abusive epithets at the head of the Kaiser'.[3]

In the event the German Emperor had relied on British neutrality, although his general staff reckoned on the British as hostile. The strange position had arisen whereby both his brother Henry and his sister Sophie, the Queen of the Hellenes, had been visiting England throughout July. Prince Henry of Prussia, a man with many friends in Britain, had been yachting at

* Plaintiffs in the High Court action which took place the following year.
† The assassination of Archduke Francis Ferdinand revived the latent Austro-Serbian conflict.

Cowes, while Queen Sophie had taken her children for a seaside holiday at Eastbourne. Prince Henry saw King George as late as 26 July and, primed by wishful thinking, gained the impression that Britain would remain neutral. He went to see his sister in her Eastbourne hotel before returning to Germany. Queen Sophie hurried back to Athens but left her children, one of whom was only a baby, in the care of their nurse at Eastbourne. Not even Emperor William would have considered leaving his young nephews and nieces locked up in a country with which he was at war.

Alexandra's immediate priority was the predicament of her relations – the Greek children and also Dagmar who was staying with her at Marlborough House. A ship was chartered to carry the former to Holland and the nurse and her charges reached the Continent under naval escort, proceeding by train to Greece.

Alexandra did her utmost to persuade her sister not to attempt the hazardous journey back to Russia, but to no avail. Dagmar was determined and, ill-advisedly, decided to travel via Berlin.

> There her train was held up, and for hours she sat in her compartment, with the windows closed, and the blinds drawn down, hardly able to breathe in the stifling heat, while the crowds on the platform jeered and hooted, or sang ribald songs, anathemizing Russia, and boasting of a speedy victory for the German armies.[4]

At long last an official from the German foreign office arrived and curtly informed her that she must return to England or go to Denmark. She chose the latter and on 6 August left Copenhagen for St Petersburg, travelling through Sweden and Finland. A Reuter telegram of the 5th from St Petersburg ran: 'The anti-German feeling has been immeasurably intensified by the treatment by the German authorities of the Dowager Empress . . .'[5] And the German press railed at her, coupling her name with the widow of that 'archfiend', Edward VII.

Alexandra now began her indefatigable efforts to help the wounded and encourage the war effort, all the time haunted by the fear that the Lady Warwick scandal would become public, thus presenting Emperor William with a heaven-sent opportunity to libel the memory of her husband. For a year that cloud hung over her and then, after a High Court action, Daisy, was silenced,* though she fared well financially. Arthur du Cros took upon his own shoulders the burden of the £16,000 she already owed him, as well as £48,000 she owed elsewhere, giving her a benefit of £64,000. 'So that amount was what she really got after all for "dear Edward's" letters. Nothing from the royal family, nothing from the American publishers, but a nice £64,000 from her intermediary, Arthur du Cros.'[6] In 1916 he received a baronetcy. For fifty years the letters from Bertie, which ended with such compromising words as – 'Goodnight & God keep you, my own adored little Daisy Wife. For ever yours, Your only Love' –[7] lay undisturbed and fading among family papers in a locked deed box in a chalet in Switzerland.

While Alexandra reserved her anger and invective of Germany for Emperor William and his leaders in Berlin, the British public loosed an emotional outpouring of hatred against everyone and everything even remotely connected with 'the Fatherland'. Dachshunds were stoned, the windows of shops bearing German names were smashed and public offices were inundated with abusive letters aimed at any employee with German connections, even by marriage or by education. The relentless hunt was on for 'Germhuns'.† To Alexandra's sadness, one victim was the First Sea Lord, Prince Louis of Battenberg, one of the outstanding sailors of all time. Although Prince Louis had been in the British Navy since 1868, he was German-bred and owned property there, and the feeling was so strong against him that he had to retire. There was some consolation to her that the man who took his place was her 'beloved Admiral', Jack Fisher. Fisher had been raised to the peerage as Baron Fisher of Kilverstone in December 1909 and retired from the office of First Sea Lord the following month. Now, at seventy-three, he was recalled to the Admiralty.

Prince Louis had been a favourite dancing partner of Alex-

---

* An injunction against the publication of King Edward's letters had been applied for 'in Chambers' and an interlocutory injunction granted. The King's identity was masked under the word 'Testator' and the point was made that the letters were copyright.

† An expression coined by Horatio Bottomley in the magazine *John Bull*.

andra's at the gay parties at Sandringham of the eighties. She had stood by him when he had a child by Lillie Langtry, at a time when most people believed that Bertie was the paramour of the famous beauty.[8] When Prince Louis's nephew, Prince Maurice, was killed in October 1914 Alexandra stood by the family, comforted his mother and attended the memorial service held at the Chapel Royal, St James's.

Alexandra herself tasted of the dangers of German attack. On 19 January 1915 Zeppelins bombed the Sandringham area. The following appeared in the *National Review*:

> Only by the Kaiser's express orders did the German aviators seek to murder our Royal Family, just as it was by Imperial orders that the Zeppelin visiting Antwerp threw a bomb on the wing of King Albert's Palace in which the Royal children were sleeping. The attack on Sandringham is, if we may be permitted to say so, a personal triumph for our Royal House, especially Queen Alexandra. Neither King George, nor Queen Mary, nor any of their children ever cottoned on to their cousin of Potsdam . . .[9]

Churchillian in her fury, Alexandra wrote to Lord Fisher: 'Please let me have a lot of *rockets* with spikes or hooks on . . . I am sure you could invent something of the sort which would bring down a few of those rascals.'[10] On 2 September 1916 the 'Zepps' came back to Norfolk again, thirteen of them, one of which was destroyed.[11] Alexandra was sitting in her daughter Victoria's room when, at ten o'clock, the threatening, reverberating rumble of the engines was heard. Victoria, ever nervous and physically weak, went as white as a sheet. The staff extinguished all lights and rushed upstairs to persuade the Queen and Princess to take shelter in the cellars. The rumble turned to a roar as one airship passed directly overhead. Alexandra and Charlotte Knollys stumbled downstairs and out into the garden. She said afterwards: 'I must confess I was not a bit afraid – but it was a most uncanny feeling . . .'[12] At four in the morning the 'Zepps', on their way home, unloaded their remaining bombs about the royal estate.

Alexandra reached her seventieth birthday in 1914. At a time when she could have expected to retire from her major duties and relax in Norfolk, she was called upon to take a leading role once more. To the general public she was the best known of the royal family, and only the very old could remember the days before the beautiful Princess of Denmark held the star role at Sandringham and Marlborough House. Now her long association with hospitals, and her pioneer work with military nursing services placed her in a key position. She was able to keep an iron hand on the administration, telling Lord Knutsford: '*Nothing* will I *allow* to be touched without *our mutual* approval and sanction'. She was also president of the British Red Cross Society. It was written of her while the memory of her was still fresh: 'Only the tabulated list of her public engagements during the war years can give any idea of her strenuous and unwearied work in those days. How at seventy and upwards she endured that self-imposed strain, is only another proof that the legend of her perpetual youth rested on something deeper than mere externals.'[13]

Photographic evidence, contemporary written reports and personal recollection prove in fact that Alexandra was far from finished. When Lord Fisher met her on his return to office he described her as being as beautiful as ever. She could still swing her stiff leg over bedside tables to demonstrate how the wounded could overcome their handicap. Certainly there was criticism of her for her financial contributions to welfare and war charities, as her lavish spending could not be supported by her income, liable as it was to taxation. Certainly there was irritation on the part of tidy-minded officials over her lengthy and unpredictable visits to hospitals. It was impossible to tie her to a schedule – 'Arrive hospital entrance at 11.17. Visit wards A, B and D. Inspect operating theatre and nurses's home. Depart 12.35' – but then the same might be said of the woman who shares with her the zenith of the love of the British people, Queen Elizabeth, the Queen Mother. When Alexandra entered a hospital she made sure that she spoke to every patient capable of chatting with her. She came as a nurse with long and real experience. For example, she was not unfamiliar with problems of lice, men returning from the trenches often being infected.[14] Sometimes the women who accompanied her drew back in horror when they saw the black specks on the pillow; Alexandra ignored them. Lord Knutsford has left a picture of a visit by her to her favourite London Hospital:

Queen Alexandra's love for 'The London' was a real passion. She wrote of it and spoke of it as 'her' hospital, and she made it so. She visited it very often indeed, and her visits were never processions, but were intimate and enjoyed by visitor and visited alike. Princess Victoria, who frequently accompanied her mother, was always very naturally anxious they should not be too prolonged, but what could I, or anyone, do – it was easy to get Queen Alexandra into a ward, but very hard to get her out of one. The visit that I remember most vividly of all was one paid during the first year of the War. She was determined that every one of the wounded men, and there were over 200 of them, should have an individual word from her.[15]

It was Alexandra's deep sympathy which led her to take interest in, and give backing to, the work of the 'Special Hospitals', originally named 'Shell-shock Hospitals', but changed as patients complained that it sounded as if they were suffering from 'cold feet'. In any case the doctors knew that the ills which they treated were often nothing to do with shells. At the outbreak of war there was no medical treatment available for cases of nervous exhaustion, trauma and shock. In all, six hospitals were established to provide such treatment, the first being opened in January 1915, and Queen Alexandra gave them priority in her programme of visits.

The difference in approach of Queens Mary and Alexandra towards hospital visits and meeting the wounded was most marked. Queen Mary was dutiful, punctual and an expert on organization and administration, but she could not make human contact with the men, mutilated physically or mentally, who lay in the beds. 'What a relief', she sighed to Queen Marie of Romania, as they left a London hospital full of wounded soldiers, 'I never know what to say to them.'[16] Her visits were more in the nature of inspection. It had been the same with her, even in her relations with her husband and her children. The contrast was noted most clearly at Sandringham, when the dreaded telegrams arrived telling of the death of a tenant or estate worker.*

Queen Mary, duly escorted, would arrive at a cottage and,

---

* The Norfolk estate knew much sadness. On 12 August 1915 the agent, Captain Frank Beck, and a detachment of Sandringham men, took part in an advance at Gallipoli and were never heard of again.

after the customary and well-worn remarks of commiseration with the widow or mother, would enquire 'what lot' the dead man had served with. On learning of the name of the unit, she would brighten: 'Oh! the 14th Blankshires! A jolly good lot! Jolly good lot!' – and then off she would go, her parasol at the ready and her mission accomplished, towards the next house of sadness. Shortly afterwards, late as usual, Queen Alexandra would drive up, hurry through the door unannounced and, grasping the bereaved woman in her arms, would whisper, 'Oh! my dear! My poor dear!'

Alexandra did not escape family anxiety as a result of the war. On the afternoon of 28 October 1915 she invited Queen Mary to tea at Marlborough House. A message arrived that the King, who was in France, had had a fall from his horse while inspecting men of the Royal Flying Corps at Hesdigneul. Although he usually carried out such inspections on foot or from a car, on this occasion Sir Douglas Haig had provided him with a mare considered to be completely crowd-trained. But the cheering of the men was so deafening that the mare shied, slipped on the wet ground and fell on the King. Fortunately the Prince of Wales was there and able to assist his father back to the small château in the woods where he was staying.[17] The doctors saw at once that the damage was more than mere bruising and, despite the pleas of Army Headquarters to move him immediately for fear of the Germans bombing the château, it was not until 1 November that they allowed him to return to England. Meantime the gravity of the accident was kept secret for security purposes and neither his wife nor his mother were informed that he had a double fracture of the pelvis. Fifty at the time, King George aged considerably thereafter, and suffered recurring pain and increased irrascibility.

Another sorrow for Alexandra was the sad condition of her grandson, John, youngest child of the King and Queen. He suffered from epilepsy. A gay and friendly little boy, he was subject to fits and his normal development was arrested. He was a particular favourite of his grandmother who saw more of him than did his parents, their visits to Sandringham being restricted owing to their many duties. At the age of twelve the doctors decided that John must have a separate establishment and he was moved to Wood Farm, Wolferton, in the care of his devoted

Queen Mary and Queen Alexandra at the wedding of Lord Louis Mountbatten and
Miss Edwina Ashley, St Margaret's Westminster, July 18, 1922

Queen Alexandra on the last of her Alexandra Rose Day drives through the streets of London

Four generations of the royal family. Queen Alexandra with her son, King George V. In the foreground are King George's daughter, Princess Mary and her son, George Henry Hubert Lascelles

Sandringham, for many years the country home of Queen Alexandra. A photograph taken in the year of her death. It was here that Queen Alexandra spent her last days

nurse, 'Lalla'. Alexandra worried that he would be lonely and the worsening of his health was an ever-present worry to her. He died in 1919.

The deaths as result of German action of two outstanding Britons hurt Alexandra deeply and intensified her hatred of everything German: those of Nurse Cavell and Lord Kitchener. She had known Edith Cavell, a Norfolk girl, since she had enlisted at the London Hospital for her training in 1896. In 1907 she had been appointed Matron of Dr de Page's Training School for Nurses in a suburb of Brussels. In November 1914 she became part of a secret organization, the object of which was to help British, French and Belgian soldiers to reach the safety of the Dutch frontier.[18] In August 1915 she was arrested. Despite strong US and other protests, she was sentenced to death on 9 October and shot three days later. Before she fell she said: 'I have no fear nor shrinking; I have seen death so often that it is not strange or fearful to me . . . But this I would say, standing as I do in view of God and eternity, *I realize that patriotism is not enough. I must have no hatred or bitterness towards anyone.'* The four words – *Patriotism is not enough* – echoed round the world, becoming as historic as the last utterance of Nelson at Trafalgar. For the funeral service in Westminster Abbey Alexandra sent a wreath of flowers. The note with them was written in her own hand: 'In memory of our brave, heroic, never-to-be-forgotten Miss Cavell.

> Life's race well run,
> Life's work well done,
> Life's crown well won,
> Now comes rest.
> From Alexandra'[19]

Although Lord Kitchener, being a bachelor, had a reputation as a 'woman-hater', this was contradicted by the friendship between himself and Queen Alexandra, a friendship which had lasted many years. Alexandra ever recalled the moment when he came to Buckingham Palace in July 1902 on his return from the Boer War to receive the Order of Merit. The great soldier knelt beside the bed of King Edward, weak from the illness which caused the postponement of the coronation, and kissed his hand.

As the King struggled to place the order around the Field Marshal's neck, the contrast between the strength of the two men overcame Alexandra and she burst into tears, something she rarely did.

When the war came Kitchener, now secretary of state for war, every day sent Queen Alexandra a special war bulletin, which she read carefully and then destroyed.[20] He helped her in many ways, agreeing to visit the London Hospital and talk to the wounded at a time when morale needed a boost and by posing, on Alexandra Rose Day, outside the War Office, setting an example by buying a rose from a pretty seller in white.[21]

In May 1916 Emperor Nicholas urged that Kitchener should visit Russia, to strengthen resistance there and carry out necessary reforms to the Russian military machine. The British Government agreed. Queen Alexandra was furious and wrote to the King saying that she considered the journey to be unnecessary and dangerous. She went to see the Field Marshal and, when handing him a letter for her sister, begged him not to go. But he would not change his mind, convinced that it was his duty. She left him sadly for, despite all the safety precautions which the navy would take in transporting such an important man, she had a premonition that he would not come back.

It was a premonition which was felt by many, and increased by a séance at which Lady Curzon, wife of the famous statesman, was present. Spiritualist Belita Hollway was in charge and questions were being asked about the war:

> When someone asked whether Lord Kitchener would remain long at the War Office as Minister for War, the pointer moved so quickly that we could not spell out the words. Then it stopped completely. At first we thought that was the end. But Belita repeated the question, saying 'Please move more slowly, we can't follow such speed.' Then the pointer began again, and moved with great deliberation . . . pausing at each letter while an unmistakable sentence was spelled out. '*Kitchener will be drowned.*'[22]

On 5 June 1916 Lord Kitchener was drowned when the cruiser *Hampshire* hit a mine on the way to Archangel. Broken-hearted, Alexandra immediately put herself at the head of a movement to raise funds for a practical and permanent memorial to 'K of K.' – Kitchener of Khartoum. Her appeal brought in gifts from every corner of the Empire and the final sum donated was nearly three-quarters of a million pounds.[23]

During the last two years of the war the scope of Queen Alexandra's work widened. When munitions became a woman's business, she often visited the shell and fuse factories. She acted as a waitress at the 'free buffets' for soldiers at London Bridge and Waterloo stations. She gave untiring backing to the Soldiers' and Sailors' Families Association. Although she had proved herself a star in the ceremonial setting since the 1860s, it was in these more humble fields that she revealed more truly the woman that she really was. And she was a continual support for her son. On 2 June 1918 he wrote to her:

> I am grateful for your prayers; they are a comfort to me and will help me to get through all these anxious days and I fear more lie ahead of us. But we must be courageous and go on to the end, however long it may take, as I shall never submit to those brutal Germans and I am sure the British Nation is of the same opinion.[24]

Then the Germans made their final lunge for victory. On 15 July Emperor William, from a camouflaged belvedere in Champagne, watched the final offensive of the German forces. He waited, in the warm summer rain, for news of victory. Three days later General Foch struck and the battle was broken off.* The Emperor climbed down from the observation post and walked slowly to his Imperial train. Before his staff he did his best to retain an air of confidence and hope, but, when he reached his coach, the pose deserted him. Dejectedly, he looked upon the photographs hanging in the corridor, reminiscent of long ago – his Aunt Alix and Uncle Bertie amid a group of guests at Sandringham, a dead stag lying on the gravel before the door of Balmoral, his house at Corfu, Queen Victoria and her family taking tea under the trees on the lawns of Osborne. The train rumbled through the night to Spa in Belgium. There, at a Crown Council, the conclusion was reached: 'We can no longer hope to break the war-will of our enemies by military operations.' On 10 November William, All Highest of Germany, went into exile in Holland.

Queen Alexandra was at Sandringham for Armistice Day,

---

* Owing to a lack of reserves, Ludendorff was forced to abandon the offensive and the initiative passed to the Allies.

but in London for the triumphant home-coming of Sir Douglas Haig in December.

Like Kitchener, Douglas Haig was a long-standing friend of Alexandra, having been ADC to King Edward. Dorothy Vivian, and her twin sister Violet, had been Maids of Honour to Alexandra. They dressed alike, were very pretty, and she called them her 'heavenly twins'.[25] When Dorothy became engaged to Douglas Haig, Alexandra arranged that they should be married at Buckingham Palace and, after the ceremony, insisted that one of her shoes should be tied to the going-away carriage, thereafter amusing the guests by hopping about on one foot. Thus in December 1918 Alexandra decided that Dorothy with her two daughters, now aged ten and eleven, should watch the triumphal drive of the Field Marshal from Charing Cross from the windows of Marlborough House. She also had another plan. This was to venture out into the roadway and congratulate Douglas Haig in person. She informed the palace of her intention, only to be told that such a course was most inadvisable, as it would upset the procession's timetable and cause problems for the police.

Alexandra, Lady Haig and the two girls took their places in a window of Marlborough House. Each held a small Union Jack and Lady Haig was unaware that anything was afoot. But as the procession approached, Queen Alexandra rose and told her guests to follow her. Out into the street she went, forcing her way through the astonished sightseers who lined the route. Haig's carriage, resplendent with its liveried royal servants, came into sight. A hush fell over the crowds as they saw Queen Alexandra, Lady Haig and the two girls standing on the processional route. The coachman, having had no orders to stop, drove on. Alexandra moved out into his path, forcing his hand. The carriage halted. A delighted, somewhat bewildered, Field Marshal stood up and Queen Alexandra took his hand. He bowed low and then the hush ended and the crowds roared their delight. They exchanged a few words,[26] Alexandra pressed a flower into his hand and, as the carriage moved on, she turned on the smile which had entranced Britain for nearly sixty years and led the way back into the quiet of her London home. Once again she had demonstrated her independence of spirit and her determination to give honour where honour was due.

TWENTY ONE

Divided Loyalties

Seldom if ever has a woman faced more divided loyalties than Queen Alexandra in World War I. Her daughter, Maud, was the Queen of Norway; her nephew, Christian, the King of Denmark; Margaret, her niece was Crown Princess of Sweden; another niece, Victoria Eugenia, the Queen of Spain; yet another, Marie, Queen of Romania; her nephew, Constantine, the King of Greece; her sister Dagmar the Dowager Empress of Russia; her nephew, Nicholas, the Emperor of Russia; her niece, 'Alicky', the Empress; and her nephew, William, the Emperor of Germany. Her sister Thyra was shut off in Austria; her nephew, the Duke of Brunswick-Luneburg, was serving with the German X Army; and her brother, Waldemar, was married to a French woman, Princess Marie of Bourbon-Orleans. Although some of these were in safety under the umbrella of neutrality, neutrality was of uncertain value in that world-wide holocaust.

Periodically came news of the death of distant relations, men who had been children when she was Princess of Wales. One such example came from the family of Vicky, Empress Frederick of Germany, King Edward's favourite sister. It was Vicky who had suggested Princess Alexandra of Denmark as Bertie's bride and who eventually brought the two together at Speyer in 1862. In spite of their differences, the two had remained close friends for forty years and when Vicky developed cancer Alexandra had shown great sympathy and travelled out to Germany to comfort her in her last days. While at Friedrichshof she had played with Vicky's grandsons.

It was a bullet from a British soldier's rifle which was to kill

277

one of those boys. On 12 October 1914, the British Third Cavalry Brigade, under Gough, was near Bailleul, in Flanders. The brigade scouts brought back news that a company of the crack German Death's Head Hussars was hiding by a monastery ahead. The brigade went out to get them. Sergeant West and Sergeant Jones rode side by side across the stubble where the dawn mist hung low. The Brigade's sweeping crossfire raked the German hideout. From behind the walls, a fair-haired German officer sprinted for the line of tethered horses. He was hit as his foot reached the stirrup. The Germans returned the fire and Sergeant Jones fell wounded at Sergeant West's side. The German officer had been badly hit. When the skirmish was over and a British doctor was tending him, he asked how long he had to live. He was told only a matter of hours. He then said that he was Prince Maximilian of Hesse and a great-grandson of Queen Victoria. He asked that the locket round his neck, containing a picture of his mother, Princess Margaret of Hesse, should be returned to her. The doctor promised that he would do his best. Next day the doctor was killed.[1] His possessions, including the locket, were forwarded to his widow. Having been informed that her husband had tended a German prince, she forwarded the locket to Queen Mary. Mary consulted Alexandra and it was forwarded to the Crown Princess of Sweden, formerly Princess Margaret of Connaught. The locket was eventually returned to Princess Margaret at Friedrichshof.

There were further developments. Sergeant Jones also died and he was buried in the same grave as Prince Maximilian. Shortly afterwards the grave was opened and the body of the German spirited away. Rumours about the identity of the prince spread among the troops and reached the British press, which began to speculate as to the name of the royal personage whose coffin had merited such particular treatment. 'THE MYSTERY OF PRINCE ———' ran the headlines, and some very bitter things were said, reminders of the link between the British and Germany royal families being most unwelcome. Maximilian's body finally reached Kronberg and was re-buried in the old castle there.

Much of the discord between Britain and Greece during the war years would have been avoided if the Greek King had not been assassinated in 1913. Britain had been responsible for making George King of the Hellenes and he always remained firmly attached to his sister's adopted home. If he wanted a pig for his farm, he ordered it from Sandringham. Just as his father had continued to treat his offspring as children until he died, so George attempted the same in Greece. But while King Christian succeeded in keeping the next generation on the leading rein, George failed. Alexandra, a firm believer in the unity of the family, had been horrified at the constant quarrels which took place between father and sons. The Greek royal children grew up in an age of quickly changing values, encouraged by the emergence of progress in the form of communication and power, transport and scientific invention. The new order broke the link of parental discipline, outdating the older generation. The sons of King George lost patience with the belief in parental omnipotence as practised at Bernstorff. Although they adored their aunt Alexandra, they regarded her as a symbol of the past, and pulled her leg without mercy.

In Greece the outbreak of war in 1914 was not only entirely unsuspected, it also came as a great shock. On 2 August Constantine received a telegram from Emperor William saying that he had concluded an alliance with Turkey and Bulgaria in case of war with Russia and that he would treat Greece as an enemy if she did not join Germany immediately.[2] But the Emperor was over-playing his hand. Although Constantine had been educated in Germany, studied at the Prussian Staff College and been appointed a Field Marshal in the Prussian army this did not commit him to Germany blindly and without question. True, he had married the Emperor's sister, Sophie, a vital link with the fatherland, as hostile opinion was soon to present it, but it was little known that Sophie and her eldest brother had been at loggerheads since the death of their father in 1888. Then William's cruel treatment of his mother had infuriated and revolted her. William was in no way responsible for the marriage of Sophie and 'Tino', Alexandra having brought them together at the time of the Diamond Jubilee. When, after her marriage, Sophie adopted the Orthodox religion, Emperor William was furious and refused to see her, even going so far as to forbid her to visit Germany.[3] While Empress Frederick continued to quarrel with her eldest son up to the day of her death, she adored her Greek son-in-law, saying of him, '. . . darling Tino, as dear to me as my own son'.[4] As we have seen, Empress Frederick had no affinity with her three eldest children, but deeply loved and understood the four youngest. But the point remained that Sophie and William were brother and sister and general opinion regarded the relationship as having the same bond as appears in the average family.

Constantine spoke his forthright comments on the German Emperor's telegram of 2 August to his brother, Nicholas:

> Does he take me for a German? Because he has given me a Field Marshal's baton, does he imagine that I am under any obligation to him? If that is so, I am ready to return it at once. He seems to forget his geography and that Greece would cease to exist within twenty-four hours of declaring herself Germany's ally. Who ever heard of such a thing! No. We are Greeks and the interests of Greece come first. For the present, at any rate, it is imperative that we should remain neutral. But as to joining Germany, such an eventuality is and always will be an impossibility.[5]

The Greek army had been strained by the recent Balkan wars and was in no state to enter a major conflict. If Greece joined Germany, the allied fleets would pound her coasts. If she joined the allies, German land forces would sweep down upon her. Greece's treaty with Serbia did not impose obligation to intervene in a war against a non-Balkan power and Constantine therefore opted for neutrality. But on 31 October 1914 Turkey entered the war on Germany's side and the situation altered. The Dardanelles were closed, thus cutting off direct communication between Great Britain and Russia. The Gallipoli campaign to force the passage was set in motion.

While Constantine remained firm in his policy of neutrality, his Prime Minister, M. Venizelos, was increasingly in favour of joining the Allies. The problem evolved into a duel between King and Prime Minister. Both Germany and France were loud and raucous in their demands that Greece should join them, but Britain played the matter down for as long as possible, partly in consideration of the links between their two royal houses, dating back for half a century.

After the disasters of the Gallipoli landings, there was no controlling the flood of hate and recrimination. Venizelos became the hero of London and Paris, Constantine the pro-German conspirator who prevented Greece giving aid to the Allies. Deeply worried, King Constantine decided to find out the true situation by sending, on separate occasions, two of his brothers to London. They were Prince Andrew and Prince Nicholas.* Prince Andrew arrived in London in July 1916 and, although he had a friendly interview with George V, was generally treated with suspicion and hostility. He was hurt and horrified to see the newspaper placards in the streets carrying such headlines as ALLIED PLANS BETRAYED TO GERMANY BY TINO–TINO'S NEW TREACHERY.[6] He returned to Athens with a gloomy picture.

Meantime the King had been harassed by Alexandra who constantly expressed her views about the deterioration of affairs in Greece. The result was a letter of 'unaccustomed emphasis' which the King sent to the Prime minister. It included the words: 'I cannot help feeling that in this Greek question we have allowed France too much to dictate a policy, and that as a Republic she may be somewhat intolerant of, if not anxious to abolish, the monarchy in Greece.'[7]

After a hazardous journey from Russia, where he had talked with the Emperor, Prince Nicholas arrived in London in October. He wrote of his arrival at Marlborough House:

> 'She greeted me with the same warm affection she had always shown me, and with that particular sweetness of which only she knew the secret. Queen Alexandra was not the person to allow her feelings of fond attachment to those she had loved in the happy days of peace to be influenced by the sordid work of calumny. Even in the darker days which were to follow, when old friends turned against us and it was considered a treasonable act to associate with us or even to acknowledge our acquaintance, Queen Alexandra never altered her affections, but remained the dearest and truest of friends.'[8]

Nicholas returned to Athens with the hope that something had been done to heal the wounds, but in his absence he found

* The fathers of Prince Philip, Duke of Edinburgh, and Princess Marina, Duchess of Kent.

that events had taken a turn for the worse. When Romania joined the Allies in August, the prime minister seceded to Salonika and there set up a provisional revolutionary government. Thereafter the Allies recognized the new Revolutionary Committee as the *de facto* government and Greece declared war on Germany, Turkey and Bulgaria. It was the end of the road for Constantine. In June he went into exile in Switzerland with his family, leaving his son, Alexander, on the throne. Thus, with abject bitterness, Queen Alexandra's long love affair with Greece came to an end; an affair which had begun in 1863 when her young brother William had learned from the newspaper in which his sandwich lunch was packed, that he was to be the King of the Hellenes.

The outbreak of hostilities brought the three Scandinavian countries closer together and, having proclaimed their neutrality, they signed an agreement to prevent any of the three taking action detrimental to another. Alexandra wrote to her nephew, King Christian X of Denmark: 'God protect the three Northern Kingdoms from their★ clutches! The courage of the three Kings was fine, and I hope to God they will maintain their neutrality.' Owing to Denmark's continuing export trade, shipowners and industrialists were able to carry messages to Alexandra's relations, and keep her in touch with their activities and welfare. It was through this channel that many of her letters to King Christian travelled. When in 1915 the Danish King suggested that the final peace conference should be held in Copenhagen, she replied that the idea was splendid – a fitting honour for the city of her birth – but added: 'We must thrash them first of all!'⁹ And always she dreamed of recapturing Schleswig-Holstein by force. In 1917 Admiral Fisher wrote to her: 'There is yet time to re-conquer Schleswig-Holstein and the Kiel Canal. It should be done now! I guarantee I could do it!'

Alexandra's main contact with Russia was through her sister, Dagmar. The shadow of Rasputin deterred her from intimate correspondence with the Emperor and Empress and rumours of the increasing influence of the latter over the Emperor as a result of Rasputin's pressure worried her deeply. In February 1915 the Dowager Empress informed her son: 'Aunt Alix wires to say that they know for certain that the Germans intend to attack

★ Germany and Austria.

Warsaw this week and she hopes we are aware of this. . . . Her information has usually been correct.'[10]

The Russian Revolution began. On 1 January 1917 the body of Rasputin was taken from the River Neva and during the month the Duma, Russian parliament, was adjourned. On 8 March the Emperor left for his military headquarters and the following day there were bread riots in Petrograd.* On the 12th the Guards' regiment mutinied and the Winter Palace was stormed. On the 15th the Emperor abdicated. On the 21st Lloyd George, the British Prime Minister, wired to the Provisional Government in Petrograd expressing the 'sentiments of the most profound satisfaction' with which the British people had received the news that Russia had adopted 'responsible government'.[11] The following day Emperor Nicholas joined his family under arrest at Tsarskoe. On 4 April Lenin arrived in Petrograd and in July the Bolshevik riots there were put down by Kerensky. In August the Emperor and his family were transferred to Tobolsk and in November came the Bolshevik Revolution.

After the abdication, the Provisional Government had inquired whether Britain would give the Emperor and his family asylum. As the request originated in Russia, the idea was approved at a meeting in Downing Street at which the prime minister was present. But King George did not agree. As a result of the criticism which had been levelled at him after meeting the Greek Princes, he did not wish to become involved and preferred that 'Nicky' should shelter in Denmark, Switzerland or France. He felt the cold winds of change. While the death of Rasputin had been greeted with relief by royalty and certain ministerial circles, to the less privileged it was fast becoming looked upon as the murder of a 'man of the people' by aristocrats. And it was largely in this light the Americans, now preparing to join the allies, saw it. Although the request for asylum had come from Russia, the public was quick to see the Romanoff arrival as a move by King George to protect his relatives. In Russia crowds were demonstrating against the Empress, 'Down with the German Woman' written large on their placards.

* During World War I the name of St Petersburg was altered to Petrograd, and, after the Revolution, to Leningrad.

The King was 'sensitive to criticism, essentially diffident and prone to discouragement'.[12] When H. G. Wells referred to his court as 'alien and uninspiring',[13] he remonstrated: 'I may be uninspiring, but I'll be damned if I'm alien!' The truth was that George had not yet realized the extremes of man's inhumanity to man. Emperor William of Germany, ever obsessed by the fear of assassination, saw the matter in a clearer light and was agreeable to giving Nicholas and his family a safe passage to England.

Meanwhile, the Emperor still clung to the hope that the family would be allowed to live in retirement in Russia, sharing the same trust in human nature as their cousin. When they at last considered taking passage to England, it was too late. A telegram came for the British Ambassador to Russia, Sir George Buchanan, and as he opened it tears came into his eyes. It announced that the Emperor Nicholas and the Empress Alexandra Feodorovna were no longer welcome in England.

Sir George's daughter, Meriel, described the arrival of the news:

> After my father had read the telegram, he paled. 'What's the matter?' I asked. 'They're refusing to allow the Czar into England. They say it would be more prudent to dissuade the Imperial Family from coming to England.' 'Why?' 'They're worried.' 'What about?' 'Of unrest in England. There could be strikes in the docks, in the munition factories and in the mines. Even a revolt may be possible if the Czar came to England . . .'[14]

It was on 24 July 1918 that confirmation of the death of the Russian Emperor and his family reached London. Two days later Queen Mary invited Queen Alexandra and Princess Victoria to Buckingham Palace – 'Mama and Toria came to tea, terribly upset at the news'.[15] Alexandra was determined that Dagmar should escape a like fate and sent as many urgent demands as the poor communications would permit, begging her to leave the country. But it was one thing to insist and quite another to make the brave and obstinate Dowager Empress obey. Another of Alexandra's relations was more discreet. Grand Duke Dimitri, serving in disgrace on the Persian front for his part in the murder of Rasputin, managed to slip across the frontier and was given

284

shelter in the British Legation at Teheran. He reached London in the late summer of 1918.

In 1917 Kiev became a centre of violence and, under pressure from the provisional government who feared for her safety, Dagmar agreed to move to a villa near Yalta in the Crimea. Then the Russian Black Sea Fleet mutinied and gangs of sailors and deserters from the army played havoc, a gang invading the villa at night, taking many of the Empress's possessions and forbidding her to leave the property.

Residents and those who had sought safety in the Crimea lived in daily terror of execution. Many were shot, then taken to the pier and thrown into the water with stones tied round their ankles. One woman, whose husband had disappeared, bribed a diver to look on the seabed. He did not give the signal to be raised and, when he was pulled up, he was found to be mad. Another diver went down to investigate. He found himself 'among a concourse of corpses' – nurses and nuns, priests and officers. The dead stood upright, held to the sand by the stones round their feet. Their hair moved with the tide like reeds upon a stream, their arms waved up and down, their clothes swayed as if they walked.[16]

Rumours of such bestiality reached London when the streets were lined with rejoicing crowds at Armistice time. For Alexandra, the contrast between joy and sadness was a shattering experience. On 23 November she took part in one of the first victory celebrations, a review of disabled soldiers and sailors. King George rode ahead, Queens Mary and Alexandra following in a landau. The King wrote: 'There were between 30,000 and 35,000 present: they were most enthusiastic & in riding down the lines they broke through & came round me to shake hands. I was nearly pulled off my horse.[17]

In April 1919 the King decided that Dagmar must be rescued and he sent HMS *Marlborough* to collect her. At first she refused to obey the captain but, under pressure, agreed, on condition that all her friends in a similar position were taken on board. There were three days of dangerous delay before the swollen party began their trip to England.

Queen Alexandra, with the King and Queen, went to Portsmouth to meet the Dowager Empress. Nearly five years had passed since they had parted and now they were reunited in the floodlight of ceremony and in the public gaze. The ship's company lined the deck. The whistles blew and Alexandra was piped on board. As the two sisters moved towards one another to embrace, it was noted that, while Dagmar was obviously excited and distressed, Alexandra was her usual unruffled, perfectly disciplined, royal self.

After a stay in England, Dagmar moved on to Denmark. There, the following year, her sister visited her.

Now at last, part of Alexandra's dream of a lifetime came true. On 7 July North Schleswig was handed back to the Danes. King Christian X arrived in the yacht *Danneborg* and, mounted on a white horse, rode over the frontier into the Duchy of Schleswig, from where his dynasty had risen. There were memories that day of Bertie's words, spoken in 1864: 'If we had sent our fleet to the Baltic at the beginning of the Danish war, all this bloodshed might have been avoided. . . .'

The Infanta Eulalia of Spain one day came across the sisters, wandering by the sound at Hvidore, searching for amber as they had always done. Dagmar's hair was silver bound and there was deep sadness and uncertainty in her eyes. She would not accept then, or ever, that her son and grandchildren had been murdered – it was more than she could bear.[18]

TWENTY TWO

❧

November Evening

The slow descent into the last phase of life is often made in shadow, a shadow thrown by the deaths of contemporaries, both friends and relations. Yet for Queen Alexandra the days were still bright with the joy of a galaxy of weddings. Inevitably she lost some old and trusted friends, outstanding among them being Lord Fisher in 1920, the Marquess of Milford Haven in 1921 and Sir Dighton Probyn, her Comptroller and Treasurer, in 1924, but in the main the gay ring of wedding bells out-peeled the tolling.

In February 1919 Princess Patricia of Connaught, was married to Commander Alexander Ramsay. The wedding was at Westminster Abbey and the service so impressed King George and Queen Mary that it led them to select the Abbey for the wedding of their own daughter. Alexandra still had star-rating:

> It is 11.50. There is an anticipatory thrill and the sound of chairs being moved an inch or two on the stone floor, as, in the nave, far beyond the organ screen, the waiting occupants are rising to their feet . . . Queen Alexandra has arrived. She had discarded her long accustomed black and silver and wears a deep shade of mauve . . .[1]

In 1920 a favourite nephew of Queen Alexandra, Prince Christopher of Greece, the last unmarried child of King George, married Mrs Nancy Stewart Leeds, an American widow. And two years later Marie, whose first husband, Grand Duke George, had been assassinated in Russia in 1919, married Admiral Pericles Joanides of the Greek Navy.

That year of 1922 was rich in weddings, outstanding among them being that of Princess Mary, only daughter of the King and

287

Queen. To Queen Alexandra's delight it was at Sandringham that Viscount Lascelles proposed to her. After the February wedding at the Abbey, Queen Mary wrote to the Prince of Wales, who was abroad: 'Grannie was wonderful & looked very nice in violet velvet wearing the Garter & fine jewels. Enormous crowds everywhere & a great reception when we stepped on to the Balcony.'[2]

Pictures from the past flooded back to Alexandra as preparations were made for a July wedding at St Margaret's, Westminster. Lord Louis Mountbatten was marrying the Hon. Edwina Ashley. The son of the young Prince Louis of Battenberg, who had sailed up the Nile with them in 1869, a close friend of her husband and herself, and the paramour of Lillie Langtry, was walking to the altar with the granddaughter of Sir Ernest Cassel – a union of memories indeed. At a luncheon at Buckingham Palace before the wedding, Alexandra and Edwina were seen in deep conversation. The old Queen was telling the young bride about past days with her grandfather. Sir Ernest had been one of the last people to talk to Edward VII and, as a memento and a wedding present, she sent Edwina a diamond pendant with the royal cypher in diamonds.[3]

The following year there was another Mountbatten wedding, Lord Louis's sister, Princess Louise, marrying Crown Prince Gustavus of Sweden.★

There was a wedding of greater interest to Queen Alexandra that November: her granddaughter, Princess Maud, marrying Captain Lord Carnegie in the Guards' Chapel at Wellington Barracks. As the couple drove away after the reception, for a Continental honeymoon travelling as 'Mr and Mrs Parker', Alexandra stood on the steps looking down at her son, the King, and her four grandsons, David, Bertie, George and Henry as they threw rose leaves. Now three of her granddaughters were married, and one grandson – the Duke of York. The Prince of Wales, remained obstinately single. She had been doing her best to encourage him to take the step since 1914, when she had produced a 'charming young princess' for him. He had refused to consider her. 'But it is a most suitable marriage in every way,'

★ Succeeded as King Gustavus VI of Sweden in 1950. Queen Louise died in 1965.

Alexandra had argued, 'and what is more, you have often admired her. What possible objection can you have?' He answered quietly: 'Only that I will never under any circumstances marry any woman unless I love her.'[4] Now he was nearing thirty.

However, Bertie's wedding in April 1923 to Lady Elizabeth Bowes-Lyon was a great compensation. At eleven o'clock on the 26th Alexandra, with Dagmar beside her, left Marlborough House. A million people jammed the streets of London and every window and balcony was full. The BBC had asked for permission to broadcast the service, but this was thought to be too revolutionary a step. The King took his place beside his mother. She was in purple and black with an ermine coat, graceful and slender as ever and with her inevitable umbrella. On their arrival at the Abbey the Prince of Wales and the Duke of York kissed her and whispered in her ear.

The Lady Elizabeth Bowes-Lyon and her maids came in by the west door. She paused by the grave of the Unknown Warrior and placed upon it her bouquet of white roses and heather. Then, as she moved on towards the Altar, to the music of 'Lead us Heavenly Father, Lead us', the sun blazed out through the spring clouds and floodlit the brilliant scene.[5]

Alexandra's 'eternal youth' lasted until she was seventy-five. Then, in the early summer of 1920, she broke a blood-vessel in her eye and for some weeks she could see little and was in great pain. Communicating with her became even more difficult. It was necessary to shout to make her hear and strangers calling at Marlborough House thought they must be involved in a family quarrel. But her determination to carry on with her duties overcame her weaknesses. Forced to postpone her Alexandra Rose Day drive, in July she was able to make her customary progress through the City and West End.

A deep worry to her was the fate of her nephew, King Constantine of the Hellenes, and his family, in exile in Switzerland – 'poor, excellent, honest Tino,' she called him. King Alexander's dog was attacked by a monkey. The monkey bit the King in the leg when he went to the dog's assistance, and he died of blood-poisoning. King Constantine was asked to return to

Greece and, after a plebiscite the result of which was overwhelmingly in his favour, he did so. Once again Alexandra was able to say, 'I told you so,' as the news of her nephew's triumphant return to Athens came in. His beflagged train slowly ploughed its way along a line packed with a seething crowd, cheering, yelling and gesticulating with delight. But Constantine went back without the recognition of Great Britain and France and he returned to a country at war with Turkey. After initial successes, disaster came for Greece and the pendulum swung once again. Insurrection broke out in the army and a revolutionary committee demanded that the King abdicate. He did so, in favour of his son George, and on 30 September 1922 he left Athens for Palermo. There, four months later, he died from haemorrhage of the brain. He was only fifty-five.

The sadness was exaggerated for Alexandra as she was relying more and more on Constantine's sister for company and was seeing much of her. Re-married and living in London, Marie was taking over in part the role of Alexandra's shadow, so long played by Princess Victoria. The health of the latter, now in her middle fifties, was becoming increasingly poor and she suffered from two serious illnesses in the early nineteen-twenties. Her doctor, Lord Dawson of Penn, was both perplexed and worried. George V, deciding that it was time that she had a break from 'Motherdear', put at her disposal an apartment in Kensington Palace. This suited the Princess well, but was not so popular with Queen Mary, as 'Princess Victoria aroused in her brother all those philistine tendencies of "the Wales cousins" from which Queen Mary had suffered so much in the first years of her marriage.'[6]

However, one source of happiness to Queen Alexandra was that Queen Olga, widow of King George of the Hellenes, came to live in London with her daughter, having been deprived of her homes in Greece and Russia. She was a frequent visitor to Sandringham and Alexandra was always sad when she left. She was also a guest at Windsor, George V being one of her favourite nephews (she called him 'Sunbeam'). She enjoyed exploring the Castle but being lame and short-sighted she was wheeled about the corridors in an invalid chair by an old retainer who had served

Queen Victoria. Seeing, as in a mist, a bronze statue of a woman on a horse, she remarked, 'Queen Victoria I presume' – unable to discern that the figure was naked. 'No, Ma'am,' replied the shocked servant. 'Lady Godiva of Coventry.'[7]

In February 1923 Alexandra became a great-grandmother again and, with Queen Mary, posed for a 'four generation' photograph which was completed by the mother, Princess Mary, and her infant son.* Then, in March, came the sixtieth anniversary of her arrival in England. She was inundated with messages of congratulation and good wishes and the magazines reprinted the illustrations which they had published in 1863. Her message of thanks to the people was broadcast:

> I am very glad upon the sixtieth Anniversary of my arrival in England to send my affectionate greetings to the British people. From the day when I received such a magnificent welcome upon landing upon these shores in 1863, up to the present time, I have always experienced the greatest kindness and consideration from all classes, and I shall ever remember with gratitude the loyal and devoted sympathy shown to me both in my joys and sorrows. With a sincere and full heart I sincerely thank them.
>
> ALEXANDRA.

On the 13 June she set off from Marlborough House on her Alexandra Rose Day drive, smiling, waving, as gay as ever. On her birthday the following December, the King commented that she was 'looking wonderfully well, one cannot realize that she is 79'.[8] But the winter tired her and she decided that she could no longer face the frequent trips to London and the strain and excitement which they involved. Visiting Denmark was out of the question and to an old friend there who wrote to say how much they missed her, she sent a message on a gramophone record[9] – her first and only recording.

The welfare of the London hospital remained a priority in her thoughts and she was particularly excited when an anonymous donor offered a gift of £80,000 provided the public would subscribe a like amount. The money came in. Early in 1924 she wrote to the organizer of the fund and her old friend, known as

* The Hon. George Lascelles.

'The Prince of Beggars':

> My dear Lord Knutsford,
>   I am most *grateful* for all you have done for *our* dear and precious Hospital, to which the public have added £80,000. You will be happy after this, and I hope to see it once more. I am not very well now and you must excuse this awful writing. I hope you and your dear family are all well and happy. Please accept this little Almanack and think of me as I used to be, now I am breaking up. Excuse this awful letter, but I am always so obliged to you and I hope to see you once more.
>   Yours, ALEXANDRA.[10]

When her eightieth birthday came round, one of the last social occasions of her life, she learned that her family and friends were planning to celebrate it in a special way. Recalling the poverty that she had known as a child, she had always been somewhat embarrassed and self-conscious about the expensive gifts showered upon her on 1 December. Now, having restricted use for jewels, Fabergé eggs and the like, she requested that her presents should consist of cheques for charity. Her well-wishers showed their feelings for her by giving both cheques and presents.

On the great day she was strong enough, with a little help, to cut her birthday cake and thereafter the King entertained her to a film show in the ballroom. After *Monsieur Beaucaire*, a great favourite at the time, there appeared on the screen movie pictures of Alexandra's life since the invention of the cine-camera. That evening the faithful Charlotte Knollys was able to read to her a special tribute appearing in *The Times*:

> Howells★ once said that to Americans England was always a land of faery, and perhaps it is not fanciful to think that when Hans Andersen used to tell the little Princess Alexandra his immortal stories, he fostered in her ardent childish imagination his own conception of a living and loving fairyland brought down to earth, a gracious, healing influence on ordinary human joys and sorrows. . . .
>
> What is certain is that in after years this is the sort of thing that often happened. A naive letter, painfully written in a child's round hand from a child's sick-bed, comes from

★ William Dean Howells, American novelist (1837–1920).

some humble address. Our Royal lady, with her quick sympathy, at once arranges a generous mass of flowers, her correspondent's name-flower if possible, in a fine gilt basket, tied with gay ribbons, and in them she tucks a prettily-worded little note. Shall the gift be taken by a messenger on foot? No, that is not our Royal lady's way. Suddenly the mean street is all lighted up, as it were, by a real Royal carriage with footmen in scarlet liveries. It stops at the tenement door, and one of the resplendent footmen descends and delivers the fragrant basket exactly as he would fulfil a similar mission in Mayfair. Is not that the authentic touch of Hans Andersen?

There was one birthday present which Alexandra prized above all others – a new pulpit for the Sandringham Church of St Mary Magdalene. The church had always been very close to her heart and interest and it was there that she had taken her first Communion at Easter in 1863. Her son, Alexander John, was buried there, as was her grandson, John. The donor was a previous benefactor, Mr Rodman Wanamaker, an American. In 1911 Mr Wanamaker had presented Queen Alexandra with the solid silver altar and reredos, and the bronze altar rails, in memory of King Edward, the gift being, in his own words, 'to commemorate the great service His Majesty rendered to the world by the manner in which he guided with great diplomacy the peaceful feelings of the English nation'. In 1915 he gave the jewelled Bible in the Sanctuary and then followed the silver processional cross which was placed in the church by Queen Alexandra in 1920 to commemorate the men of Sandringham who fell between 1914 and 1918. Now, in 1924, came the pulpit, of oak panelled in solid silver with figure work in high relief. At the foot of the pulpit steps are two silver angels, kneeling in prayer.[11]

By March 1925 Queen Alexandra was very tired and resigned to the knowledge that she had little time left. 'I feel *completely* collapsed,' she told the King. 'I soon shall go.'[12] Yet there were left to her the green and scented days of the Norfolk summer.

She visited the stables, or wandered with her Pekinese in the gardens, taking tea in the Danish dairy which she had designed, or in 'The Nest',★ a little summer-house on the lawn above the lake. She pottered among the graves of the dogs which she had loved – on one was inscribed 'Dear little faithful Swift. Belonged to Queen Alexandra, Given by Baroness Reetz-Tholt in Denmark.' She visited the Trinity House home for Aged Women and smiled with the children at the school. She took short drives with her chauffeur Stamper, to shop in King's Lynn or sit in the sun at her chalet by the sea, looking out over the waters of the Wash towards Denmark, as she had done with Bertie on her honeymoon. On Sunday mornings she was a regular attender at church, the King, whenever possible, sitting beside her and finding the places.

A visitor from the *Daily Express* called at 'the Big House' and wrote:

> I never realized what the beauty of old age could mean until I saw Queen Alexandra in the late autumn of her days. A vision of exquisite fragility, her face still that perfect oval that captivated London in the long ago, her figure slender and willowy. She sat erect in her low chair in her favourite sitting-room at Sandringham, gazing out of the window across the marshes – a view she loved. She wore a simple black gown of no fashion, of no date. The soft, elusive folds clung to the graceful, almost youthful lines of her figure. But it was her smile of greeting that I shall always remember – that wonderful smile which ravished all in the days when she came a girl-bride, and remained with her in its undying beauty.

In the first week of November she made a trip to King's Lynn. On Sunday, the 15th, she drove around the grounds of Sandringham. At three-thirty on the following afternoon came the bulletin announcing that she had had a severe heart attack and was critically ill; though she recognized King George and Queen Mary, who were constantly at her side.

The Family was sent for. David, just back from a world tour of eight months, was hunting in Leicestershire; Bertie, whose

★ The inscription inside reads: 'The Queen's Nest – A small offering to The Blessed Lady from Her Beloved Majesty's very devoted old servant General Probyn 1913 – Today tomorrow and every day God bless her and guard her I fervently pray.'

wife was expecting a baby★ in the spring, was in Cardiff. They hurried to London and next afternoon set off for Norfolk by train. David was carrying in his arms two toy dogs which he had bought as a present for his grandmother.[13]

Fog came down over the Fenlands, shrouding the signals along the line. Small groups of villagers gathered on the road outside the walls of Sandringham – two ploughmen homeward-bound, a keeper and a child, a woman with a bicycle – peering through a gap in the trees to where, scarcely visible in the fading light, the flag hung limp on its staff. In the Feathers Hotel at Dersingham the bar was packed. On the table stood the wireless set, its big, horn loudspeaker crackling out the latest bulletin.

The Princes' train arrived sixteen minutes late at Wolferton. There, in the royal waiting-room, Mr Godfrey, the stationmaster, deeply upset, passed on his sad message: 'I regret to inform your Royal Highnesses that her Majesty is dead.' A limousine swept them up the hill, past the grey banks of rhododendrons, to the Norwich Gates, wreathed in a dense white pall of fog.

'The Big House' came into view, a silhouette of darkness, as the blinds in every window had been drawn. Only a lamp showed by the main door, to guide them in, like a lone light at the end of a long jetty. It was only then that the two young men, each destined to be King, fully realized that the soul of their grandmother had slipped away on the evening tide.

★ Queen Elizabeth II.

NOTES

CHAPTER 1

1 Knutsford p. 248
2 *Dearest Mama* p. 50
3 Madol *Christian IX* p. 35
4 *Ibid.* p. 37
5 *Childhood of the Princess of Wales*
6 *Prince Nicolas of Greece* p. 61–5
7 Dangerfield p. 122
8 *Ibid.* p. 123
9 Madol p. 46
10 Trowbridge p. 46
11 Bernstorff Archives
12 *Dearest Child* p. 352
13 *Childhood of the Princess of Wales*
14 Wortham p. 94
15 *Letters of the Prince Consort* 22 July 1861
16 *Childhood of the Princess of .Wales*

CHAPTER 2

1 Corti p. 29
2 *Dearest Child* p. 245
3 Villiers p. 317
4 Trowbridge p. 303
5 Lee *King Edward VII* Vol. I p. 59
6 Bianchi *La Politique du Comte du Cavour* p. 302
7 *Uncensored Recollections* pp. 38—9
8 Eyck *The Prince Consort* p. 19

9 *Victoria Travels* p. 26
10 Battiscombe p. 17
11 Paget *Scenes and Memories*
12 *Girlhood of Queen Victoria* Vol. II pp. 188–9
13 Battiscombe p. 19
14 *Dearest Child* p. 323
15 *Ibid.* p. 339
16 Bolitho *A Century of British Monarchy* pp. 65–6
17 Kinloch Cooke Vol. I p. 369
18 *HRH Viktoria Luise* pp. 31–2
19 Anon. King Edward VII p. 52
20 Meynell p. 10

CHAPTER 3

1 *Dearest Child* p. 355
2 *Ibid.* p. 353
3 Magnus p. 73
4 *Dearest Mama* p. 39
5 *Ibid.*
6 *Hessian Tapestry* p. 76
7 *Dearest Mama* p. 82
8 *Ibid.* p. 53
9 *Ibid.* p. 98
10 *Ibid.* p. 78
11 Madol *Christian IX* p. 129
12 *Letters* 3 September 1862
13 *Ibid.*
14 Magnus p. 83
15 Paget *Embassies of Other Days*
16 Magnus p. 84
17 Holmes p. 155

18 Battiscombe p. 38
19 *Dearest Mama* p. 108
20 Holmes p. 156
21 Madol p. 76
22 *Dearest Mama* p. 126
23 *Ibid.* p. 112
24 Magnus p. 88
25 Mrs Carlyle, in a letter to
   Jane Austen
26 *Dearest Mama*

CHAPTER 4

1 *Dearest Mama* p. 172
2 Battiscombe p. 43
3 *'My Dear Duchess'* p. 212
4 Watson p. 160
5 *'My Dear Duchess'* p. 215
6 Anon. *King Edward VII*
   p. 61
7 Madol p. 133
8 Trowbridge p. 78
9 Holmes p. 160
10 Trowbridge p. 79
11 Thorndike p. 183
12 Trowbridge pp. 83–5;
   Holmes p. 161
13 Trowbridge p. 86
14 *My Reminiscences* pp. 105–6
15 *Letters* 7 March 1863
16 *'My Dear Duchess'* p. 214
17 *London Society*
18 Arthur p. 115
19 *Letters* 10 March 1863
20 *'My Dear Duchess'* p. 214
21 *Ibid.*
22 Sanderson Vol. II p. 13
23 Antrim p. 145
24 Bolitho *Reign of Queen
   Victoria* p. 198
25 Stanley *Letters* p. 286
26 *Letters* 10 March 1863
27 Churchill *Randolph Churchill*
   Vol. I p. 10

28 Stanley pp. 310–11
29 *Ibid.*
30 Holmes p. 175

CHAPTER 5

1 *Dearest Mama* p. 180
2 *'My Dear Duchess'* p. 216
3 *Ibid.* p. 217
4 Arthur p. 113
5 Battiscombe p. 52
6 Paul *Britain's King and Queen*
   p. 139
7 *Whisper Louise* p. 59
8 Battiscombe p. 55
9 Tisdall p. 63 (*Dairy of the
   Rev. B. T. Armstrong*)
10 Madol *Christian IX* p. 138
11 Hough p. 17
12 *Hessian Tapestry* p. 101
13 *Dearest Mama* p. 183
14 *Memories of Fifty Years* p. 68
15 *Journal of Benjamin Moran*
16 *Dearest Mama* p. 236
17 *Ibid.* p. 213
18 Magnus p. 113
19 Anon. *King Edward VII*
   p. 70
20 Morley Vol. I p. 546
21 *Dearest Mama* p. 289
22 Battiscombe pp. 62–3
23 Bloomfield p. 160

CHAPTER 6

1 *Further Letters* 22 July 1870
2 Longford p. 322
3 *Your Dear Letter* p. 246
4 *Dearest Mama* p. 315
5 Battiscombe p. 80
6 *Whisper Louise* p. 95
7 Marquess of Carisbrooke
8 Battiscombe p. 87
9 *Your Dear Letter* p. 200

L

10 *Ibid*. p. 186
11 Salusbury p. 6
12 Madol *Private Life of Queen Alexandra* p. 67
13 Buchanan *Victorian Gallery* p. 161
14 Madol *Private Life of Queen Alexandra* p. 68
15 Magnus p. 117
16 Madol *Private Life of Queen Alexandra* p. 66
17 Battiscombe p. 80
18 Antrim p. 102
19 *Ibid*. p. 104
20 *Letters* 10 March 1867
21 Tisdall p. 80
22 Sheppard p. 266
23 Dangerfield p. 167
24 *Your Dear Letter* p. 158
25 *Albert and Victoria* p. 225
26 Watson p. 207
27 *Ibid*. p. 208
28 Dennis p. 217
29 *Illustrated London News* 15 April 1871

CHAPTER 7

1 *Uncensored Recollections* p. 33
2 Magnus p. 122
3 Antrim p. 221
4 Battiscombe p. 138
5 Huntly p. 40
6 Lee Vol. I p. 290
7 Magnus p. 132
8 *Your Dear Letter* p. 220
9 Madol p. 91
10 Hough p. 62
11 Sanderson Vol. II p. 135
12 *Journal of a Visit to Egypt*
13 *Ibid*.
14 *Your Dear Letter* p. 221
15 *A Diary in the East*
16 Unpublished Reminiscences

17 Benson *As We Were* p. 162
18 Magnus p. 139
19 *Whisper Louise* pp. 114–5

CHAPTER 8

1 *A King's Story* p. 292
2 *Sandringham: A Guide, etc.* p. 16
3 *Whisper Louise* p. 100
4 *Sandringham: A Guide etc.* p. 16
5 24 September 1871
6 Radziwill *The Empress Frederick* p. 153
7 *Letters* 29 November 1871
8 Battiscombe p. 116
9 *Ibid*. p. 117
10 *Ibid*. p. 116
11 *Dagstelegraphen* 7 May 1868
12 Stanley *Later Letters* p. 147
13 Bullock p. 123
14 Stanley pp. 149–50
15 *Ibid*.
16 Battiscombe p. 115
17 Joseph Gwyer
18 Alfred Austin
19 Stanley p. 149
20 *Letters* 13 December 1871
21 Holmes Vol. I p. 246
22 Stanley p. 150
23 Madol p. 105
24 *Darling Child* pp. 21–4
25 Holmes Vol. I p. 244
26 *Ibid*. p. 249
27 Battiscombe p. 118
28 *Darling Child* p. 28
29 *Ibid*. pp. 30–1
30 Holmes Vol. I p. 252
31 Cresswell p. 146

CHAPTER 9

1 Trowbridge p. 139
2 Hibbert p. 178

Notes

3 Hamilton *Days Before Yesterday* p. 42
4 Madol p. 109
5 *Ibid*. p. 117
6 Gore p. 14
7 Brook-Shepherd p. 52
8 *My Fifty Years* p. 149
9 Salusbury p. 15
10 Gore p. 9
11 Tisdall p. 107
12 Bullock p. 94
13 Battiscombe p. 139
14 Cresswell
15 Brook-Shepherd p. 53
16 Nicolson p. 8
17 Bolitho *A Century of British Monarchy* p. 144
18 Nicolson p. 14
19 *Ibid*. p. 12
20 *Ibid*. p. 23
21 *Ibid*. p. 29
22 Hibbert p. 179
23 'J. P. J.' *Reminiscences* p. 50
24 Salusbury p. 20
25 Marquess of Carisbrooke
26 *Letters of Queen Victoria*
27 Anon. *King Edward VII* p. 142
28 *Uncensored Recollections* p. 201
29 Tayler *The Book of the Duffs* p. 224
30 Hibbert p. 216
31 Anon. *King Edward VII* p. 142
32 Huntly p. 14
33 *Uncensored Recollections* pp. 198–9
34 Tayler p. 86
35 Magnus p. 270
36 Kinloch Cooke, Vol. II p. 217
37 *Afterthoughts* p. 265
38 Tayler p. 225

39 *A Royal Correspondence* p. 183
40 Battiscombe p. 182

CHAPTER 10

1 Trowbridge p. 164
2 Queen Frederica *A Measure of Understanding* p. 2
3 HRH Viktoria Luise *The Kaiser's Daughter* pp. 50–3
4 Lowe *Alexander III of Russia* p. 46
5 Lyall *Life of Lord Dufferin*
6 McClintock p. 170; *The Vanished Pomps of Yesterday* p. 169
7 *The Vanished Pomps of Yesterday* p. 166
8 *Ibid*. p. 168
9 Magnus p. 217; Battiscombe p. 160
10 Massie p. 108
11 Madol *Private Life of Queen Alexandra* p. 107
12 Lowe p. 343
13 *Ibid*. pp. 338–9

CHAPTER 11

1 Macdonnell *Life of William Connor Magee* Vol. I pp. 293–4
2 Arthur *Not Worth Reading* p. 53
3 Madol p. 144
4 Lady Randolph Churchill p. 147
5 Gernsheim Illustration No. 63
6 Arthur p. 52
7 Lady Randolph Churchill p. 147
8 *Personal Letters of King Edward VII* p. 31

9 Arthur p. 51
10 Cresswell p. 147
11 Arthur p. 53
12 Madol p. 119
13 *Ibid*. p. 118
14 Cathcart *Sandringham* p. 114
15 Drew p. 103
16 Wortham p. 193
17 Drew p. 107
18 Cresswell pp. 149–50
19 *Our Queen* p. 324
20 Cresswell pp. 169–71
21 Mallet p. 19
22 F. Ponsonby p. 138
23 Knutsford p. 187
24 *Letters* 26 April 1889
25 Vacaresco Reminiscences
26 *Ibid*.
27 *Letters* 2 October 1890
28 Vacaresco Reminiscences

CHAPTER 12

1 *Victoria's Heir* p. 274
2 *A King's Story* p. 83
3 Monkswell p. 69
4 Magnus p. 227
5 Knutsford p. 362
6 Tisdall p. 132
7 Sheppard Vol. II p. 165
8 Knutsford p. 361
9 *Ibid*. p. 366
10 *Ibid*. p. 145
11 *Ibid*. pp. 145–6
12 Trowbridge pp. 216–7
13 Battiscombe p. 169
14 Bullock p. 113
15 Battiscombe p. 123
16 Gould Lee *The Empress Frederick Writes to Sophie* p. 165
17 Bullock p. 107
18 Prince Nicholas p. 171; Prince Christopher p. 214

19 *The Queen's Resolve* p. 184
20 Knutsford pp. 358–60

CHAPTER 13

1 Magnus p. 300
2 25 December 1886
3 Battiscombe p. 162
4 Magnus p. 215
5 *Ibid*. p. 225
6 Pope-Hennessy p. 192
7 Harrison p. 123
8 St Aubyn p. 239
9 *Ibid*. p. 299
10 Sheppard Vol. II pp. 160–1
11 Corti *The English Empress* p. 270
12 Battiscombe p. 174
13 Cecil *Life of Lord Salisbury* Vol. IV pp. 113, 367
14 Battiscombe pp. 176–9
15 Harrison p. 217
16 Madol pp. 155–6
17 25 December 1890
18 Pope-Hennessy p. 196
19 Lacey p. 51
20 Stephenson p. 180
21 Harrison p. 110
22 Bramsen *Huset Glucksborg*

CHAPTER 14

1 Lang p. 40
2 *Afterthoughts*
3 Hibbert p. 188
4 Magnus p. 291
5 Hibbert p. 189
6 Magnus p. 285
7 Pope-Hennessy p. 191
8 *Illustrated London News*
9 Benson *As We Were* p. 101
10 *Ibid*. p. 103
11 *Illustrated London News* 6 June 1891

Notes

12 *Ibid*. 13 June 1891

13 Magnus p. 286

14 *Illustrated London News* 13 June 1891

15 Hibbert p. 196

16 Pope-Hennessy p. 189

17 20 September 1891

18 *Illustrated London News* 28 November 1891

19 Kinloch Cooke Vol. II p. 235

20 *Illustrated London News* 5 December 1891

21 *Queen Victoria's Letters* 7 December 1891

22 Magnus p. 294

23 Pope-Hennessy p. 222

24 Ponsonby *Henry Ponsonby* p. 358

25 *Ibid*.

26 Anon. *King Edward VII* p. 153

27 Madol p. 161

28 *Queen Victoria's Letters* 2 February 1892

29 *Illustrated London News* 2 July 1892

30 Leslie p. 163

31 Nicolson p. 47

32 *Ibid*. p. 50

33 *Illustrated London News; The World*

34 Elsberry p. 19; Mahel Potter Daggett

35 *Hessian Tapestry*

36 Pope-Hennessy p. 249

37 *Ibid*.

38 Elsberry p. 25

39 *Ibid*.

40 Pope-Hennessy p. 251

41 Battiscombe p. 194

42 p. 204

43 *Illustrated London News* 12 November 1892

44 Pope-Hennessy p. 259

45 *Ibid*. p. 429

46 *Ibid*. p. 269

47 Lady Geraldine Somerset

48 Pope-Hennessy p. 270

49 Lacey p. 53

50 Pope-Hennessy p. 299

CHAPTER 15

1 Massie p. 65

2 Prince Louis of Hesse

3 Massie p. 64

4 Pope-Hennessy p. 309

5 Magnus p. 309

6 From the picture *The Last Farewell* by Melton Prior

7 Magnus p. 309

8 Massie p. 69

9 Longford p. 235

10 *Whisper Louise* pp. 150–1

11 Knutsford p. 264

12 *Ibid*. p. 249

13 Watson p. 274

14 *The Life of a Century* p. 738

15 Paul p. 343

16 *Queen Victoria's Letters* 22 June 1897

17 *Ibid*.

18 Paul pp. 342–3

19 *Queen Victoria's Letters* 29 February 1872

20 Mallet p. 159

21 Leslie p. 230

22 Hibbert p. 206

23 Battiscombe p. 209

24 *Ibid*.

25 Magnus p. 324

26 Mallet p. 103

27 Madol p. 174

28 Battiscombe p. 202

29 Beckwith p. 151

30 Brook-Shepherd p. 64

31 Magnus p. 326

32 *Illustrated London News* 11

November and 9 December
1899
33 Tisdall p. 190
34 Trowbridge p. 292
35 Magnus p. 327
36 Madol p. 171
37 Brook-Shepherd pp. 92–3
38 Tisdall p. 191
39 *Ibid.*
40 Knutsford p. 182
41 *Ibid.* p. 181
42 *Victoria Travels* p. 336
43 Dugdale p. 224
44 *Illustrated London News* 14
April 1900
45 Paoli p. 207
46 Stephenson pp. 207–8
47 *Ibid.*
48 *Prince Nicholas of Greece*
pp. 182–3
49 *Illustrated London News* 2
June 1900
50 Monkswell p. 67
51 Massey pp. 22–4
52 *Illustrated London News* 19
January 1901
53 Leslie p. 239
54 Marquess of Carisbrooke
55 Duke of Argyll
56 *Illustrated London News* 9
February 1901
57 Windsor p. 13
58 *Illustrated London News* 9
February 1901

CHAPTER 16

1 Esher Vol. I p. 279
2 *Ibid.* p. 373
3 Lee Vol. II p. 27
4 Esher Vol. I p. 318
5 Lee Vol. II p. 54
6 Knutsford p. 158
7 Monkswell p. 83

8 Madol p. 224
9 Airlie p. 107
10 Esher Vol. I p. 358
11 Lady Mallet; Epton p. 225
12 *The Girlhood of Queen
Victoria* Vol. I pp. 356–7
13 Magnus p. 366
14 Tisdall p. 204
15 *Sunday Express* 16 March
1958
16 Watson p. 79
17 Battiscombe p. 246
18 Trowbridge p. 277
19 Meynell pp. 10–12
20 Balsan p. 132

CHAPTER 17

1 Magnus p. 382
2 Esher papers; Magnus p. 476
3 Huston p. 82
4 Airlie p. 109
5 Battiscombe p. 252
6 *Ibid.* p. 177
7 Madol p. 201
8 Robinson p. 155
9 *Ibid.* p. 157
10 *Ibid.*
11 *Ibid.* p. 222
12 Madol *Christian IX*
pp. 276–8
13 Tisdall p. 217
14 Dugdale pp. 203–4
15 Wortham p. 404
16 Lee Vol. II p. 536
17 Massey p. 76

CHAPTER 18

1 Huston p. 82
2 Fischer p. 93
3 *Ibid.* pp. 307–8
4 Hibbert p. 335
5 Madol p. 195
6 Legge p. 76

7 Arthur *King George V* p. 293
8 Nicolson p. 908
9 Madol *Christian IX* pp. 276–8
10 Lee Vol. II p. 331
11 Middlemas p. 134
12 Lee Vol. II p. 332
13 Magnus p. 440
14 Fisher *Memories* pp. 4–5
15 St Aubyn p. 442
16 Battiscombe p. 231
17 *Ibid.*
18 *Ibid.* p. 232
19 Lee Vol. II pp. 543–4
20 *Ibid.* pp. 546–7
21 Madol p. 212
22 *Ibid.* p. 209
23 Battersea p. 321
24 *Rordam Memoirs*
25 Eulalia of Spain p. 213
26 Madol p. 220
27 Hibbert *Edward VII* p. 267
28 Wortham p. 387
29 Battiscombe p. 267
30 Ormathwaite pp. 144–5
31 Lee Vol. II p. 587
32 *Ibid.* p. 591
33 Tisdall p. 222
34 St Aubyn p. 361
35 Lee Vol. II p. 594
36 *Die Grosse Politik* Vol. XXV p. 479
37 F. Ponsonby p. 258
38 *Ibid.*
39 Magnus p. 526
40 *Ibid.* p. 551
41 Tschumi p. 123
42 Tisdall p. 230
43 (Report of) Lord Dawson of Penn; (repeated in) Watson p. 108
44 *Ibid.*
45 Holmes Vol. II p. 613

CHAPTER 19

1 F. Ponsonby p. 271
2 Cresswell p. 146
3 Pless p. 262
4 Windsor p. 74
5 Ormathwaite p. 192
6 Knutsford p. 266
7 Windsor p. 74
8 F. Ponsonby p. 279
9 St Aubyn pp. 380–1
10 Tschumi p. 113
11 St Aubyn p. 477
12 Cohen p. 301; Madol p. 258
13 Pope-Hennessy p. 441
14 Colville p. 111
15 Sewell p. 114
16 Pope-Hennessy p. 423
17 Battiscombe p. 274
18 Pope-Hennessy p. 423
19 *Ibid.* p. 422
20 *Ibid.*
21 *Ibid.* p. 423
22 Colville p. 113
23 Madol p. 259
24 Battiscombe p. 279
25 Pope-Hennessy p. 452
26 *Book of the Duffs*
27 Battiscombe p. 281
28 *Hessian Tapestry* p. 226
29 Madol p. 262
30 *Ibid.* p. 259
31 Gernsheim p. 153
32 Trowbridge p. 296
33 *Ibid.*
34 Nicolson p. 217
35 Pope-Hennessy p. 480
36 Dugdale pp. 250, 308
37 *Memoirs* p. 122
38 Madol pp. 265–6
39 Tisdall p. 232

CHAPTER 20

1 Lang, p. 150

2 *Political Memoirs*, p. 20
3 Battiscombe, p. 283
4 Buchanan *Victorian Gallery*, p. 171
5 Legge p. 73
6 Lang p. 259
7 *Ibid*. p. 31
8 Hough p. 97
9 February 1915
10 Battiscombe p. 284
11 Official Communiqué
12 Battiscombe p. 291
13 *Illustrated London News* 25 November 1925
14 Buchanan *Victorian Gallery* p. 183
15 Knutsford p. 361
16 Marie of Romania p. 158
17 Windsor pp. 118–9
18 Knutsford p. 282
19 Madol p. 268
20 *Ibid*. p. 266
21 *Daily Mirror* 7 June 1916
22 Curzon p. 53
23 E. B. *Kitchener*
24 Nicolson p. 323
25 Madol pp. 265–6
26 Tisdall pp. 232–3

CHAPTER 21

1 *Sunday Express* 28 January 1962
2 Telegram No. 231, Athens
3 Gould Lee p. 41
4 *Empress Frederick Writes to Sophie* p. 350

5 Prince Nicholas *Political Memoirs* p. 25
6 Buchanan *Queen Victoria's Relations* p. 183
7 Nicolson p. 282
8 *Political Memoirs* p. 183
9 Battiscombe p. 288
10 *Ibid*.
11 Nicolson p. 299
12 *Ibid*. p. 309
13 *The Times* 21 April 1917
14 *Princess Viktoria Luise* pp. 106–7
15 Pope-Hennessy p. 507
16 Madol p. 269
17 Nicolson p. 327
18 Madol p. 272

CHAPTER 22

1 *Daily Sketch* 28 February 1919
2 Pope-Hennessy p. 520
3 Masson p. 75
4 *Christopher of Greece* pp. 164–5
5 *Elizabeth of Glamis* p. 13
6 Pope-Hennessy p. 537 .
7 Nicholas of Greece *My Fifty Years* pp. 315–6
8 Battiscombe p. 301
9 Madol p. 278
10 Knutsford p. 367
11 Ashton
12 Pope-Hennessy p. 537
13 Madol p. 281

BIBLIOGRAPHY

Airlie, Mabell, Countess of. *Thatched with Gold* 1962.

Albert Victor, Prince, and George, Prince, of Wales. *The Cruise of HMS Bacchante* 1886.

Alexander, Grand Duke of Russia. *Once a Grand Duke* 1932.

Alice, Grand Duchess of Hesse. *Letters to H.M. the Queen* 1885.

Alice, HRH Princess. *For My Grandchildren* 1966.

Almedingen, E. M. *The Empress Alexandra* 1961.

Anon. *King Edward the Seventh* 1910.

Anon. *Sandringham, A Guide to the Grounds*.

Anon. *The Vanished Pomps of Yesterday* 1919.

Anon. *Uncensored Recollections* 1924.

Antrim, Louisa, Countess of. *Recollections* 1937.

Arthur, Sir George. *Concerning Queen Victoria and Her Son* 1943.

Arthur, Sir George. *King George V* 1929.

Ashton, Sir George. *H.R.H. The Duke of Connaught and Strathearn* 1929.

Ashton, Rev. Patrick. *Sandringham Church*.

Bailey, John (Ed.). *The Diary of Lady Frederick Cavendish* 1927.

Balsan, Consuelo Vanderbilt. *The Glitter and the Gold* 1953.

Battenberg, Prince Louis of. *Recollections 1854–1884* unpublished.

Battenberg, Princess Marie of. *Reminiscences* 1925.

Battersea, Lady Constance. *Reminiscences* 1922.

Battiscombe, Georgina. *Queen Alexandra* 1969.

Benson, A. C. (Ed.) *Letters of Queen Victoria 1837–1901* 1st series.

Benson, E. F. *As We Were* 1932.

Benson, E. F. *Daughters of Queen Victoria* 1939.

Benson, E. F. *King Edward VII* 1933.

Benson, E. F. *Queen Victoria* 1935.

Bernhardt, Sarah. *Memoirs* 1907.

Bloomfield, Lady. *Reminiscences of Court and Diplomatic Life* 1883.

Bolitho, Hector (Ed.). *Further Letters of Queen Victoria* 1938.

Bolitho, Hector. *The Reign of Queen Victoria* 1949.

Brett, M. V. (Ed.) *Journals and Letters of Reginald Viscount Esher* 1934.

Brook-Shepherd, Gordon. *Uncle of Europe* 1975.

Bryant, Arthur. *George V* 1936.

Buchanan, Meriel. *Queen Victoria's Relations* 1954.

Buchanan, Meriel. *Victorian Gallery* 1956.

Buckle, G. E. (Ed.). *Letters of Queen Victoria 1837–1901* 2nd and 3rd series.

Burghclere, Lady (Ed.). *A Great Lady's Friendships* 1933.

Christopher, Prince, of Greece. *Memoirs* 1938.

Cohen, Lucy. *Lady de Rothschild and Her Daughters* 1935.

Collier, E. C. F. *A Victorian Diarist* 1946.

Colville, Lady Cynthia. *Crowded Life* 1963.

Connell, Brian. *Manifest Destiny* 1953.

Cornwallis-West, Mrs G. *The Reminiscences of Lady Randolph Churchill* 1908.

Corti, Egon Caesar Conte. *The English Empress* 1957.

Cowles, Virginia. *Edward VII and His Circle* 1956.

Cozens-Hardy, Harry. *The Glorious Years* 1953.

Crawford, Emily. *Victoria Queen and Ruler* 1903.

Curzon, Marchioness of Kedleston. *Reminiscences* 1955.

Dangerfield, George. *Victoria's Heir* 1941.

Dugdale, Edgar T. S. *Maurice de Bunsen* 1934.

Eckardstein, Baron von. *Ten Years at the Court of St James'* 1921.

Emden, Paul H. *Behind the Throne* 1934.

Eulalia, Infanta of Spain. *Court Life from Within* 1915.

Bibliography

Fischer, Henry W. *The Private Lives of William II and His Consort* 1904.

Fisher, Lord, Admiral of the Fleet. *Memories* 1919.

Fisher, Lord, Admiral of the Fleet. *Records* 1919.

Fulford, Roger. *Darling Child* 1976.

Fulford, Roger. *Dearest Child* 1964.

Fulford, Roger. *Dearest Mama* 1968.

Fulford, Roger. *Your Dear Letter* 1971.

Gernsheim, Alison. *Edward VII and Queen Alexandra* 1962.

Gore, John. *King George V* 1941.

Gould Lee, A. *The Royal House of Greece* 1948.

Gould Lee, A. (Ed.). *The Empress Frederick Writes to Sophie* 1955.

Gower, Lord Ronald. *My Reminiscences* 1895.

Hamilton, Lord Frederick. *The Days Before Yesterday* 1920.

Harrison, Michael. *Clarence* 1972.

Hibbert, Christopher. *Edward VII: A Portrait* 1976.

Hibbert, Christopher. *The Court at Windsor* 1964.

Hohenlohe, Prince. *Memoirs* 1906.

Holmes, Sir Richard. *Edward VII* 1911.

Hough, Richard. *Louis and Victoria* 1974.

Huntly, Marquis of. *'Auld Acquaintance'* (undated).

Jagow, Dr (Ed.). *Letters of the Prince Consort, 1831–1861* 1938.

'J.P.J.'. *Reminiscences* 1929.

Kennedy, A. L. (Ed.). *'My Dear Duchess'* – Letters to the Duchess of Manchester 1956.

Kerr, Mark. *Prince Louis of Battenberg* 1934.

Kinloch Cooke, C. *H.R.H. Princess Mary Adelaide, Duchess of Teck* 1900.

Knutsford, Viscount. *In Black and White* 1926.

Lacey, Robert. *Majesty* 1977.

Lang, Theo. *The Darling Daisy Affair* 1966.

Langtry, Lillie. *The Days I Knew* (undated).

Lee, Sir Sidney. *King Edward VII* 1925.

Lee, Sidney. *Queen Victoria* 1902.

Legge, Edward. *The Public and Private Life of Kaiser William II* 1915.

Longford, Elizabeth. *Victoria R.I.* 1964.

Lowe, Charles. *Alexander III of Russia* 1895.

Madol, Hans Roger. *Christian IX* 1939.

Madol, Hans Roger. *The Private Life of Queen Alexandra* 1940.

Magnus, Philip. *King Edward the Seventh* 1964.

Makin, W. J. *The Life of King George the Fifth* 1936.

Mallet, Victor (Ed.). *Life with Queen Victoria* 1968.

Marie Louise, Princess. *My Memories of Six Reigns* 1956.

Martin, Theodore. *The Life of the Prince Consort* 1877.

Massey, Gertrude. *Kings, Commoners and Me* 1934.

Massie, Robert K. *Nicholas and Alexandra* 1968.

Masson, Madeleine. *Edwina* 1958.

Maurois, André. *King Edward and His Times* 1933.

McClintock, Mary Howard. *The Queen Thanks Sir Howard* 1946.

Metternich, Princess Pauline. *Souvenirs 1859–1871* 1922.

Meynell, Lady Mary. *Sunshine and Shadows* 1933.

Middlemas, Keith. *The Life and Times of Edward VII* 1972.

Nevill, Lady Dorothy. *My Own Times* 1912.

Nevill, Ralph. *The Reminiscences of Lady Dorothy Nevill* 1906.

Nicholas, Prince of Greece. *My Fifty Years* 1926.

Nicolson, Harold. *King George the Fifth* 1952.

Oman, Sir Charles. *Things I have Seen* 1933.

Ormathwaite, Lord. *When I was at Court* 1937.

Paget, Lady Walburga. *In My Tower* 1924.

Paoli, Xavier. *My Royal Clients* (undated).

Paul, Thomas. *Britain's King and Queen* 1904.

Pless, Daisy, Princess of. *From My Private Diary* 1931.

Ponsonby, Arthur. *Henry Ponsonby: His Life from His Letters* 1942.

Ponsonby, Sir Frederick (Ed.). *Letters of the Empress Frederick* 1928.

Ponsonby, Sir Frederick. *Recollections of Three Reigns* 1951.

Bibliography

Pope-Hennessy, James. *Queen Mary* 1959.

Pope-Hennessy, James (Ed.). *Queen Victoria at Windsor and Balmoral* 1959.

Radnor, Helen, Dowager-Countess of. *From a Great-Grandmother's Chair* (undated).

Radziwill, Princess Catherine. *The Royal Marriage Mart of Europe* 1915.

Redesdale, Lord. *Memories* 1915.

Rendel, Lord. *The Personal Papers* 1931.

Robinson, Sir Henry. *Memories: Wise and Otherwise* 1923.

Russell, G. W. E. *Collections and Recollections* 1903.

St Aubyn, Giles. *Edward VII, Prince and King* 1979.

St Aubyn, Giles. *The Royal George* 1963.

St Helier, Lady. *Memories of Fifty Years* 1909.

Salusbury, F. G. H. *King Emperor's Jubilee* 1935.

Sanderson, Edgar. *King Edward VII* 1910.

Sewell, Lieut.-Col. J. P. C. (Ed.). *Personal Letters of King Edward VII* 1931.

Sheppard, Edgar (Ed.). *George, Duke of Cambridge* 1907.

Shore, W. Teignmouth. *The Baccarat Case* 1931.

Smyth, Dame Ethel. *Streaks of Life* 1920.

Stephenson, John (Ed.). *A Royal Correspondence* 1938.

Stoeckl, Baroness Agnes de. *When Men had Time to Love* 1953.

Tayler, Alistair and Henrietta. *The Book of the Duffs* 1914.

Thorndike, Russell. *Children of the Garter* 1937.

Tilney Bassett, A. *Gladstone to His Wife* 1936.

Tisdall, E. E. P. *Unpredictable Queen* 1953.

Topham, Anne. *Memories of the Kaiser's Court* 1914.

Trowbridge, W. R. H. *Queen Alexandra 1921*.

Tschumi, Gabriel. *Royal Chef* 1954.

Victoria, Queen. *Leaves from the Journal of Our Life in the Highlands* 1870.

Victoria, Queen. *More Leaves from the Journal of a Life in the Highlands* 1885.

Viktoria Luise, Princess of Prussia. *The Kaiser's Daughter* 1977.

Warwick, Frances, Countess of. *Afterthoughts* 1931.

Watson, Vera. *A Queen at Home* 1952.

Wheeler-Bennett, John W. *King George VI* 1958.

Williamson, David. *Before I Forget* (undated).

Windsor, Dean of, and Bolitho, Hector (Eds.). *Letters of Lady Augusta Stanley* 1927.

Windsor, Duke of. *A King's Story* 1951.

Woodham-Smith, Cecil. *Queen Victoria* 1972.

Woodward, Kathleen. *Queen Mary* (undated).

Wortham, H. E. *The Delightful Profession: Edward VII* 1931.

INDEX

320

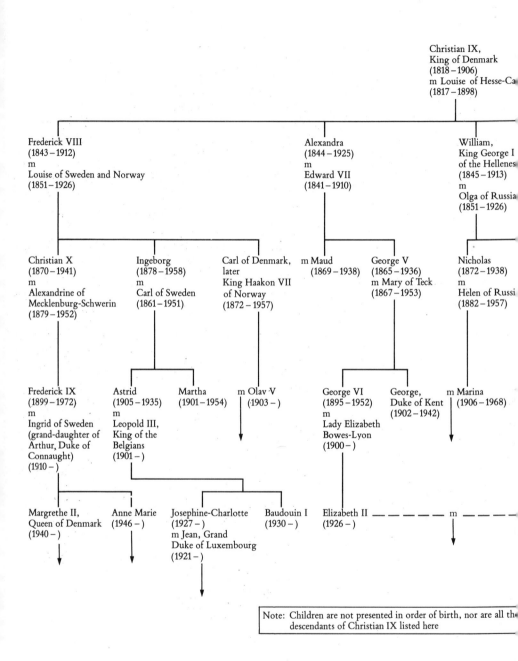

Christian IX,
King of Denmark
(1818 – 1906)
m Louise of Hesse-Ca
(1817 – 1898)

Frederick VIII
(1843 – 1912)
m
Louise of Sweden and Norway
(1851 – 1926)

Alexandra
(1844 – 1925)
m
Edward VII
(1841 – 1910)

William,
King George I
of the Hellenes
(1845 – 1913)
m
Olga of Russia
(1851 – 1926)

Christian X
(1870 – 1941)
m
Alexandrine of
Mecklenburg-Schwerin
(1879 – 1952)

Ingeborg
(1878 – 1958)
m
Carl of Sweden
(1861 – 1951)

Carl of Denmark,
later
King Haakon VII
of Norway
(1872 – 1957)

m Maud
(1869 – 1938)

George V
(1865 – 1936)
m Mary of Teck
(1867 – 1953)

Nicholas
(1872 – 1938)
m
Helen of Russia
(1882 – 1957)

Frederick IX
(1899 – 1972)
m
Ingrid of Sweden
(grand-daughter of
Arthur, Duke of
Connaught)
(1910 –)

Astrid
(1905 – 1935)
m
Leopold III,
King of the
Belgians
(1901 –)

Martha
(1901 – 1954)

m Olav V
(1903 –)

George VI
(1895 – 1952)
m
Lady Elizabeth
Bowes-Lyon
(1900 –)

George,
Duke of Kent
(1902 – 1942)

m Marina
(1906 – 1968)

Margrethe II,
Queen of Denmark
(1940 –)

Anne Marie
(1946 –)

Josephine-Charlotte
(1927 –)
m Jean, Grand
Duke of Luxembourg
(1921 –)

Baudouin I
(1930 –)

Elizabeth II
(1926 –)

m

Note: Children are not presented in order of birth, nor are all the
descendants of Christian IX listed here